Tanais (Don) R.

ster R.

LAKE MAOTIS
(Sea of Azov)

CASPIAN SEA

40°

PITYUS

EUXINE SEA

ARMENIA

PAPHLAGONIA   PONTUS

BYZANTIUM   CHALCEDON
Propontus   NICAEA
CYZICUS

CE

ANCYRA   CAPPADOCIA
(Angora)

NISIBIS

Tigris R.

MYSIA
SARDIS   PHRYGIA
LYDIA
EPHESUS
CARIA

TYANA

CARRHAE   MESOPOTAMIA

DURA

LYCIA   CILICIA   SYRIA

Euphrates R.

BAGHDAD

CTESIPHON

RHODES

ANTIOCP

EMESA

CYPRUS

PALMYRA

BABYLON

30°

TYRE
CAESAREA
JERUSALEM
GAZA   PALESTINE

BABYLONIA

ALEXANDRIA

PELUSIUM

Jordan R.

30° E G Y P T

40°

Nile

ARABIA

ZOSIMUS: HISTORIA NOVA

ZOSIMUS:
HISTORIA NOVA

The Decline of Rome

Translated by
James J. Buchanan
Tulane University
and
Harold T. Davis
Trinity University

TRINITY UNIVERSITY PRESS
SAN ANTONIO, TEXAS
1967

INTRODUCTION

Little more is known for certain concerning Zosimus the historian than what is supplied in the title of *Codex Vaticanus* 156, "Zosimi Comitis et Exadvocati Fisci Historia Nova"; that is, Zosimus was a count (*comes*) of the imperial consistory by virtue of having served a two-year term as advocate of the fisc in one of the prefectures, and he composed a history of "modern" times. Two attempts to enlarge upon this bald statement of facts have proved unavailing:

(1) In the year 468 the Emperors Leo I and Anthemius excluded pagans from serving as advocates of the fisc (Cod. Just. II.vi.8). Because the tone of Zosimus' work is so patently pagan the assumption has been made that he must have been a fiscal advocate prior to 468. Yet it is quite conceivable that Zosimus outwardly professed the Christian faith while inwardly remaining anti-Church. Indeed, together with his thoughts he may well have kept his *scrinia* hidden, just like the later writer Procopius, the publication of whose *Secret History* would have led to his execution for lese majesty.

(2) To read into the word "nova" the notion that Zosimus wrote not long after the year 410, at which point his history comes to an end, is futile for the simple reason that that end is an abrupt one. It need not be doubted that he died in the midst of his labors, Book VI barely begun. Indeed, his *scrinia* may well have been recovered by his heirs and their contents published posthumously.

The name Zosimus was common enough in the Eastern Empire. For example, there existed in Egypt an alchemical school of Zosimus, one of whose members was

Olympiodorus of Thebes.   Olympiodorus, too, wrote a
''historia nova'' down to the year 425, the latest work
referred to by our author.[1] Again, the Souda s. v. ''Zosimus'' refers to his place of origin as being either Gaza or
Ascalon.   Now, actually the Souda is here conflating two
other writers of the same name: Zosimus of Gaza was a
sophist who was active during the reign of Anastasius
(491-518)[2] , while Zosimus of Ascalon was a grammarian
of whose output there is extant a life of Demosthenes. This
biography is couched in a style entirely different from that
of our author, who can hardly have written it. Our author's
style is for the most part pedestrian, embodying so few
purple patches that it is safe to say he cannot be the sophist
of Gaza either. Strange as it may seem that no notice of his
native city should have come down to us, at least it is clear
from Book II.30 that he was thoroughly at home in the
capital city of Constantinople.

Just as uncertainty must remain with regard to Zosimus'
place of birth so it must remain with regard to his date of
birth.   But the date of composition of his work may be
placed between a *terminus post quem* of *ca.* 450[3] and a
terminus ante quem of 503, the year in which Eustathius of
Epiphania published his universal history, citing Zosimus
as one of his sources. Within this spread of something over
half a century it is tempting to pinpoint the time of composition later rather than sooner for three reasons: (1) the

---

[1]With the possible exception of the Athenian Neoplatonist Syrianus,
whose *floruit* was probably 430 A.D.; cf. below, Book IV.18.

[2]It is disconcerting to realize that the reputedly careful lexico-
grapher Hesychius, from whom the Souda's entry s. v. "Zosimus"
derives and whose *floruit* likewise was Anastasius' reign, did not
identify our author more precisely. But apparently Zosimus' history
had no more of an impact shortly after its publication than it has had
since.

[3]See below, Book II.38n., concerning the abolition of the *follis*.

theme of "gloom and doom" is so pervasive that a date
subsequent to the deposing of Romulus Augustulus seems
called for; (2) a careful reading of Book V.23 yields the
impression that it was written considerably after Honorius'
reign[1]; and (3) the work shows signs of carelessness, as
though it were the hastily dashed off product of a crabbed
old man, old in sentiment if not in age.

Zosimus had an axe to grind, and grind it he did. He was
the last of the pagan historians, and his history thus lay
neglected throughout the middle ages (its anti-Christian
stance caught the eye of the great Gibbon, who used it perhaps injudiciously). The question arises whether it should
continue to lie neglected in our own era, and because we
feel that it should not we have made this translation. For,
having remarked on our author's demerits in matters of
style, of carelessness, and of prejudice, we shall now list
his merits:

(1) Zosimus' fuddy-duddy attitude has prompted some
interesting antiquarian information, such as his account of
the *Ludi Saeculares* (II.1-7, the longest extant on the subject) and of the *Pontifices* (IV.36).

(2) Zosimus' bias against the Church acts as an antidote
to the overly favorable "press" enjoyed, in both ancient
and modern times, by the so-called Christian Emperors
Constantine and Theodosius I, however unfair passages like
II.32ff. with regard to the former and IV.27ff. with regard
to the latter may be. "And diff'ring judgments serve but to
declare That truth lies somewhere, if we knew but where."

(3) Zosimus' perpetuation of the later Neoplatonist
philosophy of history (as presented in, e.g., I.1, V.35, and
V.41) is of value for the student of historiography. Nevertheless, the canard (going back as far as Photius, the great
ninth-century patriarch of Constantinople) that Zosimus did

---

[1]Cf. also I.57f., III.32, and IV.21.

nothing more than abridge the work of the Neoplatonist historian and biographer Eunapius should at long last be laid to rest. For —

(4) Zosimus may not have handled his sources skillfully, but he handled a good many of them. He employed the Athenian Dexippus for the period 238-270, excerpting the best continuous history of that period. Thereafter, having given us our only trustworthy portrait of Queen Zenobia, he relied on Eunapius, whose work came down to the year 404, primarily but not exclusively (to take but one example, Ludwig Mendelssohn[1] showed conclusively Zosimus' debt to Magnus of Carrhae in his glowing narrative of the Emperor Julian). After Eunapius, Zosimus made use of the aforementioned Olympiodorus as his main source.[2]

(5) More important, however, than the actual sources Zosimus followed is the tradition he emulated, the tradition of the man of action (rather than of style) who wrote history. That Zosimus was no armchair historian is evident from the opening words of his history: ''Polybius of Megalopolis...'' As Polybius wrote of Rome's rise, which yet contained the seeds of Rome's fall, so Zosimus would dilate upon ''the good old days'' in Polybian vein. By and large he failed in his endeavor, although an occasional passage is worthy to be compared with Polybius: IV.57ff., V.4ff., V.27ff., V.38ff. (this last with a neat reminiscence of Thucydides). Such passages as these should serve to satisfy one's curiosity as to why Zosimus' history ever got published in the first place and why it managed to survive, right alongside the contemporaneous ecclesiastical histories of Sozomen and Socrates, down through the ages of the Faith.

---

[1] In the preface to his Teubner edition (Leipzig, 1887), pp. XXXIX ff.

[2] Not very deftly: see below, V.34n. In fact, from the point where it picks up Olympiodorus to the point where it runs out, Zosimus' text stands in sore need of a redactor.

The translation is based on the Mendelssohn edition already referred to, which is definitive in every respect. The few places where we have admitted readings at variance with Mendelssohn's are duly noted.

The problem of literalness has, as it must all translators, perplexed us. However, since the book was designed for the reader who is interested in the later Roman Empire but has little or no Greek, we have eschewed any inclination to manufacture silk purses. One practice adopted by us perhaps requires a word of explanation. Zosimus follows in the train of the great Greek and Roman historians in that he inserts a goodly number of speeches in his narrative of events. Most of them are in *oratio obliqua*, and these we have reproduced by enclosing them within single quotation marks.

The authors wish to acknowledge with appreciation the help given them by several people. They are especially indebted to Miss Marjorie L. A. Davis, who provided preliminary translations of Books II and III and supplied a number of useful notes. Miss Davis, who holds a master's degree from Indiana University, has taught in the classical departments of Illinois College, St. Olaf College, and the Centennial High School of Pueblo, Colorado.

The authors are also much indebted to Mrs. Adelynne Pope, managing editor of the Trinity University Press. She has given devoted attention to the arduous editorial duties incident to publication of the book. Nor should one neglect to mention the skillful work of the members of the Trinity Printer, who have turned the manuscript into type. The authors appreciate especially the help of Mrs. Doris Caylor, manager of the Trinity Printer, and Miss Mary Ashbrook, who corrected the proofs.

ZOSIMUS: HISTORIA NOVA

TABLE OF CONTENTS

THE DECLINE OF ROME

BOOK I

P olybius of Megalopolis, having undertaken to set down
the events of his own time that were worthy of remembrance, thought it correct to show through the evidence of
the facts themselves that the Romans, though they had
fought with their neighbors for 600 years after the founding of the city,[1] had not attained great power. But then,
having gained dominion over a certain part of Italy, which
they in turn lost after Hannibal's passage through it and
after their defeat at Cannae, and having seen the enemy
pressing upon their very walls, they were raised to such
great fortune that in scarcely fifty-three years' time they
had acquired not only Italy but all of Africa as well, while
in the West they had subdued the Spaniards. They sought
yet more: they crossed the Ionian Gulf, conquered the
Greeks and dissolved the Macedonians' realm, capturing
alive him who was currently their king[2] and taking him
back to Rome. Now of such things no one would attribute
the cause to human strength, but rather to the Fates' necessity, or the stars' revolutions, or God's will, which is attendant upon those pursuits of ours that are righteous. For
these agents impose a certain sequence of causation upon
future events, making them appear in such a way as to im-
plant in people who judge human affairs aright the opinion
that their administration is prescribed by providence: thus
spirits thrive during periods of productivity but, when

---

[1]Actually, Polybius begins his *Histories* with the 140th Olympiad
(220 B. C.), only 533 years after the traditional date of Rome's founding.   [2]Perseus, who reigned from 179 to 168 B. C.

sterility predominates, they decline to that condition which is now observed. What I am saying will of necessity be made manifest by the facts.

2. After the Trojan expedition until the battle of Marathon nothing worthy of telling appears to have been done by the Greeks in relation either to themselves or to any other people. But when Darius, through the agency of his lieutenants, marched against them with many myriads of troops, 8,000 Athenians, possessed of some divine impulse, armed themselves with what weapons came to hand and ran to do battle with the enemy. They won such a victory that they slew 90,000 men and drove the rest from their country. In and of itself this battle made Greece more conspicuous in world affairs. After Darius' death Xerxes provided himself with a much greater force (he filled the sea with ships and the land with foot soldiers in an attempt to lead all Asia against the Greeks). Inasmuch as he had to cross from Asia into Europe, as if the elements would not suffice to receive his army unless they robbed each other of their primary uses, the Hellespont was bridged over to provide passage for the foot soldiers and Athos was tunnelled through to receive the ships along with the sea. In the meantime, although Greece was terrified at the very news of the matter, she still armed as best she could and in the sea battles, first at Artemisium and secondly at Salamis, she gained a victory so much more illustrious than her previous one that Xerxes was glad to get away with his life. He had lost most of his army, and the rest were utterly destroyed at Plataea, bequeathing great glory to the Greeks, who thereby restored their fellow Greeks living in Asia to freedom and gained control over almost all the islands.

3. Indeed, if they had been constant allies, content with their present circumstances, and if the Athenians and Lacedaemonians had not had a mutual falling-out while contending with one another over the hegemony of the Greeks,

then Greece would never have experienced foreign over-
lords. But the Peloponnesian War diminished the Greeks'
fighting forces and reduced the city-states to poverty.
Thus arose for Philip an opportunity to expand the kingdom
to which he had succeeded — a kingdom the equal in
strength of no one of his neighbors — by certain cunning
devices: for he won over by means of money his own troops
and those of such allies as joined themselves to him, and
so from small beginnings became great enough to contend
in arms against the Athenians at Chaeronea. After his victory he showed himself mild and gentle to all. He was
already contemplating an invasion of the Persian kingdom
and was in the midst of collecting a suitable force for this
enterprise when he died.

4. Alexander assumed the kingdom and, having settled
matters in Greece on the spot, crossed over into Asia with
a goodly army in the third year of his reign. After he had
defeated without difficulty the satraps who opposed him, he
advanced against Darius himself, who with a vast army
occupied sites near Issus. There he engaged the Persians
and, having won a victory surpassing all belief and having
routed Darius, kept to the direct route to Phoenicia, Syria
and Syria Palaestina (the things he did in Tyre and Gaza
one may find out from the writings of the Alexander-histo-
rians). Thence he made his way into Egypt, where he paid
homage to Ammon and in right good fashion took the necessary steps for the founding of Alexandria. He then returned to make an end of his war against the Persians and,
finding all men friendly, he crossed into Mesopotamia.
After having learned that Darius had provided himself with a
much bigger army, he set out with what troops he had and
joined battle with him at Arbela. He came off so much superior that he killed almost all the enemy and, although
Darius did escape with a few men, the realm of the Persians was dissolved.

5. Thereafter Bessus killed Darius, and Alexander after his exploits in India returned to Babylon, where he departed this life. The government of the Macedonians was now divided into provinces and thus weakened by continual internecine wars. Fortune placed the remainder of Europe under the Romans, who indeed crossed into Asia and waged war against the kings of Pontus and against Antiochus, and later also against the rulers of Egypt. As a result they kept adding something to their empire year in and year out (so long as the authority of the aristocracy was maintained), because their consuls strove to outdo one another in feats of valor. But when the civil wars of Sulla and Marius and thereafter of Julius Caesar and Pompey the Great had destroyed the Republic, they abandoned the aristocracy and chose Octavian dictator. To his discretion they committed the entire administration without realizing that they had riskily entrusted this great power to the impulse and license of a single individual. For even if he should undertake to rule with rectitude and justice, he would not be able to do the right thing for everybody: e. g., he could not succor readily those who were separated from him by a very great distance. Again, he would not be able to discover enough magistrates who would be ashamed not to live up to a vote of confidence placed upon them. Moreover, he would not be able to accommodate so many diverse customs. If on the other hand he transgressed the limits of his power and got carried away into tyranny, upsetting the magistrates' offices, overlooking hanky-panky, thwarting justice with bribes, reducing subjects to the status of slaves (such has been the case with most autocrats, in fact almost all of them with few exceptions), then of course it followed of necessity that the brute power of him who got possession of authority spelled calamity for the public at large. For flatterers are plied at the hands of such a man with gifts and honors and attain the highest

offices, while gentlemen who prefer the life of leisure to the busy life naturally resent the fact that they do not enjoy the same benefits. And so it comes to pass that the cities are filled with sedition and riots: since civil and military offices are handed out to men who are not above corruption the results are to render civilian life unpleasant and distasteful for men of refinement and to weaken the soldiers' zeal in times of war.

6. Indeed, that these results are the case experience of events has clearly shown in itself. These events began in Octavian's reign, when the pantomimus' dance was introduced for the first time[1] by its co-promoters, Pylades and Bathyllus, as well as other things which have been responsible for much mischief right up to the present. Nevertheless Octavian appears to have wielded his power with moderation, especially after he heeded the precepts of Athenodorus the Stoic; but Tiberius, who succeeded to his realm, resorted to extreme cruelty and, having seemed intolerable to his subjects, was banished. He went into hiding on a certain island,[2] where he died. Thereafter Gaius Caligula, surpassing Tiberius in every form of unnatural conduct, was murdered by Chaereas, who through so daring a deed freed the state from bitter tyranny. Then Claudius, having committed the administration of his affairs to eunuchs who were freedmen, perished shamefully.[3] Next Nero and then his successors attained sole rule; concerning them I have decided to say nothing whatsoever, that there may be no record extant of their unbridled and monstrous actions. When Vespasian and his son Titus had been more temperate in the use of their power, Domitian, outdoing all in savagery, licentiousness and avarice, despoiled the State

---

[1]The year was 22 B. C.   [2]Capri, where Tiberius repaired (at the suggestion of the treacherous praetorian prefect Sejanus) in 26 A. D. and lived until his death eleven years later.

[3]In 54 A. D., reportedly from a dish of poisoned mushrooms handed him by his fourth wife (and niece) Agrippina.

for all of fifteen years until, killed by one of his freedmen, Stephanus, he was seen to pay the full penalty for his wickedness.

7. Thereafter good men assumed the principate: Nerva and Trajan and then Hadrian and Antoninus Pius and the pair of brothers Verus and Lucius.[1] They set right many wrongs, and not only did they regain what their predecessors had lost but also they made some new acquisitions. Then there assumed power Marcus' son Commodus, who was addicted both to tyranny and to unnatural acts. When he had been murdered by his concubine Marcia, who had adopted a manly spirit, Pertinax was chosen to rule. But the praetorian soldiers could not endure his strictness concerning military training and discipline as well and killed him in unseemly fashion. Rome almost underwent a revolution as the soldiery designated to guard the palace appropriated to themselves the right of setting up a monarch, having violently taken the decision in this matter away from the Senate. When the throne was put up for sale Didius Julianus, at the instigation of his wife and out of folly rather than soundness of mind, produced the money and bought it, presenting a spectacle the likes of which the world had never before seen. For he was led into the palace, not by the Senate nor by any other legitimate escort of attendants, but merely by the soldiers who had set him up in this position, forcibly delivering over to him the palace and all its contents. But he was simultaneously exalted and destroyed by those who led him there, having survived no longer than a dream lasts.

8. The Senate again convened for the purpose of considering whom the rule ought to be bestowed upon, and Severus was declared Emperor. But when Albinus and

---

[1]The adopted sons of Antoninus Pius; Verus is better known as Marcus Aurelius while Lucius (his junior by nine years) is better known as L. Aurelius Verus.

Niger pretended to the same rule there arose over them far from insignificant civil wars: cities split apart, some living upon one side, some on the other. After a big stir was caused throughout the East and Egypt and the Byzantines (who, favoring Niger's cause, had received him) ran a tremendous risk, Severus' side won out. Niger was killed first, and then Albinus departed his life along with his realm, leaving the sole command of affairs to Severus. Thereupon he turned his attention to correcting matters which had been handled sloppily, and first of all he prosecuted sharply those soldiers who had murdered Pertinax and committed the Empire to Julianus. Secondly, he addressed himself diligently to military matters; attacking the Persians, he took Ctesiphon and Babylon with one onset and then, running over the nomadic Arabs, he subdued all of Arabia. Many other things he managed nobly: he was inexorable towards delinquents and, confiscating the property of those who stood accused of outrageous acts, (9) he adorned many of the cities with sumptuous buildings.

He appointed his own son Antoninus[1] Emperor and, when about to die, designated both him and his other son Geta as heirs to the throne, leaving as their guardian Papinian, a very just man and one who excelled all the Roman jurisconsults before and after him in both knowledge and interpretation of law. This man, who was praetorian prefect, Antoninus regarded with suspicion, for no other reason than that Papinian, perceiving Antoninus' hostile intent against his brother Geta, was impeding his plots insofar as he could. Therefore, wishing to remove this impediment, he contrived Papinian's slaughter through the agency of his soldiers. The way was now[2] clear for him

---

[1]Commonly known as Caracalla.   [2]Zosimus alone of our sources (which here include Dio and Herodian) — almost surely mistakenly — places Papinian's death before Geta's.

to kill his brother; not even their mother,[1] to whom his brother had run, was able to rescue him.

10. Not long afterward indeed Antoninus paid the penalty for fratricide, at the hands of an unknown assassin. Now the soldiers at Rome named Macrinus (who was praetorian prefect) Emperor, while those in the East named a young man from Emesa who was related by birth to Antoninus' mother.[1] When each army held out for its own nominee civil discord ensued: the supporters of Antoninus of Emesa were leading him to Rome while the soldiers of Macrinus set out from Italy. The armies fell to with each other at Antioch in Syria and Macrinus was thoroughly beaten. Having abandoned his camp in flight, he was captured at the strait between Byzantium and Chalcedon and died, his body lacerated.

11. After Antoninus' victory he proceeded against the partisans of Macrinus as though they were enemies. He lived a shameless, disgraceful life, particularly in that he consorted with magi and vagabonds and profaned things sacred. The Romans could not stand his extravagant licentiousness; they murdered him and dismembered the corpse. They then designated as Emperor Alexander, who also was descended from the family of Severus. Being still youthful and well endowed by nature, he caused everybody to hold high hopes for the Empire. Flavianus and Chrestus were appointed praetorian prefects, men not unskilled in military matters and singularly competent to manage civil affairs. However, when the Emperors' mother Mamaea appointed Ulpian as his overseer and partner in power, as it were (for he was both a most excellent jurisconsult and capable of regulating the present and divining the

---

[1]Geta's and Caracalla's (i. e., Antoninus') mother was the remarkable Julia Domna. A Syrian, she was also the great-aunt of the future Emperor Marcus Aurelius Antoninus (Elagabalus), a native of Emesa.

future keenly), the soldiers took offence at this and secretly contrived his destruction. But Mamaea got wind of this plot and anticipated it by immediately doing away with its authors. Ulpian was now made sole holder of the praetorian prefectship. Nevertheless, because he had come under the army's suspicion (why exactly, I cannot say, for differing stories have been handed down concerning his character) a riot was started and he was killed, and not even the Emperor was able to come to his aid.

12. Afterwards the soldiers little by little backed away from their earlier good will toward Alexander and revealed themselves as less enthusiastic to obey his orders. Then fearful lest they suffer for their indolence, they incited sedition: they conspired to place Antoninus in power. But he, not being able to stand up under the weight of the office, disappeared in flight; and a certain Uranius[1] of servile descent was designated and, decked out in the purple, was immediately led before Alexander. As the hatred of the Emperor kept increasing, he was perplexed about the turn of events. Both physically and mentally he was a changed man: he was afflicted with the disease of avarice and devoted himself to the collection of funds, which he deposited with his mother.

13. His affairs being in this unhealthy state, the armies stationed in Pannonia and Moesia, which even earlier had been averse from him, were now the more ready for revolt. Taking a revolutionary course they raised to power Maximinus, who at the time was commander of the Pannonian troops. And Maximinus, having collected the forces around him, started for Italy, thinking that he would rather easily set upon the Emperor unprepared. But Alexander, who was sojourning among the peoples along the Rhine, when he learned of the revolutionary movements, made straight for

---

[1]Zosimus is confused: Antoninus and Uranius are actually one and the same man, Uranius Antoninus.

Rome. He promised the soldiers and Maximinus as well forgiveness if they would desist from their undertaking but, since he was unable to win them over, he jettisoned all hope and gave himself up in one way or another to slaughter. When Mamaea left the palace along with the prefects for the purpose of putting down the tumult she was herself killed, and with her the prefects.

Now that Maximinus' hold upon the Empire was secure, all were repentant because they had exchanged a moderate rule for a bitter tyranny. For Maximinus was of obscure lineage and, upon assuming office, what gains had naturally accrued to him he immediately forfeited by his licentious use of power. To all he was intolerable; not only did he insult magistrates but he also conducted affairs with all manner of savagery. Sycophants alone he cultivated, those sycophants who informed against men that preferred to stay out of the limelight - as if these latter owed the imperial treasury something. Eventually, owing to his lust for their money, he even resorted to men's death without trial, and he appropriated to himself all the cities by divesting their inhabitants of their own property.

14. The nations subject to the Romans were oppressed by his excessive cruelty and upset by his manifest graspingness. The inhabitants of Africa designated as Emperors Gordian and his son of the same name, and sent legates to Rome, among whom was Valerian, a man of consular rank who later reigned as Emperor. The Senate was well pleased with this act and was preparing the ejection of the tyrant, both inciting the soldiers to rebellion and reminding the people of the wrongs done each privately and all publicly. Since there was general accord, they selected twenty Senators who were skilled in military strategy and from this number singled out two, Balbinus and Maximus, as commanders-in-chief. Then, having blockaded the roads leading to Rome, they stood ready for insurrection.

15. But Maximinus, after these things had been reported to him, set out for Rome with his Moorish and Celtic troops. When those who had been assigned to guard Aquileia closed their gates to him they were besieged. Then his own partisans, at long last embracing the cause of the commonwealth, gave their blessing to those who wanted Maximinus killed. Reduced to a state of extreme peril, he presented his son as a suppliant before the soldiers, as if he might be able owing to his age to change their anger to pity. But they were roused to greater wrath and slew the young man in lamentable fashion and then at once slaughtered the Emperor. Some one seized the head, severed it from the body and brought it to Rome, exhibiting it as a sure sign of victory. Thus liberated from fear, they now awaited the arrival from Africa of the Emperors.

16. However, they had perished in a storm while sailing. The Senate now handed over the administration of affairs to Gordian III, son of Gordian II.[1] In this Emperor's reign the Roman people recovered from their former dejection as he diverted them with theatrical and gymnastic contests. But when all had been resuscitated from a deep torpor, as it were, a clandestine plot was laid against the Emperor, Maximus and Balbinus [2] putting certain soldiers up to it. Following its detection both those who had started

---

[1] Zosimus has been employing an inferior source since Chapter 14. Herodianus orders the events of the year 238 (through which he lived and at which he ended his *Histories*) as follows: (1) proclamation of the two Gordians as Emperors; (2) death of the two Gordians (but not at sea: Gordian II was slain by Capellianus at Carthage, and his father committed suicide shortly thereafter); (3) murder of Maximinus and his son; (4) appointment by the Senate of Balbinus and Pupienus Maximus, who were assassinated after a reign of two months; (5) salutation by the praetorian guard of Gordian III (the nephew, not the son, of Gordian II).

[2] Once again Zosimus is in error, as Maximus and Balbinus were already dead: cf. the preceding footnote.

the mischief and the many who were privy to it were killed.

17. Not much later even the Carthaginians became alienated from the Emperor's good will and promoted Sabinianus for the throne. But when Gordian called up his African forces their wills were reconciled to him and, having delivered up the man who aimed at the tyranny, they received pardon and release from imminent peril. Meanwhile Gordian married the daughter of Timesicles, a man celebrated for his learning. By making him praetorian prefect he appeared to make up for his own deficiencies, owing to his tender age, in the administration of affairs.[1]

18. Now that his hold on the Empire was secure, the Persians were expected to make an attack upon the nations of the East, since Sapor had just succeeded Artaxerxes, the King who had recovered the government from the Parthians and restored it to the Persians. For after the time of Alexander the Great and of the Diadochs, when Antiochus ɪɪ was ruling over the upper satrapies, the Parthian Arsaces, incensed at the spiteful treatment of his brother Tiridates, made war against Antiochus' satrap and furnished occasion to the Parthians to eject the Macedonians and to claim the kingdom for themselves. Accordingly the Emperor was now going against the Persians with all his resources. Although the Roman army was seen to have conquered in the first engagement, the death of Timesicles the praetorian prefect greatly weakened the Emperor's confidence in the security of his throne. Indeed, after Philip had been appointed to succeed Timesicles, gradually the soldiers' good will towards the Emperor evaporated. For Philip was a native of Arabia, a worthless nation, nor did he progress, along with his fortune, for the better: as

---

[1]Gordian was a mere sixteen years of age when (241) he appointed his father-in-law (whose real name was Timesitheus, not Timesicles) praetorian prefect.

soon as he had assumed his office he developed a lust for
the Empire and made friends of those soldiers who were
inclined toward revolution. He discerned that an abundance
of military supplies was being brought in and the Emperor
was still staying with the army in the vicinity of Carrhae
and Nisibis. Philip himself ordered the ships which held
the soldiers' provisions to move up-country, so that the
army, oppressed by hunger and the lack of necessities,
might be provoked to sedition.

19. Events turned out according to his plan. The soldiers, using as pretext their want of necessaries, in disorderly fashion surrounded Gordian and killed him as if he
were responsible for the wasting away of the army and, as
per their agreement, they draped the purple around Philip.
He swore a treaty of friendship with Sapor and, the war
over, set out for Rome. Courting the soldiery with great
largesse, he dispatched messengers to Rome to announce
that Gordian had died of a disease. Having reached Rome
and having wooed the senatorial order with plausible words,
he felt he should grant the highest offices to his own relatives. He placed his brother Priscus in command of the
Syrian forces and entrusted the troops in Moesia and Macedonia to his brother-in-law Severianus.

20. Thus supposing his Empire secure, he himself
marched against the Carpi, who were at the time laying
waste the regions around the Danube. In the ensuing battle
the barbarians did not withstand the assault, but fled to a
certain fortress and there were besieged. As soon as they
observed that their side, which had been scattered hither
and yon, was again assembled, their courage revived and
they went out to meet the Roman army. But they could not
sustain the charge of the Mauretanians and sued for peace.
To this Philip consented quite affably and withdrew, as
many disturbances were at this very moment upsetting his
affairs. On the one hand the Eastern provinces, vexed

because of the tribute exactions and because Priscus, who had been placed in command of the nations there, was intolerable to one and all, resorted to revolution and promoted Jotapianus for the imperium; on the other hand the troops in Moesia and Pannonia promoted Marinus.

21. Perturbed by these things Philip asked the Senate either to assist him in such troubles or at any rate, if displeased with his rule, to release him from it. No response whatsoever was made, whereupon Decius, a man of distinguished family and rank besides being adorned with every virtue, said that 'he was foolish to be anxious over these things, which would of themselves disappear the more readily because they could gain backing from no quarter.' Though matters fell out in the way Decius on the basis of his own experience had conjectured, Jotapianus and Marinus being removed with no great effort, nevertheless Philip continued to be afraid, conscious as he was of the soldiers' hatred toward his commanding officers in those places. Accordingly he invited Decius to take over the command of the forces in Moesia and Pannonia, but the latter begged off in the belief that this would be of no advantage either to himself or to Philip. Employing the so-called Thessalian persuasion [1] Philip dispatched Decius to Pannonia to chastise those who there had sided with Marinus. But the soldiers there, seeing Decius prosecuting the offenders, believed it would be in their own best interests if they could shake off the danger confronting them and simultaneously set up as Emperor one who would both look after the commonweal better than Philip and would effortlessly surpass him in political excellence and military experience.

22. Therefore they threw the purple around Decius and, although he shuddered at the prospect, they pushed him against his will into the administration of affairs. When this appointment was proclaimed to Philip he collected

[1] The English Hobson's choice.

his army and moved to the attack. Decius' cohorts, although they realized that the enemy was numerically much greater, were nonetheless confident, relying on Decius' skill and foresight in everything. When the two armies clashed, the one superior in number, the other in generalship, many on Philip's side fell; among the casualties was he himself, together with his son, whom he had elevated to the rank of Caesar.[1] And thus Decius gained control of the Empire.

23. Now owing to Philip's sloth everywhere things were in utter disarray. The Scythians had crossed the Tanais and were plundering places in the vicinity of Thrace. Decius went out against them and in every encounter was victorious. In addition he recovered the booty they had taken. He was endeavoring to prevent their retiring homeward, intending to wipe them out altogether lest they regroup their forces and make a new irruption. Having stationed Gallus on the bank of the Tanais with a sufficiently large force, he himself with the remainder of his men went against the enemy. As matters were succeeding for him according to plan Gallus devoted himself to revolution and sent legates to the barbarians inviting them to join in his plot against Decius. When the barbarians welcomed Gallus' proposal most heartily, he kept at his watch on the bank of the Tanais while they split themselves into three divisions, of which the first was drawn up in a place shielded in front by a swamp. After Decius' destruction of many from this first division the second came up; it too was routed. Of the third division only a few men revealed themselves hard by the swamp. When Gallus signaled Decius to rush through the swamp against these, in ignorance of the lay of the land he proceeded imprudently and got stuck in the mud together with the forces he had with him. He and they alike, no one being able to escape, perished as the barbarians

---

[1] Actually, this son (Philip II) had been elevated to the rank of Augustus in 247, two years before his death.

rained javelins upon them from every angle. Such was the end of Decius, who had been a very good Emperor.

24. Gallus succeeded to the Empire and designated as his colleague his son Volusianus, all but shouting aloud that it was by his contriving that Decius and his army were destroyed. The condition of the barbarians now began to prosper. For not only did Gallus permit them to return with their loot inside their borders, but he also promised to pay them annually a certain sum of money and granted them license to lead away the most nobly born of the captives, the majority of whom had been taken at the sack of Philippopolis in Thrace.

25. Having settled matters thus Gallus arrived at Rome, priding himself upon the peace struck with the barbarians. At the outset indeed he kept making favorable mention of Decius' reign, even adopting that one of his sons who was still alive. But with the passage of time, having grown fearful lest some of those who were accustomed to revolutionary projects, recapitulating the virtues of Decius as Emperor, might deliver the Empire over to his son, he plotted his death, taking no account either of his adoption or of honorableness.

26. Since Gallus handled his office in negligent fashion the Scythians first terrorized the nations in their neighborhood and then proceeded down the line to lay waste those as far as the sea; as a result not a single nation subject to Roman sway was left unpillaged by them, and almost every unwalled town was captured, along with a majority of those that were fortified. Yet with the war pressing upon them from every direction a plague besides hit the towns and villages and destroyed whatever human life was left. Never before, indeed, in the preceding centuries had so great a loss of human beings been suffered.

27. Thus matters stood: the Emperors were in no wise able to defend the State but neglected all affairs outside of

Rome and once more the Goths, Borani, Urugundi, and
Carpi were sacking the cities of Europe, appropriating whatever remained in them. Meanwhile the Persians invaded
Asia, occupied Mesopotamia, and progressed into Syria
even as far as Antioch itself. They seized this metropolis
of the entire East, killing some of the inhabitants and taking
others captive. Then, having razed absolutely every building, private and public, in the city with no one whatsoever
interfering, they returned home with an untold amount of
booty. And in truth all Asia would have been acquired
easily by the Persians had they not, overjoyed at the immense quantity of their plunder, in their zeal been concerned only about getting it back home safely.

28. Likewise all the Scythians of Europe, living in complete security, had now crossed over into Asia and laid
waste everything as far as Cappadocia, Pessinus, and
Ephesus. Aemilianus, leader of the Pannonian contingents,
having emboldened insofar as he could the soldiers under
his command, who lacked the courage to stand up against
the barbarians in their prosperity, and having reminded
them of the Romans' reputation, made a surprise attack
on the barbarians found in those regions. Having killed a
great part of them, he now even led his soldiers into their
territory, cut down whatever he came upon of a sudden,
liberated the Roman subjects contrary to their every expectation from the barbarians' madness, and was hailed
as Emperor by his own soldiers. Thereupon collecting his
forces, who had become more courageous as a result of
their victory over the barbarians, he moved on Italy,
wanting to engage Gallus in battle unprepared. The latter,
ignorant of what had happened in the East, was arming
himself with what was conveniently near; he dispatched
Valerian to fetch the Celtic and Germanic legions. When
Aemilianus had marched into Italy with great speed and
the armies were close to each other, Gallus' soldiers,

keeping in view the facts that their leader was far inferior in manpower and besides that he was a slothful, careless man, killed him along with his son. They joined Aemilianus' ranks and appeared to strengthen his regime.

29. Valerian, however, was leading his vast number of trans-Alpine troops into Italy and was eager to fight it out with Aemilianus. When the latter's men saw that their leader approached matters in the manner of a soldier rather than of an Emperor, they killed him as being unsuitable to reign.

Valerian, having by common consent succeeded to the imperial power, took pains to administer affairs well. But the Scythians had emerged from their abodes, and the Marcomanni besides, and they were assaulting and despoiling places bordering upon the Roman Empire. Thessalonica stood in utmost peril: her siege was raised with difficulty and great effort owing to the staunch resistance of those inside, but all Greece was harassed with troubles. Indeed, the Athenians began to fix their wall, of which no care had been taken ever since its destruction by Sulla; the Peloponnesians were fortifying the Isthmus, and from all of Greece there sprang up a common guard for the safety of the region.

30. Valerian, observing the peril that threatened all parts of the Roman Empire, appointed as his partner in government his son Gallienus. With matters pressing everywhere, he himself headed for the Orient to oppose the Persians and handed over the European forces to his son, exhorting him to use these in resistance to the barbarians, who were making irruptions from all quarters. Gallienus, noting that the German tribes were more troublesome than the rest and that they were a quite vexatious annoyance to the Celts who dwelt around the Rhine, personally took the field against them there; while against those who were bent on plundering property in Italy, Illyria,

and Greece he instructed his generals with armies in
those places to wage war. He positioned himself as best
he could to guard against crossings of the Rhine in one way
or another. But he was up against it, fighting a vast host
with a greatly inferior force. By making a treaty with one
of the chiefs of the German tribes he appeared in turn to
diminish the danger, for this man prevented the other
barbarians' constant crossing of the Rhine and obstructed
attackers. Such, then, was the condition of those dwelling
along the Rhine.

31. Meanwhile the Borani and Goths and Carpi and Urugundi (these are the peoples who live around the Danube)
would leave no part of Italy or of Illyria immune from devastation, but ranged over everything with no one to stop
them. Indeed, the Borani tried to cross over into Asia, and
succeeded in the attempt rather easily thanks to the inhabitants of the Bosporus, who through fear rather than any
inclination gave them boats and conducted their passage.
For as long as they had a monarchy transmitted from
father to son, because of either friendship for Rome or
commercial facility or the gifts sent them annually by the
kings, they continued to thwart the Scythians' desire to
cross into Asia. But with the royal line extinct certain
worthless and abject persons had become established in
power; they were fearful for themselves and granted the
Scythians passage into Asia via the Bosporus, transporting
them in their own boats, first outward and then homeward
bound.

32. While the Scythians were plundering everything in
sight those who lived along the shore of the Euxine retreated inland to places heavily fortified. The barbarians
first attacked Pityus, a place with a very large protective
wall and a harbor affording very safe anchorage. Successianus, who had been placed in charge of the soldiery there,
with his force resisted the barbarians and chased them off.

The Scythians were afraid lest the men in the other fortresses might find out what had happened, take their stand beside the soldiers of Pityus, and completely destroy them. They got hold of as many boats as they could and at very great peril returned home, having lost many of their own in the war over Pityus. Then those living on the Euxine Sea, having been preserved by Successianus' leadership as we have described, did not expect the Scythians (they who had been repulsed in the manner aforesaid) ever to repeat the voyage. However, when Valerian had summoned Successianus to him, appointed him praetorian prefect, and discussed with him the affairs of Antioch and its restoration, the Scythians again took boats from the people of the Bosporus and made the crossing. But this time they kept the boats, not as before allowing the people of the Bosporus to take them back home. They anchored off Phasis, where there is said to be located the shrine of Phasian Diana and the palace of Aeëtes. Having tried but failed to seize the shrine, they made straight for Pityus.

33. They took the stronghold with the greatest of ease, stripped it of its garrison, and moved on ahead. Being well supplied with boats, using as sailors the captives who knew how to row, and enjoying calm weather during nearly the entire summer, they made for Trapezus, a large and populous city which besides the customary soldiery had taken in an additional force of 10,000 men. When they began to besiege the city, they did not even dream, much less hope, that they would conquer it, surrounded as it was by two walls. But, observing that the soldiers, given to indolence and drunkenness, no longer bothered to climb to their posts as they let nothing interfere with their wanton drinking-parties, they moved trees which they had long ago gotten ready for the purpose against the wall wherewith to scale it. Little by little in the nighttime they climbed up these and took the city. The soldiers within

were struck dumb by the sudden and unexpected nature of
the assault. Some of them slipped out of town by another
gate; the rest were destroyed by the enemy. The city
having been captured in this manner, the barbarians gained
mastery over untold amounts of money and captives; for it
so happened that nearly all those in its vicinity had flocked
into it as being a stronghold. Having destroyed the temples,
edifices, and everything else fashioned for beauty or im-
pressiveness, and having overrun to boot the entire countryside, with their very great fleet of ships they went back
home.

34. When the neighbors of the Scythians saw the wealth
brought by them, they became desirous of accomplishing
similar feats. They started to build boats, the work on
which was done by those who were their captives or else
who had commercial dealings with them. But they decided
not to make the voyage in the same way as had the Borani,
on the grounds that it would be long and hard and through
areas already sacked. Thus, having waited for winter, with
the Euxine Sea on their left and their infantry force keeping
up by running as fast as they could on the shore to their
right, they passed by Istrus, Tomi, and Anchialus and came
to Lake Phileatina, which lies near the Euxine in a westerly
direction from Byzantium. Realizing that fishermen lay
in hiding along with their boats in the marshes adjacent
to the lake, they came to terms with them, embarked their
infantry in their boats, and made their way through the
strait separating Byzantium and Chalcedon. Now there was
a garrison in Chalcedon itself and as far out as the shrine
near the sea's entrance that greatly outnumbered the invaders; but some of the soldiers left as if forsooth desirous of
meeting a general sent by the Emperor, while others were
seized by such trepidation that as soon as they heard the
news they fled at full tilt. When this happened the barbarians at once made the crossing and, taking Chalcedon

without resistance, they gained possession of money and armor and other paraphernalia in the greatest quantity.

35. They made for Nicomedia, a very great and prosperous city, well-known for its riches and resources of all kinds. When its inhabitants had gotten advance notice about the barbarians they anticipated their arrival by running off, carrying as much wealth as they were able; nevertheless, the barbarians were astonished at the total of what they found, and they paid their best respects to Chrysogonus, who had long since been urging them to go to Nicomedia. Having assaulted, in much the same way and with the same results, Nicaea and Cius and Apamea and Prusa, they sought Cyzicus. However, the Rhyndacus River was swollen owing to heavy rains, and they could not cross it. They then turned back and burned Nicomedia and Nicaea. Having thrown their spoils aboard wagons and boats they were purposing to journey homeward, thus bringing to a close the second invasion.

36. Although Valerian had heard about the situation in Bithynia, in no one of his generals did he have the confidence to undertake a war of vengeance upon the barbarians. He sent Felix to guard Byzantium and removed himself from Antioch to Cappadocia. After having merely afflicted the cities along the way he made an about-face. But, vhen the plague hit camp and wiped out the greater part of his men, Sapor invaded the Eastern frontier and there was a mass upheaval. Valerian owing to his effeminate, loose way of life despaired of retrieving a situation that had become critical and, wanting to terminate the war by a payment of money, he sent ambassadors to this end to Sapor. The latter dismissed them, their mission unaccomplished, and demanded that the Emperor come in person and treat of those matters which he thought required negotiation. To this request the Emperor imprudently consented and, accompanied by only a few men, recklessly went to Sapor.

Suddenly, as he started to converse with him about a truce, he was seized by the enemy. Reduced to the rank of a prisoner of war he died among the Persians, bequeathing the Roman name a heritage most shameful to future generations.

37. Such was the situation over-all in the East: confusion, defenselessness. But the Scythians had formed into one league all their peoples and nations: one part of them was pillaging Illyria and sacking the cities there while another part had reached Italy and was advancing on Rome itself. With Gallienus quartered beyond the Alps intent upon the German wars, the Senate, seeing Rome driven to the brink of disaster, armed as many soldiers as were in the city and gave weapons also to those of the populace who were in the best of health, thus assembling an army which outnumbered the barbarians. This was the very thing the enemy feared, and they left R o m e; but they attacked and afflicted almost all of Italy. The situation in Illyria likewise was serious as a result of the Scythians' invasion.

With the entire Roman Empire reeling in the direction of ultimate annihilation, a plague the likes of which had never throughout all time occurred broke out in the cities. It lightened the calamities inflicted by the barbarians, and caused those who were become sick to account happy both themselves and the cities that, having already been captured, were altogether destitute of men.

38. Disturbed by all these things, Gallienus was journeying back to Rome in order to dispose of the war visited upon Italy by the Scythians. Meanwhile there rose up against him Memor the Moor and Aureolus and Antoninus and many more men, almost all of whom were brought to punishment; Aureolus continued of hostile mind towards the Emperor. In addition Postumus, who had been entrusted with the military command among the Celts, was induced

to lead a revolution. With the soldiers who were his fellow conspirators he marched on Agrippina, a very great city situated on the Rhine. There he besieged Saloninus, Gallienus' son, insisting that unless he surrendered to him the siege would not be stopped. The soldiers under pressure of the siege delivered over not only Saloninus but also Silvanus, whom the Emperor had appointed his son's guardian. Postumus, having slain them both, was now autocrat among the Celts.

39. Now the Scythians were despoiling Greece, having stormed Athens itself. Gallienus was on his way to battle against those who had already occupied Thrace. The situation in the East being desperate, he ordered to come to its rescue Odaenathus of Palmyra, a man whose ancestry had been held in honor by the Emperors. This man, when he had mixed in as many of his own men as he could with the army that had been left there, attacked Sapor in force. He recovered the cities then held by the Persians, including Nisibis, which had been taken by Sapor and favored the Persian cause; Odaenathus attacked it, seized it and leveled it. When he had advanced as far as Ctesiphon, not once but twice, he confined the Persians within their own fortifications; they were happy just saving their children and their wives and themselves. He now took personal charge of righting affairs throughout the devastated land, insofar as he could. Thereafter, when he was staying at Emesa and celebrating a friend's birthday, he was slain by treachery. Zenobia succeeded to the management of affairs. The wife of Odaenathus, she was endowed with a man's mind and, with the help of her husband's friends, exercised equal diligence in administration.

40. Such being the condition in the East, it was now announced to Gallienus as he persevered in his warfare against the Scythians that Aureolus, commander of the entire cavalry, who had been stationed in the city of Med-

iolanum to watch Postumus' passage into Italy, had resorted
to revolution and was ambitious to become Emperor. Upset
by this news, Gallienus at once made ready for the journey
to Italy, leaving in charge of the war with the Scythians
Marcianus, a man thoroughly trained in military affairs.
While this man handled the war successfully, Gallienus
en route to Italy encountered the following plot. Heraclianus
the praetorian prefect was laying plans for Gallienus'
death, having taken into his confidence Claudius, who appeared to be second to the Emperor in the administration
of affairs. He commissioned to perpetrate the deed a man
most ready for such matters who was commander of a
squadron of Dalmatians. This man, standing over Gallienus
while he was at dinner and reporting that one of the scouts
had announced the approach of Aureolus and his troops, by
such talk caused alarm. Thereupon the Emperor, calling
for arms and springing aboard his horse, passed the word
to the soldiers that they arm themselves and follow, and
off he rode without even his bodyguard. The squad commander, seeing him thus unprotected, killed him.

41. When the soldiers at their leaders' bidding had
quieted down, Claudius succeeded to the supreme power,
which indeed had been given him even before this time by
common consent. Aureolus, who for a long period of time
had stayed out of Gallienus' clutches, at once sent an embassy concerning peace to Claudius. Having given himself
up he was slain by the Emperor's guards, who were still
angry with him on account of his defection.

42. At this point as many of the Scythians as had survived, encouraged by their earlier successful expeditions,
allied with themselves the Heruli, Peuci and Goths and
mustered by the Dniester River, which discharges itself
into the Euxine Sea. Having built 6,000 boats and having
embarked on these 320,000 men, they sailed to Tomi, a
walled city. In their attempt to take it they were repulsed

and, putting to sea, proceeded as far as Marcianopolis, which is in Moesia. Failing to take it also, they sailed on, having the wind at their stern. When they reached the narrows of the Propontis, their great number of ships could not withstand the swiftness of the current: the transport vessels collided with one another while the light boats were scattered in disarray. The steersmen let go their rudders, so that some ships sank men and all. some ran aground abandoned by their men. Over-all, a multitude of men and vessels were destroyed.

43. For this reason the barbarians retired slowly from the strait of the Propontis and navigated toward Cyzicus. Nothing accomplished there, they slipped away and sailed via the Hellespont through to Mount Athos, where they repaired their boats. They laid siege to Cassandrea and Thessalonica and by bringing machines up against their walls came within an ace of capturing them. But when they learned that the Emperor was approaching they went up into the interior and started plundering the countryside around Doberus and Pelagonia. In these parts they lost 3,000 men because they fell in with the Dalmatian cavalry; with their remaining men they fought the Emperor's troop. Battle having been joined and men having fallen on both sides, the Romans were in the act of fleeing by unfamiliar roads when they came upon 50,000 barbarians unexpectedly and slew them. A portion of the Scythians, sailing about Thessaly and Greece, were devastating scattered places there. Not being able to invade towns, since these had taken the precaution of building walls and other defenses, they were abducting the men they found in the fields.

44. The Scythians, then, were dispersed as I have recounted and had lost a great part of their men. Zenobia meanwhile, desirous of bigger things, sent Zabdas into Egypt, where a certain Timagenes was seeking the dominion

over his country for Palmyra. An army numbering upwards
of 70,000 Palmyrenes, Syrians, and barbarians was collected, against which were pitted 50,000 Egyptians. After
a fierce battle the Palmyrenes were victorious by a large
margin; they set up a garrison of 5,000 men and withdrew.
Now Probus, who had been appointed by the Emperor to
rid the sea of pirates, when informed that Egypt was occupied by the Palmyrenes, with his own force plus as many
of the Egyptians as did not favor the Palmyrene cause set
upon the garrison and ejected it. The Palmyrenes took
the field once again, and Probus collected an army of
Egyptians and Africans which conquered and drove the
Palmyrenes from the bounds of Egypt. But when Probus
occupied a mountain in the neighborhood of Babylon, thus
shutting off the enemy's passage into Syria, Timagenes,
as he had knowledge of the region, gained the top of the
mountain together with 2,000 Palmyrenes, attacked the
Egyptians unawares, and destroyed them, including Probus
who when taken captive committed suicide.

45. With Egypt now in the hands of the Palmyrenes,
the barbarian survivors of the battle fought at Naissus[1]
between Claudius and the Scythians were making their way
into Macedonia, protecting themselves with their wagons.
However, being famished owing to a scarcity of provisions,
they and their draft animals together were perishing. The
Roman cavalry went to meet them as they proceeded,
killed many, and made the rest betake themselves to the
Haemus Range[2] where, surrounded by the Roman army,
they suffered great losses. After this, the Emperor's infantry and cavalry being at variance with each other, he
decided that the former should fight it out with the bar-

---

[1]A town in Moesia; the battle is that mentioned in chapter 43
above, in which 50,000 barbarians reportedly were slain.

[2]These mountains separate Moesia and Thrace.

barians; a strenuous battle ensued in which the Romans were routed. When not a few had been slain the cavalry put in an appearance and moderated the infantry's sense of failure.

46. The Scythians kept marching further on and the Romans kept pursuing them. Meanwhile the barbarians who had sailed around Crete and Rhodes retired, having accomplished nothing worth the telling. Plague took them all, some dying in Thrace, some in Macedonia. Those who came through safely either were received into the Roman legions or, having received land, devoted themselves to agriculture. The plague seized the Romans as well: many in the army died, as did Claudius, outstanding in every virtue, whose death produced much mourning among his subjects.

47. Claudius' brother Quintillus was now declared Emperor. He lived only a few months, accomplishing nothing noteworthy, whereupon Aurelian ascended the imperial throne. According to certain of the historians Quintillus was advised by his friends, at the time of learning that the imperial power had been made over to Aurelian, to withdraw and voluntarily stand aside from office in favor of a far better man. He is reported to have done so: a vein being opened by one of his physicians, he bled to death.

48. Aurelian, secure in his power, went on the march from Rome to Aquileia and thence to the people of Pannonia, whom he had learned the Scythians were set to attack. He sent scouts telling them to convey inside their cities grain and cattle and everything else that would be useful to the enemy; he thus intended to increase the hunger which pressed upon the enemy. After the barbarians had crossed the river into Pannonia a well-matched battle was fought, such that when night came on the victory was a toss-up between the two sides. But that same night the

barbarians recrossed the river and at daybreak sent legates to sue for peace.

49. Having heard that the Alemanni and their near neighbors had decided to assail Italy, the Emperor, naturally more concerned about Rome and its vicinity than about Pannonia, left behind a sizable garrison and headed for Italy. Having joined battle at the border of Pannonia near the Danube, he killed many myriads of the barbarians. Meanwhile the situation around Rome had also been in turmoil as certain Senators were brought to trial on the grounds of plotting together against the Emperor and were sentenced to death. Rome was now surrounded with a wall, having previously been unwalled; the task, although begun by Aurelian, was completed during Probus' reign. And now there came under suspicion of revolutionary activity Septimius and Urbanus and Domitianus; they were immediately apprehended and punished.

50. Affairs throughout Italy and Pannonia having been handled in this manner, the Emperor was planning an expedition against the Palmyrenes, who now held dominion over the nations of Egypt and the entire East as far as Ancyra in Galatia and would have laid claim to even more, namely, as far as Chalcedon in Bithynia, had not the people there, upon learning that Aurelian had been made Emperor, shaken off the Palmyrene faction. Thereupon, as the Emperor advanced with his army, first Ancyra was added to the Romans' realm and then Tyana and one after the other all the cities as far as Antioch, where he discovered Zenobia with a large army ready to do battle; he himself stood ready to oppose her just as he was. But, noting that the Palmyrene cavalrymen boasted heavy defensive armor and had far more experience in horsemanship than did his own men, he drew up his infantry apart across the Orontes River. Then he passed along word to the Roman horsemen 'not to engage the cavalry of the Palmyrenes

at the outset while it was fresh but, having awaited its attack, to appear to take flight, doing this until they should see riders and horses alike giving up the chase beneath the burning heat as well as the weight of the armor.' The Emperor's cavalry observed these orders to the letter; as soon as it saw the enemy worn out and lying motionless on their exhausted horses, it pulled up short, attacked, and trampled them under foot as they fell from their mounts of their own accord. Then there was promiscuous slaughter, some being destroyed by the sword, others by the horses, both their own and the enemy's.

51. As many as were able to flee having entered Antioch, Zabdas, Zenobia's general, was afraid lest perchance the inhabitants of Antioch might hear of the battle's adverse outcome and attack his men. Having found a middle-aged man who appeared to bear some resemblance to the Emperor, and having dressed him in such fashion as Aurelian probably wore in battle, he led him through the center of the city as though he had captured the Emperor alive. And having deceived the Antiochenes by this clever trick he got out from the city by night and removed to Emesa, leading with him the rest of his army and Zenobia also. Now, the Emperor had intended, as soon as day broke, to pick up his infantry force and attack from both sides an enemy that had already been routed; but when he learned of Zenobia's flight he entered Antioch, whose citizens received him gladly. Having discovered that many a citizen had left through fear of experiencing some woe for having sided with Zenobia, he issued proclamations in every direction recalling the fugitives and attributing their circumstances more to constraint and necessity than to free choice.

52. After the exiles saw these proclamations they came on the run and enjoyed the welcome extended by the Emperor, who, having settled the city's affairs, marched towards

Emesa. But, when he found that a detachment of Palmyrenes was occupying a hill above the suburb of Daphne
(from this vantage-point it supposed it could shut out the
enemy's passage), he enjoined his soldiers 'to lock
shields together and make the ascent straight uphill in
close battle array, which by its very thickness would
shake off any missiles or stones that might happen to be
thrown at them.' And to this instruction he had ready obe-
dience. When as ordered they climbed uphill they put
themselves on a par in all respects with their adversaries.
These they straightway routed: some of them were torn
to pieces as they slid down the steep crags while some
were slain by their pursuers either from atop the hill or
down below. Securing by this victory safe passage. . .[1] the
Emperor went his merry way as Apamea, Larissa and
Arethusa welcomed him. Having spied the army of the
Palmyrenes mustered 70,000 strong (counting both themselves and as many others as had chosen to join their
expedition) in the plain before Emesa, he took the field
opposite them with his Dalmatian cavalry and the Moesians
and Pannonians and besides the Noricans and Raetians,
which are Celtic legions. In addition to these there were
the men of the imperial brigade, selected according to
merit out of the entire body, the most distinguished of
all. Along with these there were drawn up the Moorish
cavalry and, from Asia, troops out of Tyana, Mesopotamia,
Syria, Phoenicia, and Palestine, ranks of the bravest of
men. Those who came from Palestine in addition to their
other equipment had brought with them clubs and cudgels.
    53. When the armies had engaged, the Roman cavalry
was seen to give ground to a certain extent in order that
the Roman army might not fall into a trap and be encircled
by the cavalry of the Palmyrenes as it rode around with

---

[1]The passage is mutilated.

its great advantage in number. The Palmyrene horse thereupon chased after those who were retreating, thus disrupting its own lineup, but things turned out the opposite of what the Roman cavalrymen planned. For they were being pursued by an enemy to whom they were actually far inferior, and since very many indeed fell the result was that all the fighting rested upon the infantrymen. They, seeing the line of the Palmyrenes broken as their cavalry devoted itself to the chase, wheeled their ranks around and attacked the enemy thus confused and scattered. Thereupon there was a huge slaughter as they came on with the customary weapons, except in the case of the Palestinians, who brandished their clubs and cudgels against those who were outfitted with iron and bronze corselets. And this as much as anything else was responsible for the victory, the enemy being unacquainted with and terrified by the cudgels' impact. The Palmyrenes now fled headlong, in the process trampling their own men under foot, and were also slain by the enemy, so that the plain was filled with corpses of both men and horses. Those able to make a getaway betook themselves to the city.

54. Zenobia, naturally much disheartened by her defeat, took counsel concerning what should be done; it was the best judgment of one and all 'that they give up on the situation at Emesa because the inhabitants there were alienated from her and sided with the Romans and that they occupy Palmyra, entrusting their own salvation to that secure city where they could deliberate in more leisurely fashion concerning their affairs.' No sooner said than done: they went along with what had been decreed. Moreover, Aurelian, informed of Zenobia's flight, entered Emesa, whose citizens enthusiastically received him. Possessing himself of the resources which Zenobia had not been able to carry out with her, he forthwith hastened with his army to Palmyra. There he halted, ringed the

city wall around and began a siege, provisions being furnished his camp by the neighboring tribes. The people of
Palmyra jeered that it could not be taken, and now some
one let loose foul words against the Emperor's very person. A certain Persian who stood by the Emperor's side
said, ''If you so command you shall see this insolent man
a corpse.'' When the Emperor did so command, the Persian stationed some men in front of himself for conceal-
ment, stretched his bow, fitted an arrow thereon, and let
it fly. It lodged itself in the fellow as he was peeping out
over the parapet, still hurling insults. He was thrown down
from the wall a dead man and was thus presented to the
army and the Emperor.

55. Now the besieged kept up their resistance, expecting the enemy to give way owing to the lack of supplies;
but finding them resolute and themselves pressed hard for
want of food, they resolved to make a dash for the Euphrates, there to win aid from the Persians and foment revolution against the Romans. Having decided upon this course,
they put Zenobia on board a she-camel... [1] (they are swifter
than the male, outstripping even horses in speed) and led
her secretly out of the city.   Aurelian, disgusted at Zenobia's flight, did not let flag his natural vigor but immediately dispatched horsemen to pursue her. They caught up
with her as she was just about to cross the Euphrates,
led her down from the boat and took her to Aurelian. He
was overjoyed at the unexpected spectacle, but then, being
ambitious by nature, he got it into his head that there
would be no glory for him among posterity for having conquered a woman, and he bore it with bad grace.

56.   Among the Palmyrenes shut up within the city
there was a difference of opinion: some were willing to
bear the brunt of a full-scale, all-out war in the city's

---

[1]The passage is mutilated.

behalf against the Romans, others were holding out olive branches from the wall and begging forgiveness for past offenses. When the Emperor accepted their supplication and bade them to be of good courage, they poured forth from the city bringing gifts and sacrificial victims. Aurelian honored the victims and took the gifts and dismissed the citzens unhurt. He now became lord and master of the city, its movable and immovable wealth and votive offerings. Having returned to Emesa, he brought to trial both Zenobia and her accomplices. In the process of setting forth her case and freeing herself from blame, she implicated many others as having led her, a woman, astray; included among these was Longinus, whose writings are of great assistance to those who lay claim to learning. When he had been convicted oi those things of which he had been accused, the Emperor at once inflicted upon him the death penalty, which Longinus endured so nobly that he consoled even those who inveighed bitterly against his suffering. Others likewise whom Zenobia had denounced underwent punishments.

57. Now what happened prior to Palmyra's demolition is worth relating, even though I appear, in accordance with the purpose stated in my introduction, to have been composing my history in summarized form. For just as Polybius narrated how the Romans acquired their sovereignty within a brief period of time, so I am going to tell how they lost it through their own blind folly within no long period of time. But more of this when I shall have come to the later portion of my history. Now as for the Palmyrenes, when they had obtained no small part of the Roman Empire, as I have recounted, many announcements portending their ultimate destruction were made by heaven; what these were I shall say. At Seleucia-in-Cilicia stood a temple to Apollo (who is there called Sarpedonius), wherein there was an oracle. The things said about this

god, even how that to all those annoyed by the damage of
locusts he would make delivery upon request of Seleuciades
(these were birds living in places around the temple),
which would flit about the locusts, seize them in their
beaks, consuming a countless multitude of them on the
spot in a jiffy, and thus rid mankind of loss resulting from
them — these things I resign to the blessed age of mankind,
our own generation having repudiated all divine benevolence.   But when the Palmyrenes consulted the oracle as
to whether they would hold the supremacy of the East, the
god responded in these words:

"Leave my sanctuary, deceitful, baneful men,
You who cause the glorious stock of the gods pain."

And when certain men made inquiry concerning Aurelian's
campaign against the Palmyrenes, the god gave this
answer:

"A single hawk is the precursor of chill woe
For many doves; they shiver at this murderer."

58. Moreover, another similar thing befell the Palmyrenes.   There is a place between Heliopolis and Byblus,
Aphaca, where stands a shrine to Aphrodite Aphacitis.
Near it there is a pool similar to a man-made reservoir.
Now around the temple and the area adjacent there appears
in the air fire after the manner of a torch or a ball, whenever at stated times meetings are held in the place; and it
has continued to appear right down to our present era.
Those who assembled at the pool used to bring in honor
of the goddess gifts fashioned of gold and silver, and in
addition goods woven of flax and of linen and of other more
costly material. And if these were seen to be acceptable,
equal in weight with other pieces of cloth they would sink;
but if unacceptable and to be rejected, one might see them
swimming above the water, whether they were fabrics or

whether they were made of gold and silver and other mate-
rials which by nature do not float on water but submerge.
Now the year before their destruction the Palmyrenes
convened at the season of the feast and threw in honor of
the goddess into the lake gifts of gold and silver and tex-
tiles, all of which sank to the bottom; but at the following
year's festival season all their gifts were seen to float,
the goddess thereby signifying what the future would bring.

And, indeed, the benevolence of providence towards
Rome was of such sort so long as the sacred rites were
observed. But when I shall have arrived at those times in
which the Roman Empire gradually became barbarized and
shrank to a smaller size (and that, too, disabled), then,
to be sure, I shall present the reasons for its misfortune
and shall add, insofar as I can, the oracles which disclosed what would take place. (59) But meanwhile it is
high time that I return to where I digressed, lest I appear
to forsake, undone, the order of my history.

Now they say that, as Aurelian marched toward Europe
leading with him Zenobia together with her son plus all
those who had taken part in their rebellion, Zenobia died
either contracting illness or abstaining from food,[1] and the
rest outside of Zenobia's son were drowned in the middle
of the strait between Chalcedon and Byzantium. (60) But
Aurelian kept on his way to Europe, and as he went a
message caught up with him to this effect, that 'some of
those left in Palmyra had associated with themselves
Apsaeus, who had been responsible for their actions in
the past as well, and they were working on Marcellinus,
whom the Emperor had made prefect of Mesopotamia and
entrusted with the administration of the East, if perchance

---

[1]Zosimus prefaces this statement with a qualifying φασίν, "they
say"; all our other sources state that Zenobia, having been exhibited at Aurelian's triumph in Rome, was granted a pension and a villa
at Tibur (modern Trivoli).

he might allow himself to be invested with the imperial regalia. However, he kept putting them off, in order that he might deliberate as to what should be done. Although they troubled him in similar fashion again and again and again, he kept making ambiguous replies until he could inform Aurelian of his decision himself. But now the Palmyrenes had placed the purple robe around Antiochus, and were staying put at Palmyra.'

61. Having heard these things Aurelian at once, just as he was, set off for the East. He reached Antioch as a horse race was being run off and, appearing before the populace unexpectedly, terrified everybody. Then he marched to Palmyra. He took the city without a struggle and razed it to the ground, but he let Antiochus go, considering him because of his meanness to be unworthy even of retribution. Furthermore he subdued with dispatch the Alexandrians, who, distracted by faction, had contemplated revolt. He led a triumphal procession into Rome, where he got a very big reception from the people and the Senate. At this time also he constructed the sumptuous temple of Sol, embellishing it with adornments from Palmyra, and consecrated therein statues to both Sol and Belus. Having arranged these things thus, he overcame without hard work Tetricus and other rebels and visited them with fitting vengeance. And now he distributed new silver in the name of the State, having made the people surrender the adulterated coinage; in this way he redeemed promissory notes from breach of contract. Furthermore, he gratified the Roman populace with a dole of bread. Having disposed of all these matters, he departed from Rome.

62. While he was sojourning at Perinthus (now called by a new name, Heraclea) a plot was organized against him, as follows. There was at court a certain man named Eros, appointed to publish abroad imperial legal opinions.

On account of some delict the Emperor had threatened
this man and intimidated him. And so, fearful lest action
be added to the threats, he took counsel with certain
members of the guard whom he knew to be extremely
daring. Having produced letters which he personally had
forged to conform with the Emperor's (indeed, he had
been practicing this type of forgery for a long time), he
persuaded those who suspected that their death was imminent (this conclusion indeed was to be inferred from the
letters) to compass the Emperor's murder. Having watched
the Emperor leave the city without enough of a bodyguard, they all charged him with swords unsheathed and
killed him. Then he was buried on the very spot by his
army, in magnificent style on account of the works and
the dangers he had undergone in behalf of the commonwealth.

63. Tacitus now took in hand the supreme power at
Rome, as the Scythians, having crossed Lake Maeotis,
were making incursions throughout Pontus as far as Cilicia. Tacitus went out against them: some he personally
wore down and wiped out, others he consigned to Florianus
his praetorian prefect. Then he started for Europe but,
encountering a plot, he was killed for the following cause.
He had bestowed the government of Syria upon his kinsman
Maximinus. who, having treated the chief men in the
country harshly, had excited both envy and fear. These
things having bred hatred. the end result was treachery.
Associating themselves with those who had slain Aurelian,
they set upon Maximinus and butchered him; then they
went in pursuit of Tacitus and killed him as he was breaking
camp for Europe.

64. These events precipitated a civil war, as those in
the East chose Probus, those in Rome Florianus, to be
Emperor. Now Probus was holding Syria, Phoenicia,
Palestine. and all of Egypt, Florianus the territory from

Cilicia to Italy; to the latter also belonged the trans-Alpine
nations, Gaul and Spain, together with the island of Britain, and, besides, the whole of Africa and the Moorish
tribes. Both having prepared for war, Florianus came to
Tarsus resolved to pitch camp there; he had left his victory
over the Scythians on the Bosporus half-completed, in
that he allowed them, encircled though they were, to regain
their homes without fear. Meanwhile Probus procrastinated the war inasmuch as he had undertaken it with far
fewer troops. At Tarsus in the course of the summer a
heat wave developed; the soldiers aligned with Florianus
were unaccustomed to heat (for the greater part of his
army was European) and were wasting away with a dread
disease. Having learned this, Probus decided to attack in
due season. There were skirmishes in front of the city,
Florianus' soldiers indeed exerting themselves far beyond
their strength; but no deed worth telling about was done
before the armies separated from each other. Thereafter
certain men of those serving with Probus came and deposed
Florianus. Henceforth he was kept in custody for a time;
but as it was reported that what had been done to him was
not of Probus' choosing Florianus was allowed to assume
the purple once again until the return of those who, indicat-
ing how Probus really stood in this matter, caused Florianus to be slain by his own henchmen.

65. The Empire now devolved upon Probus, who as he
marched ahead made his first official act in the State's
behalf an object of praise: he decreed that those who had
murdered Aurelian and set upon Tacitus should be punished. However, he did not do openly what he had decided
upon, for fear that it would result in some disturbance,
but, having set up a company of men to whom he might
confide this matter, he invited the assassins to a banquet.
They congregated in the expectation of partaking of the
imperial board. Probus had withdrawn to one of his upper

rooms, from which the proceedings were visible, and gave the signal to those selected to perpetrate the deed. They attacked the assembled guests, who were unarmed; all were slaughtered except one, whom not long afterwards they arrested and burned alive as having caused them danger.

66. After Probus had done this, Saturninus, a Moor by race, being a very close friend of the Emperor's and for this reason having been entrusted with the government of Syria, renounced his allegiance to the Emperor and entertained thoughts of insurrection. Probus heard of this undertaking and intended to deal with it, but was anticipated by the soldiers in the East, who extinguished together the man and the attempted tyranny. Probus put down yet another rebellion, plotted in Britain, through the agency of Victorinus, a Moor as to race who had prevailed upon him to put in charge of Britain the man who had revolted. For when he had summoned Victorinus to himself and had reproved him for the advice he had given, he dispatched him to remedy the fault. The latter, hastening straightway to Britain, destroyed the tyrant by a skillful strategem.

67. Having disposed of these matters in the manner aforesaid, Probus against the barbarians as well secured large-scale victories, having fought two wars, at one of which he was present in person, for the other of which he had appointed the general. Since he was obliged to give assistance to the cities in Germany that had been molested by the barbarians near the Rhine, he marched in person towards that river. The war had just begun when a famine broke out everywhere there. Then a tremendous storm burst forth, pouring down grain in addition to raindrops, such that heaps of it automatically piled up in certain places. All were stunned by this marvel, and at first did not dare touch the grain and thus appease their hunger. But when necessity became stronger than every kind of terror, they baked loaves and devoured them; at one and

the same time they shook off their hunger and very easily won out in the war, thanks to the Emperor's luck.

He was successful with little effort in other wars as well. He fought fierce battles, first against the Longiones, a German nation, against whom he prevailed, taking alive their leader, Semno, together with his son, whom he received as suppliants. Having recovered what captives and booty they had, he dismissed them upon stated terms of surrender, even giving back Semno long with his son. (68) Secondly, he fought a battle against the Franks, whom he conquered by force through the agency of his generals. Thirdly, he fought personally against the Burgundians and the Vandals. When he saw that his own forces were inferior in number, he planned to draw aside a certain portion of the enemy's men and fight it. And somehow fortune seconded the Emperor's resolve. For when the armies were alongside both banks of the river the Romans kept challenging to battle the barbarians opposite, who got provoked at this and, as many as were able, crossed over. And, after the armies had clashed, some of the barbarians were slain and some came alive into the hands of the Romans; the rest sued for peace and obtained their request on condition that they return both the booty and the captives that they happened to be holding. But when they did not hand over everything the Emperor was incensed; he attacked them as they were retreating and exacted fitting punishment by slaughtering several and taking their leader Igillus captive. As many as he was able to bring back alive he shipped over to Britain. They settled down on the island and proved useful to the Emperor thereafter when any insurrection arose.

69. These wars having been waged by him thus near the Rhine, the Isauri now committed acts which should not be passed over in silence. A certain Lydius, an Isaurian by birth who had been inured to robbery from childhood on,

had procured a pack of men like himself and was assailing
all of Pamphylia and Lycia. However, when soldiers assembled for the purpose of capturing the robbers, Lydius,
not being able to oppose himself to a Roman army, went
to Cremna, a Lycian[1] town situated on a precipice and in
part made secure by very deep gullies. In this town, since
it was so safe and was enclosed by walls, he found that
many had taken refuge. When he saw that the Romans
were intent upon beleaguering it and were patiently enduring
the delay involved, he razed buildings, made the land arable
and, planting grain. was maintaining the people within the
town. But perceiving that those in need of support constituted a great number he forcibly evicted from the town
those of useless age, male and female alike. However,
the enemy saw through Lydius' design and forced those
who had been ejected to return to the town; whereupon he
pitched them into the gullies round about, killing them.
Having dug a tunnel, an amazing piece of construction.
from inside the town to outside it and then having extended
it to a point beyond the enemy camp, he sent out from the
town via it some men to seize cattle and other victuals.
By means of this he supplied the besieged well enough for
a time, until a woman disclosed it to the enemy. But not
even so did Lydius give up: he little by little curtailed
his associates' wine and measured out less than the customary ration of grain. Still and all the food was failing,
and he was reduced to the necessity of destroying everyone in the town save for a few men who were both his intimate friends and seemed to suffice for keeping watch. He
retained also some women, whom he bade to be shared
by all for the necessary function of nature.

70. When he had determined to go on wrestling against
every peril, an incident took place after all as follows.

---

[1]Pisidian, according to Strabo XII.6.

There was with him a certain man who knew how to assemble engines of war and could discharge arrows from them so accurately that whenever Lydius ordered him to shoot at one of the enemy, he did not miss the mark. But now it happened that, when he commanded him to wound one of the adversary, he discharged an arrow (either accidentally or on purpose) which missed; and Lydius had him stripped of his clothing and whipped unmercifully, even threatening him with death. The man was both enraged at the torture and terrified by the threats. He stole out of town when the opportunity presented itself and, chancing upon some men from the camp, he explained to them what he had done and what he had suffered. Then he pointed to a window in the wall through which Lydius was wont to spy the goings-on in the camp, and promised to shoot him with an arrow while he was peering through it in his accustomed fashion. The leader of the expedition thereupon welcoming him, he set up an engine, stationed men in front to prevent his being seen by the adversary, spotted Lydius stooping through the peephole, and with his missile struck him a mortal blow. The latter raged most cruelly indeed after this blow against some of his associates and, having bound the survivors by oaths never ever to yield to the siege, he finally expired. But they could not longer endure the siege of the city and gave themselves up to the army. And in this manner the brigandage met its end.

71. The Ptolemais which is located in the Thebaid revolted from the Emperor and undertook a war against the Coptites for a brief period of time. Probus, through the agency of those who were currently commanding his forces, caused both it and its allies the Blemmyes to surrender. He received the Basternae (a tribe of Scythians) when they cringed at his feet. and colonized them in parts of Thrace. where they lived consistently with Roman laws and mores. Likewise the Franks approached the Emperor

and obtained abodes from him; but a part of them defected and, having collected a large supply of ships, disturbed all of Greece. Then they bore down upon Sicily and landed at Syracuse, where they wrought great slaughter. Presently they came to anchor even in Africa, where they were repulsed by a force raised at Carthage; however, they were able to get back home after having suffered no loss.

Also during Probus' reign there occurred the following event. Upwards of eighty gladiators formed a conspiracy, destroyed those guarding them, set out from the city, and were plundering everything in their path; they were joined by many men, as usually happens. But these too the Emperor wiped out by dispatching troops.

These things were accomplished by Probus, who conducted the affairs of state brilliantly and justly.[1] And now news of an uprising was reported from the West, where the armies in Raetia and Noricum had placed the purple upon Carus. The Emperor sent a force to oppose Carus, but they transferred their allegiance to him and, attacking Probus, who was now destitute of aid, they slew him without opposition. He had reigned six years and four months.

72. The Emperor Carinus, the son of Carus, accomplished nothing for the good of the commonwealth. He gave himself up to a riotous, undisciplined mode of life. upon which he made useless expenditures. He effected the murders of men who had done nothing wrong but were deemed to have given offense in one way or another. All men were vexed at his harsh tyranny combined with his rashness: everything he did he did unrestrainedly and unreasonably.....

---

[1] Zosimus' text ends abruptly here. What follows in the Mendelssohn edition from here to the end of Book I is a series of excerpts almost all of which are drawn from other sources, including John of Antioch (probably 7th century) and Eunapius, the early 5th century historian whose work was used by Zosimus extensively.

73. As Carinus, the son of Carus, reigned and was doing everything unrestrainedly and unreasonably, when the news of Numerianus' death reached those in Italy, the leaders of the armies there, irritated at Carinus' carelessness in all respects and his savagery, placed the imperial garb on the prefect Sabinus Julianus and were intending to fight it out together with him against Carinus. The latter, having gained knowledge of the insurrection, was traveling to Italy. Then the soldiers, having brought over to their way of thinking those who had returned from fighting the Persians, led Diocletian, who had already put on the purple robe at Nicomedia, through Italy. While he was still on the way, Carinus engaged the soldiers of Sabinus Julianus in battle, routing them. However, some of his companions attacked him suddenly and he was murdered by one of his tribunes, whose wife, as it happened, he had corrupted.

BOOK II

(There is a gap in our text down to the year 303, the twentieth year of Diocletian's reign. Book II begins in the midst of an account of the Secular Games (*Ludi Saeculares*), the longest that we possess of the ceremonies. A celebration of the Games was scheduled for the year 304 but was cancelled — with, according to Z o s i m u s, dire consequences).

... As a result the longest life a man lives will embrace the time between celebrations of this feast. For what we call an age the Romans call a *saeculum*. Moreover, it is of help in curing plagues and pestilences and diseases. It got its start for the following reason. Valesius, from whom is descended the Valerian gens, was an illustrious man among the Sabine folk. In front of his house there was a grove of very tall trees which were struck and burned by thunder and lightning, the significance of which event was a moot question. Thus, when his children fell sick, besides the medical practitioners he conferred also with the soothsayers, who concluded from the manner of the fire's falling that the gods' wrath was at work. Naturally Valesius tried to appease heaven by sacrificial offerings. And since both he and his wife were overcome with fear expecting that the death of their children would occur momentarily, he prostrated himself before Vesta and promised to give her in exchange for the children two unblemished souls, his own and that of their mother. When he looked back at the grove that had been struck by lighning, he seemed to hear a voice bidding him to take the children to Tarentum and there give them water from the Tiber to drink, having heated it upon the hearth dedicated to Dis and Proserpina. After hearing this he the more despaired of his children's safety, 'for Tarentum was in a truly remote part of Italy wherein water from the Tiber would not be found. Besides, it gave him no good hope to have heard that the water was to be heated on an altar of the nether divinities.' (2) Thereupon the soothsayers also were in a quandary; but he, having heard the same things a second time, decided he must obey the god. He put the children on board a river boat and carried the fire along with him. But when the children lay prostrate under the heat, he navigated toward the side of the river where the water's flow seemed peaceful. Having bivouacked at a shepherd's hut together with his children, he heard that he must land at Tarentum (for this was the name of the place, which was homonymous with the Tarentum near the Iapygian Promontory). Accordingly, having worshiped heaven for this happy event, Valesius instructed the pilot to pull ashore and, having disembarked, told all to the shepherds. He drew water from the Tiber, heated it upon a hearth which he constructed on the spot, and gave it to his children to drink. And, sleep coming upon them as soon as they had drunk, they were restored to health. They dreamt that they had offered black victims to Proserpina and Dis and spent three straight nights in festival, singing and dancing. They told the dream to their father, relating that a big man of divine appearance had laid a strict charge upon them to perform these things upon the Campus Martius at Tarentum, where there is a place reserved for the exercising of horses. However, when Valesius wished to construct an altar there, the marble-workers upon excavating the place found an altar already built, on which had been inscribed "To Dis and Proserpina." Thereupon, since he was now more clearly informed as to what should be done, he offered black victims on this altar and there kept the nightlong vigils.

3. Now this altar and the institution of the sacrifice had their origin from the following cause. There had once been a war between Rome and Alba Longa. Both being under arms, there came into view a certain prodigy clad in a black skin and shouting that Dis and Proserpina enjoined them, before engaging, to make a sacrificial offering beneath the earth to them. Having thus spoken, it vanished. Accordingly the Romans, confounded by the apparition, both consecrated an altar and, having sacrificed thereon, concealed it underground at a depth of twenty feet so that it would not be known to any others except themselves. Valesius, when he had discovered this altar and completed the sacrifice and the all-night vigils, was called Manius Valerius Tarentinus: the Romans' word for the gods of the underworld is *manes* and for being hale is *valere,* while he was given the name *Tarentinus* because the sacrifice was performed at Tarentum. Later, in the first year following the expulsion of the Kings, a pestilence having come upon the city, Publius Valerius Poplicola sacrificed upon this altar to Dis and Proserpina a black ox and a black heifer and freed the city from the plague, inscribing on the altar these words: "I, Publius Valerius Poplicola, have dedicated the fiery plain to Dis and Proserpina and have staged spectacles in honor of Dis and Proserpina because of the liberation of the Roman people."

4. Following these events, when in the 502nd year after the city's founding diseases and wars had broken out, the Senate, desirous of finding relief from these woes, ordered the *decemviri sacris faciundis,* who were charged with keeping the Sibylline Books, to investigate the oracles. When the oracles declared that the evil would cease if sacrifice were made to Dis and Proserpina, they searched out the spot and hallowed it by fire, just as instructed, to

Dis and Proserpina, in the fourth consulship of Marcus Popillius.[1] And, having completed the sacrifice and having rid themselves of the ills that beset them, they again concealed the altar, laying it to rest in some far corner of the Campus Martius. This mode of sacrifice was neglected for a period of time, but Octavian Augustus revived the ceremony once more after certain unhappy events....[2] Lucius Censorinus and Manius Manilius Puelius being consuls.... Ateius Capito explained the ordinance concerning the games as well as the times when the sacrifice should be performed and the spectacle held, the *quindecemviri sacris faciundis*,[3] who were charged with keeping the Sibylline Books, having made their investigation. After Augustus, Claudius held the celebration, not observing the defined number of years intervening.[4] Thereafter Domitian, paying no heed to Claudius' reckoning but counting up the number of years from the date when Augustus staged the

---

[1] The text here may be corrupt, or Zosimus may just have been in error. He would appear to be speaking of the year 252 B. C. (502 A. U. C.), yet M. Popillius Laenas was consul for the fourth time in either the year 350 B. C. or the year 348 B. C., almost a century earlier.

[2] Here both the text is corrupt and Zosimus is in error. Having mentioned Augustus' renewal of the games, he backtracks to the year 149 B. C. when the consuls were L. Marcius Censorinus and M.'Manilius (the cognomen Puelius, found in the text, is spurious). Actually, the best-attested dates for the Secular Games are as follows: 348 B. C., 249 B. C., 146 B. C. (not 149, as here), 17 B. C. (the Augustan Games for which Horace composed his well-known *Carmen Saeculare*), A. D. 47 (Claudius), 88 (Domitian), 204 (Septimius Severus), and 248 (Philip, purporting to celebrate Rome's millenium, a celebration not mentioned by Zosimus).

[3] Here Zosimus is accurate. The *decemviri* mentioned at the beginning of this chapter became *quindecemviri*, probably in Sulla's time, certainly no later than 51 B. C. (Cicero, *ad Familiares* viii.4.7).

[4] The antiquarian Claudius, treating a *saeculum* as precisely a century, decided to celebrate Rome's 800th birthday.

festival, was seen to maintain the institution as tradition-
ally handed down. One hundred and ten years later Severus
together with his sons Antoninus and Geta set up the same
festivities, in the year when Chilo and Libo were consuls.

5. The mode of the festival as recorded is as follows.
Heralds used to make the rounds inviting everybody to
gather for a spectacle which they neither had seen before
nor would ever see again. In summertime, a few days
before the games were held, the *quindecemviri,* seated
upon a temple podium on the Capitoline or the Palatine,
distributed the lustral articles to the people: these are
torches and brimstone and bitumen, and slaves do not
partake of them, but freemen only. After the entire populace has convened at the aforesaid places or at the temple
of Diana located on the Aventine Hill, one and all bearing
wheat and barley and beans, they solemnly keep the nightlong vigils to the Fates on....[1] nights. The time of the
feast being now at hand, which they celebrate over a period
of three days and as many nights in the Campus Martius,
the sacred rites are performed at Tarentum on the bank
of the Tiber. They sacrifice to these gods: Jupiter, Juno,
Apollo, Latona, Diana; also the Fates and the goddesses
of childbirth and Ceres and Dis and Proserpina. At the
second hour of the ceremonies' first night the Emperor
along with the *quindecemviri* slaughters three lambs upon
three altars set up at the riverbank and, having stained
the altars with blood, he burns the offerings whole. A
theatre-stage having been constructed, fires are kindled
and lit up, a hymn, newly composed, is sung, and sacred
pageants are put on. The performers receive as their
wages the firstfruits of the wheat and barley and beans
(for these, as I have said, are distributed to all the people
alike). On the first day thereafter, having ascended the

---

[1]The text is mutilated.

Capitoline, where they offer the usual victims, they move thence to the theatre that has been prepared for the performance of the games in honor of Apollo and Diana. And on the second day, at the hour designated by the oracle, noble matrons congregate on the Capitoline, supplicating and hymning the god [1] as is meet and right. And on the third day, in the temple of Apollo on the Palatine, twenty-seven remarkable boys and as many girls, all of them flourishing on both sides (i. e., having both parents alive), sing hymns and paeans in both the Greek and the Latin languages, by which the cities subject to the Romans are kept safe. Likewise other things used to be performed in the way divinely ordained; so long as these services were discharged the Roman Empire continued intact. Furthermore, that we may believe this to be the very fact of the matter, I shall set forth Sibyl's oracle itself, seeing that it has already before us been recited by others:

6. ''Indeed, whenever man's longest span of life
Comes round its cycle of one hundred ten years,
Remember, Roman, however forgetful,
Remember to do all these things, for the gods
Undying, on the plain washed by Tiber's wave
Where narrowest,[2] when night steals over the earth,
The sun having hid its light. Then do you make
Offerings to the procreant Fates, both lambs
And dark she-goats. Gratify the goddesses
Of childbirth with incense fit. Next, for Tellus,
Teeming everywhere,[2] slaughter a black sow.
Let all-white bulls be led to Jupiter's stand
By day, not night: for to the gods celestial

---

[1] The text is corrupt here: "god" should read "goddess," as Juno is meant.

[2] The text is corrupt at this point.

Daytime sacrifices alone are pleasing.[1]
Let Juno's shrine accept from you a heifer
Immaculate. And let Phoebus Apollo,
Son of Latona, invoked also as Sol,
Get like offerings. May the Latin paeans
Sung by boys and girls at once fill the temple
Of the gods. But let the girls keep their chorus
Separate, as the boys. Let all their parents
On both sides be still alive and flourishing.
On that day married women on bended knee
Alongside Juno's celebrated altar
Will pray the goddess. Give purgations[1] to all,
Men and women, especially the latter.
Let all bring from home whatever is proper
For mortals to offer the gods as firstfruits,
Propitiation to dwellers in heaven
Mild and blessed. Let all these things lie heaped up,
That women and men seated as suppliants
You may remember to serve. Both day and night
Let a vast throng continually attend
The gods' chairs. Mix solemnity with laughter.
May these things always be in your hearts and minds,
And all the land of Italy and Latium
Will ever submit to your sovereignty."

7. Now, events themselves have proven to us the fact
that, as long as all the above was performed precisely in
accordance with the oracle's direction and the demands
of the situation, the Romans kept their Empire and continued to hold under their sway nearly the entire civilized
world; but, the rites having been neglected near the time
of Diocletian's abdication, the Empire gradually ebbed and

---

[1]The text is corrupt at this point.

has escaped notice becoming for the most part barbarized. That this statement is true I indeed mean to demonstrate chronologically. For from the consulship of Chilo and Libo, when Severus celebrated the Secular Games, until Diocletian was made consul for the ninth time and Maximinian for the eighth, 101 years elapsed. And then Diocletian became a private citizen, with Maximian following his example. But when Constantine and Lucinius were consuls for the third time the interval of 110 years had now come full circle: the games ought to have been held conformably to custom. Since this was not maintained affairs necessarily have come to the unhappy state that currently oppresses us.

8. Diocletian in fact died three years later. Those who had already[1] been made Emperors, Constantius and Galerius Maximianus, designated as their Caesars Severus and Maximinus, the latter being the son of Galerius' sister. Severus was granted Italy, Maximinus the provinces in the East. Matters were in good shape; the barbarians everywhere were gladly keeping still because the right actions had been taken beforehand regarding them. And now Constantine, who had been begotten out of wedlock by the Emperor Constantius and had designs upon the imperial throne for himself, was the more covetous after Severus and Maximinus had attained the rank of Caesar. He decided to leave his present surroundings and to set out for the trans-Alpine peoples, amidst whom his father Constantius lived, more often than not in Britain. Fearing, however, least he be apprehended in flight (as the love for Empire which possessed him was already manifest to many), he would upon arriving at a stable hobble and render useless as many horses as were kept there at the public expense, and would employ the re-

---

[1] That is, in 305, following Diocletian's and Maximian's abdication (Diocletian's death is probably, as Zosimus would have it, to be dated to the year 316).

mainder for the next stage of the journey. Time after time he did this, thus impeding his pursuers' progress, until he reached the nations among whom his father was.

9. However, at just this point it happened that the Emperor Constantius died. The praetorian soldiers judged that none of his legitimage children was worthy of reigning, but noted that Constantine was hale of body. They conferred upon him the rank of a Caesar, as soon as their hopes of splendid rewards had been raised. When his image was displayed at Rome in the customary fashion, Maxentius, the son of Maximian Herculius, regarded it as intolerable that Constantine, born of an ignoble mother, should get his heart's desire while he himself, the son of so great an Emperor, should remain aimlessly supine as others obtained his father's imperium. Having allied with himself to assist in his undertaking the tribunes Marcellianus and Marcellus, plus Lucianus (the dispenser of the hog's-flesh which the public treasury furnished to the Roman populace) and the soldiers at court that are called praetorians, he was seated by these men upon the imperial throne after he had made a contract that they would receive in exchange for this grant great emoluments. Indeed, they started off upon their business after first killing Abellius because he in his rôle as urban prefect appeared to oppose their adventures.

10. Galerius Maximianus, having learned of these things, dispatched his Caesar, Severus,[1] from Mediolanum with a body of Moorish soldiers to make war upon Maxentius. But Maxentius, having corrupted with money the majority of his men and having presently attached to himself even the praetorian prefect Anullinus, conquered Severus upon his approach most easily. The latter slipped off to Ravenna, a very secure and populous city possessing a sufficient supply of provisions for himself and for his

---

[1]Actually Severus had been made Emperor of the West, succeeding Constantius Chlorus, upon the latter's death in 306 A. D.

soldiers. Having gained knowledge of this, Maximian Herculius was, naturally, solicitous in his son's behalf. From Lucania, where he was at the time, he rushed to Ravenna. Realizing that S e v e r u s could not be moved against his will out of this city since it was both fortified and adequately stocked with food, he beguiled him with oaths and persuaded him to go to Rome. Thereupon, as Severus on his journey came to a place called the Three Taverns, he was seized in an ambush set up by Maxentius and hanged by the neck until dead. Galerius Maximianus did not take calmly these things that had befallen his Caesar, Severus. He resolved from the East to make for Rome, there to inflict upon Maxentius a punishment that fit his wrongs. But when he had arrived in Italy, sensing that his own soldiers were not loyal, he marched back East without engaging in one battle.

At this particular point in time Maximian Herculius, taking umbrage at the turmoils that were vexing the polity, went to Diocletian, who was staying at Carnutum, a Celtic town.[1]   He tried to persuade him 'to take up again the sovereign power and not allow that, which had been preserved for so long a time and also by their own hard work, to be tossed about and exposed to the distraught and deranged rashness of those who had intruded upon it.' But Diocletian did not assent to this request, preferring retirement to the distraction of public business (indeed he may just have foreseen the confusion that would grip affairs, inasmuch as he was ever most devoted to religious observances). Herculius, frustrated in his attempt, proceeded as far as Ravenna and then marched back again into the Alps to meet Constantine, who was sojourning there. Being officious and treacherous by

---

[1] This town (modern Chartres) Zosimus undoubtedly nas confused with Carnuntum in upper Pannonia, where tne conference of the Emperors was held in 308.

nature, he fulfilled a promise to give Constantine his daughter Fausta and then endeavored to deceive him and persuade him to leave Italy, pursue Galerius Maximianus, and set a trap for Maxentius. Since he found Constantine docile as regards these things he departed, zealous to assume the imperium once again and hopeful that he would set over against each other his son-in-law Constantine and his son Maxentius.

11. However, while he was at work on these matters, Galerius Maximianus made his dear old friend Licinius Emperor, intending that he take the field against Maxentius. While Galerius was pondering these plans he perished of an incurable wound, and Licinius now tried to gain possession of the Empire. But Maximian Herculius, having undertaken (as I have said) to regain his imperium, was eager to alienate the affections of Maxentius' soldiers. Having drawn these soldiers to his side by gifts and piteous supplications, he attempted to lay a plot through their agency against Constantine. But Fausta nipped the undertaking in the bud by informing Constantine about it, and Herculius, being in despair about the way everything had fallen out, died of an illness at Tarsus.[1]

12. Maxentius, having escaped this piece of treachery and believing that he now had a secure sovereignty, dispatched men to display his image around Africa and, in particular, Carthage. There the soldiers prevented this from taking place, owing to their fond remembrance of Galerius Maximianus. When they learned that Maxentius was going to campaign against them on account of their opposition, they removed to Alexandria. But they encountered a considerable force which they could not with-

---

[1]Zosimus has confused Maximian (Herculius) with Maximinus Daia, who died at Tarsus four years later (314; see chapter 17, below). Maximian was captured at Massilia and committed suicide.

stand, and sailed back again to Carthage. Upset by these wrongful acts, Maxentius decided to sail to Africa and punish those who had committed them. But, after the soothsayers had made sacrifice and said that the omens were not favorable, he shrank from the voyage not only because the entrails appeared inauspicious but also because he feared that Alexander, who held the post of acting praetorian prefect in Africa, might stand in his way. To effect for himself a passage from Italy into Africa which would be free from all suspicion, he addressed himself to Alexander, asking that his son be given him as a hostage (for Alexander had a son in the full bloom of manhood and of handsome appearance). Suspecting, however, that Maxentius asked that the son be given him not for security reasons but so as to deal treacherously with him, he rejected the embassy sent on this mission. Maxentius now dispatched other men to take him off by cunning, but this contrivance was betrayed and brought to light. Thereupon the soldiers, having found an occasion suitable for rebellion, bestowed the purple upon Alexander, a Phrygian by birth, craven, cowardly, slow to undertake any labor, and advanced in age as well.

13. At this time a fire started in Rome either from the air or from the earth (this is uncertain), and the temple of Fortuna was ablaze. As everybody hurried to put out the fire a certain soldier who had uttered blasphemies against providence was attacked and killed by the populace out of religious zeal. This stirred the soldiers to insurrection. They would have come within an ace of destroying the city had not Maxentius quickly tamed their fury.

14. Thereafter Maxentius kept looking for excuses to wage war against Constantine. With the pretense that he was distressed over his father's death, a death of which Constantine was the cause, he was intending to march to Raetia, as this province is near the regions of both Gaul

and Illyria. For he dreamt of gaining Dalmatia and also Illyria through the agency of the military commanders in those places and of the forces of Licinius. Although Maxentius had these things in mind, he thought he ought first to settle matters in Africa and so, having collected troops of men over whom he put as commander Rufius Volusianus, the praetorian prefect, he dispatched them to Africa. Along with Rufius he sent Zenas, a man celebrated for his military experience and his clemency alike. At the first assault the soldiers of Alexander wheeled in a kind of mass maneuver, and Alexander joined them in their flight. This maneuver having been overcome by the enemy, he himself was seized and strangled.

The war having been finished in this manner, great leeway was granted the sycophants to inform against practically everyone in Africa who was wellborn or well-to-do as being a partisan of Alexander. And positively no one was spared: some lost all the property they possessed, others lost their lives as well. Indeed, a triumph was held in Rome on account of the evils perpetrated at Carthage. Thus did Maxentius administer these affairs, and thus did matters stand throughout Italy and Rome proper as he addressed himself to them with all cruelty and wantonness.

15. And now Constantine, who even earlier had been suspicious of him, made more preparations to do battle against him. Having gotten together forces from the barbarians he happened to have won by the spear and Germans and other Celtic peoples, besides some raised from Britain — altogether circa 90,000 infantry and 8,000 cavalry — he marched from the Alps into Italy. Those towns which submitted to an armistice he left undamaged, but those which took up arms he subdued. Maxentius had made ready a far larger army. There fought on his side

a grand total of 170,000 infantry and 18,000 cavalry, as follows: upwards of 80,000 Romans and Italians, and as many Etruscans as dwelt along the entire coastland; in addition the Carthaginians furnished a company of 40,000 men as did the Sicilians besides.

Both being fitted out with an armament of such size, Maxentius built a bridge over the Tiber. The bridge was not completely hooked up from the one bank which faces the city to the other, but was divided into two parts so that in the midst of the river the pieces connecting one part with the other could be assembled somehow with iron pins, pins which could be pulled asunder whenever somebody wanted the bridge uncoupled. He gave orders to the engineers that, when they should see Constantine's army standing at the bridge junction, they pull out the pins and disconnect the bridge so that those standing thereon would fall into the river. These things Maxentius was contriving.

16. Meanwhile Constantine, having proceeded with his army as far as Rome, encamped in front of the city in a plain that spread out and was suitable for deploying cavalry. Maxentius, having shut himself up within, was offering victims to the gods and consulting the soothsayers about the war's fortune; he also was searching the Sibylline Books. Now, when he discovered an oracular sign to the effect that one who did the Romans some harm must perish by a woeful death, he took it that the oracle referred to himself, as one who would ward off those that attacked Rome intent upon her capture — which very thing turned out to be true. For when Maxentius had led his forces out of Rome and crossed the bridge which he himself had joined, owls in endless number flew down and covered the wall. Upon observing this, Constantine ordered his men to form in order of battle. When the armies stood with wings opposite each other, Constantine sent in his

cavalry, which charged and conquered the enemy horse.
The signal having been given for the infantry also, they
moved against the enemy in due order, and a fierce battle
ensued. The Romans themselves and their Italian allies
were reluctant to venture into danger, wishing as they did
to find release from bitter tyranny. However, of the rest of
the soldiers an untold multitude fell, being both trampled by
the cavalry and slain by the infantry. Indeed, as long as
Maxentius' cavalry offered resistance there seemed to be
some hope left for him. But when his horsemen gave up he
took to flight along with the rest and made for the city via
the bridge across the river. The timbers could not sustain
the pressure of the host, but broke; and together with all
the others Maxentius himself was borne downstream.

17.   When the victory was announced to those in the
city no one dared to display any rejoicing at what had been
accomplished, as some believed the report to be untrue.
But when the head of Maxentius was brought back on a
spear they put aside their fear and exchanged their faint-
heartedness for joy.

At this turn of events Constantine exacted penalties
from only a few of Maxentius' very close associates, but
he wiped out the praetorian soldiers and demolished the
garrisons where they had been quartered. Having settled
affairs in Rome he set out for the Celts and Gauls. He
summoned Licinius to Mediolanum and gave him his sister
Constantia in marriage; he had promised to do so earlier,
when he wished to have him as a partner in his hostility
against Maxentius. This done, Constantine departed for
the Celts. Now civil war flared up between Licinius and
Maximinus and a fierce fight took place in Illyria. At first
Licinius appeared to be beaten but upon renewing battle he
forthwith routed Maximinus, who leaving for Egypt via the
East in the hope of recruiting battlewise troops died at
Tarsus.[1]

---

[1]See above, chapter 11, note 1.

18.   In this way the imperial power devolved upon Constantine and Licinius.   After a very brief passage of time a disagreement arose between them — not that Licinius had given occasion for it but Constantine, as was his custom, had proved faithless in connection with his agreements and sought to detach certain nations belonging to Licinius' jurisdiction.[1] Thereupon their enmity broke out into the open: both men rallied their forces for the purpose of fighting.   Now, Licinius mustered his army at Cibalis, a town of Pannonia situated on a hill.   There is a narrow (i.e., five-eights of a mile wide[2]) road leading up to the town.   Adjoining the greater part of this road is a deep swamp, while the remainder, including the hill upon which the town lies, is mountainous.   From here an open plain extends, a great one, indeed, and of boundless prospect. On this plain Licinius pitched camp, spreading out his phalanx lengthwise under the hill that his wings might not appear weak.   Constantine meanwhile had drawn up his troops near the mountain, with the cavalry in the van; for this arrangement seemed to him more advantageous, that the enemy might not burst in upon his infantrymen, who moved more slowly, and prevent them from advancing owing to lack of maneuvering space.   This done, he quickly commanded the first charge; with standards raised he was immediately on top of his adversaries.   There ensued a battle fiercer than any other, so to speak, for after both sides had exhausted their arrows they fought for a long time with javelins and spears.   The battle began at dawn and continued along until evening, when the right wing under the command of Constantine was victorious and put its opposition to flight.   When Licinius' legions observed that he also was astride his horse and poised for flight, they dared

---

[1]Our only other source, the *Anonymus Valesii*, whose author (a pagan?) apparently was Constantine's contemporary, states that it was Licinius who acted in bad faith.

[2]Obviously there is trouble with the text.

hold their ground no longer, even to eat. They abandoned
their cattle and draught animals and all the rest of their
equipment and, taking only as much food as was sufficient
to stay their hunger that night, in all haste they reached
Sirmium along with Licinius. Sirmium is a city of Pannonia washed on both sides by the Savus River, which
flows into the Danube. Licinius, having passed through
this city on the run and having wrecked the bridge over
the river, moved forward with the intent of levying a force
from the Thracian countryside.

19. Constantine, having seized Cibalis and Sirmium
and everything else the fleeing Licinius had left behind,
sent 5,000 heavy-armed men in pursuit of the latter. They,
however, being ignorant of the road by which Licinius had
fled, were unable to overtake him; but Constantine, having
repaired the bridge on the Savus which Licinius had broken
up, kept his army on the move close behind. Having crossed
over into Thrace, he arrived at the plain where Licinius
was found encamped. On the very night of his arrival he
drew up his line of battle and instructed his troops to be
ready to fight at dawn. When day came Licinius, having
caught sight of Constantine and his army, himself drew
up a counter line of battle. He had as his fighting partner
Valens, whom he had appointed Caesar following the flight
from Cibalis. When the two armies first engaged they
employed bows, an interval separating them; but when
their arrows were spent they rushed in with spears and
daggers. While the armies were still fiercely pressing
the battle, those whom Constantine had ordered to chase
Licinius came down from a certain vantage ground upon
them. They turned round a hill, thinking they must join
their own side from a lofty location and thus surround the
enemy completely. But Licinius' men were on their guard
and struggled valiantly against all, and when countless
numbers had fallen on both sides and the contest had be-

come a draw the armies at a given signal broke off the fighting.

20. On the next day a truce was made. Both parties agreed to an offensive and defensive alliance on these terms: 'that Constantine rule over the Illyrians and all the nations beyond them; that Licinius hold Thrace and the East and the regions beyond it; but that Valens, Licinius' appointed Caesar, be put to death' as the alleged cause of the evils that had occurred. This done, oaths were given by each side that these conditions would be conscientiously kept. To make more binding the obligation to abide by their agreements, Constantine appointed as Caesar Crispus, his son by a concubine named Minervina and still a youth; also Constantinus, born not many days before in Arelate; and as a third Caesar proclaimed along with them Licinianus the son of Licinius, now twenty months of age. Thus ended the second war.

21. When Constantine learned that the Sarmatae who dwelt beside Lake Maeotis had crossed the Danube in ships and were ravaging his territory, he led his forces against them. At the same time the barbarians, together with their king Rausimodus, went to meet him head on. First the Sarmatae assailed a town defended by a sufficiently large garrison; that part of its wall which rose straight off the ground was built of stone, but the upper part was of wood. The Sarmatae accordingly, supposing they would take the town quite easily if they burned the entire wooden part of the wall, set fire to it, the while shooting at those standing upon the walls. But as these latter kept throwing down missiles and rocks from their higher stations and killing the barbarians, Constantine came up and fell upon the barbarians from behind; he killed many, captured alive still more, and caused the remainder to flee. Rausimodus, having lost the greater part of his troops, took ship and crossed the Danube, intending once again to plunder the

Romans' domain. When Constantine heard this, he made pursuit, crossing the Danube in person. They had taken refuge on a hill covered with dense forests; there he set upon them and killed many, among them Rausimodus himself. Having taken many captives, he graciously received the rest of the multitude upon their surrender; and so he returned to his headquarters with a large number of prisoners.

22. These he distributed to the cities, and then he went to Thessalonica, which he provided with a harbor (there had not been one there before). He made preparations for a fresh war against Licinius: upwards of 200 triaconters were readied and more than 2,000 merchantmen were assembled, as well as an army of 120,000 foot soldiers and 10,000 marines and horse. Licinius, having heard of Constantine's preparations, sent messengers hither and yon bidding the nations make ready men-of-war and forces of both infantry and cavalry. Right away the Egyptians dispatched eighty triremes, as did the Phoenicians, while the Ionians and Asiatic Dorians sent sixty, the Cyprians thirty, the Carians twenty, the Bithynians thirty and the Africans fifty. His infantry force was about 150,000, and his cavalry 15,000; these were furnished by Phrygia and Cappadocia. Constantine's fleet was anchored in the Piraeus, Licinius' in the Hellespont. Thus were each man's naval and infantry forces arrayed. Licinius was encamped at Adrianopolis in Thrace; meanwhile Constantine summoned from the Piraeus his ships, which had been collected in greater part from Greece, and, having set out with his infantry from Thessalonica, took up a position on the bank of the Hebrus River, which washes Adrianopolis on the left. Licinius, indeed, drew up his forces 200 furlongs distant from the mountain which commands the town, where the Tonoseeius [1] River flows into

---

[1] Undoubtedly the Tundja is meant.

the Hebrus. For many days the armies sat still opposite one another, but then Constantine, having noted where the river was narrowest, devised the following stratagem. He ordered his soldiers to bring timber down from the mountain and to bind it with ropes as though he were going to bridge the river and thus transport his army. He thereby deluded the enemy and, having climbed a certain hill thickly wooded enough to hide troops, he planted there 5,000 infantry armed with bows and 800[1] horse. Next, accompanied by twelve cavalrymen, he went across the Hebrus River at the narrow place where one could cross most easily and unexpectedly fell upon the enemy. As a consequence some were killed, many fled headlong, while the others stood agape, astounded by the surprising suddenness of the crossing. In the meantime the rest of the cavalry and then the entire army had made it safely across, and there arose a great slaughter in which about 34,000 men fell. Towards sunset Constantine took the camp. Licinius, however, having collected as many of his men as he could, drove through Thrace to get to his fleet. (23) At daybreak as many of Licinius' army as had taken refuge in the mountains or ravines gave themselves up to Constantine; along with them were those whom Licinius had abandoned in his hasty flight.

When Licinius fled to Byzantium Constantine tailed him and laid siege to the city. Now the fleet of Constantine, having, as I said, sailed forth from Piraeus, had its anchorage in Macedonia; he sent for the captains and gave orders for the ships to come to the mouth of the Hellespont. The fleet having come as directed, Constantine's commanders decided to fight with only eighty triaconters, the fastest sailers, inasmuch as the place owing to its straitness was unsuitable for a large number of ships.

---

[1]The text reads 80, but it is conjectured that the figure should be 800.

But Abantus, Licinius' admiral, was sailing up with 200 ships, exceedingly scornful of the small size of the opposition's fleet, which he believed he would intercept easily. When the ensigns had been raised on both sides and the lookout men were going at each other, Constantine's admirals bore down upon the enemy in an orderly fashion but Abantus sailed against the opposition haphazardly. The latter's ships, being so many in so narrow a place, were dashed against one another and thus ways and means were provided to the enemy to sink or otherwise destroy them. After many sailors and marines had been plunged into the sea nightfall ended the naval engagement; one side anchored at Eleus in Thrace while the other put into the Aeantian Harbor.

24. The next day a strong north wind was blowing as Abantus advanced out of the Aeantian Harbor and made preparations for a battle at sea. But because those penteconters [1] which had been staying at the mouth of the Hellespont had now at their leaders' command come to Eleus, Abantus, terrified by the great number of the enemy ships, was hesitant about sailing against them. Around noon the north wind died down and a strong south wind arose. It hit Licinius' fleet hard by the Asiatic shore, causing some ships to run aground, dashing others against the rocks, and sinking yet others men and all. As a consequence there were destroyed 5,000 men and 130 ships with their crews, ships in which, as it happened, Licinius had dispatched part of his army from Thrace to Asia because quarters were too tight in Byzantium for the multitude of those who were with him lying under a state of siege. Moreover, when Abantus with four ships had taken refuge in Asia, thus calling a halt to the naval engagement, and when boats transporting all sorts of wares and a very great supply

---

[1] Obviously Zosimus means the triaconters referred to in chapters 22 and 23 above.

of provisions for Constantine's leaders had landed at the Hellespont, these set sail with their entire expeditionary force to join the party besieging Byzantium and encircle the city by sea. Licinius' infantry could not endure the mere sight of such a naval force but took ship and sailed off to Eleus.

25. Constantine, pressing the siege, raised a mound equal in height to the wall and on it placed wooden towers higher than the wall; from these its defenders were shot down upon with arrows. Consequently he could without risk move battering rams and other machines up against the walls with the intention of capturing the city. Because of these things Licinius did not know what to do and decided to abandon Byzantium. Leaving the weaker part of his army there, he hurried to Chalcedon in Bithynia with those men who were well-disposed and had already evinced their good will toward him. Indeed, he was confident that he would be able to renew the fighting after recruiting an army from Asia. Therefore, having sailed across to Chalcedon, he took as a partner in his venture Martinianus, leader of the palatine ranks (whom the Romans style *magister officiorum*): he appointed him Caesar and sent him off with an army to Lampsacus to prevent the enemy's crossing from Thrace into the Hellespont. As for himself, he stationed his own forces on the hills and gullies in the vicinity of Chalcedon.

26. While Licinius was about these matters Constantine with a large number of ships, both merchantmen and men-of-war, wanted to gain the shore opposite. However, fearing that the Bithynian coast was difficult of access, especially for transport ships, he constructed skiffs and fast sailers and put out to sea bound for the so-called Sacred Promontory, which is situated at the mouth of the Euxine 200 furlongs from Chalcedon. There he landed his troops and climbed up certain hills, from which he selected a

place to draw up his line of battle. Licinius, although
he saw Bithynia in enemy hands, nevertheless, schooled
as he was in every sort of danger, summoned Martinianus
from Lampsacus and having emboldened the soldiers,
over whom he promised to take personal command, he
arranged the ranks for battle. Having proceeded forth
from the city he encountered an enemy that was all prepared for the fierce battle that ensued in a location midway
between Chalcedon and the Sacred Promontory. Constantine's side clearly got the upper hand, falling upon the
opposition with great force and wreaking such great havoc
that out of 130,000 men scarcely 30,000 escaped. As soon
as these events had occurred the Byzantines threw open
their gates and received Constantine, and the Chalcedon-
ians did likewise; but the defeated Licinius removed to
Nicomedia with the remnant of his cavalry and a few
thousand infantry.

27. At this time a Persian of royal descent named
Hormisda deserted to the Emperor Constantine for the
following reason. Once while his father, the Persians'
reigning Monarch, was celebrating his birthday in the
Persian manner, Hormisda entered the palace bringing
much game. When the feasting guests paid him no honor
nor did they rise as was fitting, he angrily threatened to
inflict upon them Marsyas' doom.[1] This allusion being
foreign, the majority did not understand it. But a certain
Persian who had lived in Phrygia and heard the tale of
Marsyas explained to his fellow banqueters the import of
Hormisda's threat. They retained this in their memory
and, when Hormisda's father met his death, the Persians,
reminded of his boastful words, selected his younger
brother King regardless of the law which conferred the

---

[1]The Phrygian satyr Marsyas was flayed alive by Apollo because
he arrogantly challenged that god to pit his lyre against his own
flute and lost.

supreme power upon an elder prince. Hormisda they bound in fetters and kept under guard on a certain hill situated in front of the city. Some time having elapsed, his wife contrived his escape in the following fashion. She caught a fish, inserted a large iron file in its stomach, sewed it up, and gave it to her most trustworthy eunuch. Him she commanded to tell Hormisda 'to eat the fish when no one was present and use for his own deliverance what he should find in its stomach.' Having hit upon this course she dispatched camels laden with wine and abundant food, providing a feast for her husband's guards. And when they applied themselves thereto Hormisda, who had torn open the fish and found the file, severed the fetters that bound his feet, seized the eunuch's stole and made his departure through the midst of the already intoxicated guards. Taking with him one of the eunuchs, he reached his friend and host the King of the Armenians. Through his agency he hurried safe and sound to Constantine, who deemed him worthy of every honor and attention. These things I have narrated exactly as they happened.

28. As Constantine besieged Licinius in Nicomedia too, the latter, his hopes dashed because he knew that he had no force adequate for battle, came forth from the city in suppliant state. He both brought Constantine the purple and hailed him as lord and master, begging his pardon for the events of the past; for he was confident that he would remain alive, his wife having secured oaths to this effect from Constantine. Martinianus was delivered up to Constantine's spearbearers to be killed, while Licinius was sent away to Thessalonica as if he would live in security there. But not much later the oaths were trodden under foot (a customary action on Constantine's part) and Licinius was hanged. [1]

---

[1] The circumstances of Licinius' death are uncertain.

29. The universal sovereignty having devolved upon Constantine alone, no longer did he conceal his innate badness of disposition but he indulged himself in every licentious act. Still, he made use of the ancestral rites, not so much out of respect as out of necessity. And therefore he had faith in soothsayers of whom he had made trial, just as though they had truly foretold all the things that had prospered for him. When he had arrived at Rome he was altogether full of vainglory, and he thought he should make a beginning of impiety with his own household. For he put to death his son Crispus, whom he had honored with the rank of Caesar as I have related earlier,[1] for having come under suspicion of being intimate with his stepmother Fausta; no consideration was accorded natural law. When Constantine's mother, Helena, bore with irrepressible bad grace the pathetic destruction of one so young, as if consoling her Constantine cured the evil with a greater evil: he ordered an extraordinarily hot bath to be prepared, put Fausta in it, and removed her only after she had died.[2]   Feeling guilty about these crimes as well as about his scorned oaths, he approached the priests asking for lustration. They replied that no method of purification had been handed down capable of cleansing such abominations.   But a certain Spaniard named Aegyptius, who had entered Rome and become a close friend of the women in the palace, in a conversation with Constantine maintained confidently that 'the doctrine of the Christians could wash away any crime and held out this promise, namely, that the unrighteous who accepted it would immediately stand free and clear of all sin.' Constantine most readily re-

---

[1] Chapter 20, above.

[2] Zosimus is the sole authority for this mode of Fausta's execution, an execution which was an imperial scandal however it may have been handled.

ceived this word and laid aside the ancestral rites in favor of those which Aegyptius imparted to him. He now initiated his impiety by holding divination as suspect for, since through it many pieces of good fortune had been predicted and had come to fulfillment for him, he was afraid lest, in the case of others' consulting it against him, that which it should predict would likewise come to pass. In keeping with his decision he directed his efforts towards abolishing things of this kind. Thus, when there fell the ancient feast day on which the army had to ascend the Capitoline and discharge the customary rites, Constantine, fearful of the soldiery, participated in the celebration; but at a sign sent by Aegyptius they let loose a torrent of abuse against the march up the Capitoline. Constantine, having apostatized from the sacred service, incurred the hatred of the Senate and the People.

30. Since he could not abide the execrations proceeding from all sides, so to say, he kept seeking after a city to counterbalance Rome in which to build his own palace. Consequently, when he was in the Troad, between ...[1] and ancient Ilium he found a site suitable for establishing a city. He both laid foundations and raised a section of wall to a height such that to this day those sailing toward the Hellespont can see it. But he had a change of heart and, leaving the work unfinished, went to Byzantium. Marveling at the site of this city, he decided to expand it as much as possible and render it suitable for an imperial residence; for the city is situated on a hill and extends over a part of the isthmus which is bounded by the so-called Horn and the Propontus. Formerly, indeed, it had a gate at the point where the porticoes built by Severus end (that Emperor did lay aside his anger against the Byzantines for admitting his enemy Niger into their city[2]). Again, a wall

---

[1] Probably Sigeum has here dropped out of the text.

[2] Cf. Book I, chapter 8 above

leading down the hill from the west side extended as far as Venus' temple and the sea over against Chrysopolis, while one from the north side of the hill in similar fashion descended to the port (which they call the Dockyard) and beyond to the sea which lies straight ahead at the mouth through which one sails out into the Euxine. This strait has a total extent out to the Euxine of about 300 furlongs. Such, then, was the original size of the city.

In the place where the gate had formerly been Constantine constructed a circular forum which he encompassed with two-storied porticoes. He built two very high arches of Proconnesian marble facing one another; through these one may both enter the porticoes of Severus and leave the old city. Wishing to make the city much larger, he surrounded it, at a distance of fifteen furlongs beyond the old wall, with a new one that cut off the entire isthmus from sea to sea.

31. And when in this way he had encompassed a city far larger than its predecessor he constructed a palace not much smaller than the one in Rome. In addition, he decked out with every finery a hippodrome, a part of which he made a shrine to the Dioscuri; their statues even now may be seen standing in the porticoes of the hippodrome. Also, in another part of the hippodrome, he set up the tripod of the Delphic Apollo, which had on it the very image of the god. There being in Byzantium a very great forum with four porticoes, at the end of one of these, to which there are not a few steps leading up, he constructed two temples and set therein cult-statues. One was of Rhea, mother of the gods, which Jason's sailing companions had once upon a time placed upon Mount Dindymus overlooking the city of Cyzicus. They say that Constantine, out of indifference to divine objects, treated this despitefully, removing the lions on either side and changing the attitude of the hands; for formerly the goddess appeared to be

holding the lions, but now her gesture was changed to
that of one praying, as she vigilantly looked out over the
city.   In the other temple he set up a statute of Fortuna
Romana.   Moreover, he built homes for certain Senators
who had followed him from Rome.   He waged no further
successful warfare: even as the Taifali, a Scythian people,
were attacking with 500 horse, not only did he not line up
against them but, having lost the greater part of his army
and having seen the enemy plundering everything right up
to his camp, he was glad to save himself by flight.[1]

32. With no war on his hands he devoted himself to
luxurious living.   He distributed to the Byzantine populace maintenance which has continued in existence up to
this day.   Expending public money upon a great many useless structures, he built some which a bit later were demolished as being unsafe owing to hasty construction.   He
also threw into confusion the long-standing magistracies.
For there had been two praetorian prefects sharing the
office jointly: they were empowered and authorized to
attend not only to the palatine ranks but also to the city
guards and those stationed in every remote outpost. Indeed,
the prefects' office was considered next in importance to
the imperium; it also disbursed the doles of grain and dis-
pensed retributive punishments for offences against military discipline.

33. Constantine upset this established order and divided
the one office into four commands.   To one prefect he
assigned all of Egypt along with the African Pentapolis;[2]

---

[1]This episode is obscure, if not vicious. If the invasion of the
Taifali took place at all, it certainly had no lasting effect: their next
appearance in Zosimus' narrative is at the outset of Theodosius I's
reign (Book IV, chapter 25 below).

[2]This comprised the five cities of Cyrenaica, namely, Apollonia,
Barca, Berenice, Cyrene, and Ptolemais.

the East as far as Mesopotamia; and in addition the Cilicians, Cappadocians, Armenians, the entire seacoast from Pamphylia to Trapezus, and the fortresses beside the Phasis. To the same man were entrusted also Thrace (bounded by the Moesian town of Asemus and the Rhodopean town of Topirus[1]) and, furthermore, Cyprus and the Cyclades Islands (though not Lemnus, Imbrus, and Samothrace). To the second prefect he assigned Macedonia, Thessaly, Crete, Greece and the islands thereabout, and both Epiruses; also, besides these, the Illyrians and Dacians and Triballi; and Pannonia as far as Valeria, plus upper Moesia. To the third prefect he assigned all Italy and Sicily and the neighboring islands, as well as Sardinia and Corsica and Africa from the Syrtes to (Mauretania-) Caesariensis.[2] To the fourth prefect he assigned the trans-Alpine Celts, Spain, and Britain besides. Having made this division of power among the prefects, he was eager to lessen their influence in other ways too. For there had been everywhere in command of the soldiers not only centurions and tribunes but also *duces* (for such were those called who in any place held the post of general); he instituted *magistri,* one for the cavalry, one for the infantry, and to them transferred the power of ordering the soldiers and punishing offenders. In this way did he detract from the prefects' authority, thereby doing harm to the affairs of both peace and war, as I shall immediately explain. For while the prefects had exacted the revenues everywhere through their agents and paid for their military expenses out of these; and while they had had the soldiery under control, submitting to punishment for whatever seemed to them to be an offense; naturally the sol-

---

[1] There may be trouble with the text: neither Asemus nor Topirus are identifiable.

[2] This is Mendelssohn's conjecture; the text is corrupt.

diers, realizing that he who supplied their provisions was also he who punished delinquents, would not dare do anything contrary to their duty, out of fear partly that their rations would be cut off, and partly that they would be punished forthwith. But at the present time, with one man as paymaster and another as arbiter of discipline, the soldiers act as they please in all respects, and to boot the greater part of the provisions falls to the gain of the general and his agents.

34. Constantine also did something else that afforded the barbarians free access into the Roman people's domain. Thanks to Diocletian's foresight all the frontiers of the Roman Empire had been fortified in the manner already described[1] with towns and citadels and towers where the entire soldiery lived. Thus the barbarians could not effect passage anywhere as forces would encounter them and repel invasions. Constantine abolished this security by removing the greater part of the soldiery from the frontiers to cities that needed no auxiliary forces. He thus deprived of help the people who were harassed by the barbarians and burdened tranquil cities with the pest of the military, so that several straightway were deserted. Moreover, he softened the soldiers, who treated themselves to shows and luxuries. Indeed (to speak plainly) he personally planted the first seeds of our present devastated state of affairs.

35. Having already[2] appointed as Caesar his son Constantinus, together with whom he designated his other two sons Constantius and Constans, he enlarged Constantinople to the size of an excessively great city, such that many of his imperial successors, upon taking up residence there,

---

[1] This description must have occurred in the gap intervening between Books I and II.

[2] Cf. chapter 20 above. Constantinus was appointed Caesar in 317, Constantius in 323, Constans in 333.

enticed an unnecessarily large throng gathering from all
parts of the world for the purpose of military service or
trade or other pursuits. Consequently they surrounded it
with other walls far greater than the ones Constantine
built. They permitted dwellings to be chockablock, so
that the city's inhabitants, both stay-at-homes and market-
ers, are pressed for space and proceed at risk owing to
the plethora of men and animals. In addition, no mean
part of the surrounding sea has become land, where stakes
were driven and edifices raised upon them, edifices which
by themselves are enough to make up a goodly city.

36. Indeed, I have often wondered how, since the city
of Byzantium has grown so great that no other can compare with it in prosperity or size, no divine prophecy
about its developing good fortune was given to our fore-
bears. Having meditated long on this matter and having
unrolled many historical works and collections of oracles
(spending time also in perplexity over these latter), I
have finally come across a certain oracle (reportedly
that of the Erythraean Sibyl or of the Epirote Phaenno,
who is said to have delivered oracles as one possessed
herself), upon which Nicomedes the son of Prusias relied
and, interpreting it to his own advantage, declared war upon
his father at the behest of Attalus.[1] And this is the oracle:

(37)   "Thracian King, you'll leave your city to the sheep
       And raise a lion, huge, crooked-clawed, dreadful,
       That will snatch the treasure of your native land
       And seize the earth without toil. And yet, say I,
       You'll not long enjoy the rights of the scepter
       But fall from majesty as dogs surround you.
       A sleeping wolf you'll rouse, crooked-clawed,
                    dreadful,

---

[1]Nicomedes II, son of Prusias II, at the behest of Attalus II. The
year was 149 B. C.

That won't place his neck beneath the yoke gladly.
Then will a pack of wolves Bithynia's land
Infest on Jove's advice. Soon the rule will pass
To men who inhabit the seat of Byzas.[1]
Thrice-blessed Hellespont, walls built by gods for
men,
. . . . .[2] at divine command.
The horrid wolf will be constrained to cower.
For they who dwell in my settlement know me.
No more shall I hide my father's mind, but sing
Clearly to mortals the deathless oracles.
Thrace will soon bring to birth a great bane, a child
Sowing evil . . . . [2]
A grave sore will rise on the continent's flanks
And will swell until, bursting, it oozes blood."

This oracle really tells all, so to say, however indirectly
and enigmatically, both of the evils that would befall the
Bithynians in later times owing to the heavy burden of
taxes imposed upon them, and of the fact that the rule
would soon "pass to men who inhabit the seat of Byzas."
And just because the events foretold have occurred over
no little extent of time let no one assume that the prophecy pertains to some other matter. For all time is brief
to God, who always both is and shall be. These things,
then, have I gathered from what the oracle said and from
what has happened. If the oracle seems to anyone to imply
something else, let him be minded in this way.

38. Having brought about these things, Constantine persevered in his unnecessary gifts to worthless and useless
men, exhausting the tribute money. Thus he became bur-
densome to the taxpayers while enriching those who had no

---

[1] The mythical Megarian founder of Byzantium (traditional founding
date: 667 B. C.).

[2] The text is mutilated.

contributions to make, for he considered prodigality to be liberality. He also imposed an excise of gold and silver upon all those who conducted business enterprises anywhere in the world, right down to the most paltry merchandise: not even the unfortunate courtesans did he let avoid this impost. As a consequence it was possible to perceive every four years, when the period was almost at hand within which this tax had to be paid, wails and lamentations throughout the entire city. And when the appointed time arrived scourges and tortures were applied to the bodies of those who, on account of extreme poverty, could not pay the fine. What's more, mothers even sold their children as slaves and fathers prostituted their daughters; they were obliged to give the exactors of the tribute money out of the traffic of such things. Indeed Constantine, wishing to contrive something really painful for the men of conspicuous wealth, would name each to the office of praetor and, using this honor as a blind, would dun each of a great weight of silver. Therefore one could see, as often as those commissioned to make this appointment came to the cities, the flight abroad of all those in fear lest they obtain the honor with the loss of their fortune. He had the net worth of the most illustrious men registered, and imposed a tax which he personally dubbed the *follis*.[1] With such assessments Constantine impoverished the cities, for long after his time the exaction continued.[2] The wealth of the cities little by little is being drained off, until the majority are now bereft of their inhabitants.

39. Having grieved the State in all these ways, Con-

---

[1] This Latin word originally meant a pair of bellows, later a leathern money pouch, finally a small bronze coin, 1/144 of Constantine's standard *solidus* and undoubtedly the rate of the Senatorial property tax now imposed.

[2] The *follis* was abolished about 450, the *terminus post quem* of Zosimus' work.

stantine died of a disease. His three surviving children
succeeded to the imperium (they were born not of Fausta,
the daughter of Maximian Herculius, but of another woman
whom Constantine had charged with adultery and put to
death[1]). They managed the affairs of state, giving way to
the inclinations of youth rather than to the general welfare.
For in the first place they distributed the nations among
themselves. Constantinus, the oldest, with Constans, the
youngest, gained the entire trans-Alpine region and Italy
and Illyria besides, as well as the country around the
Euxine Sea and Africa as far as Carthage. To Constantius
were committed the regions of Asia and the East and Egypt.
In a sense they shared the Empire with Dalmatius, who
had been appointed a Caesar by Constantine, with his
(Constantine's) brother Constantius, and with Hannibalianus; these wore a purple robe with gold fringe and were
styled *nobilissimi*, having received this title from Constantine himself out of respect for kinship.[2]

40. However, when the Empire had been divided up into
these separate parts Constantius, in his zeal not to take
a back seat, as it were, to his father in impiety, wished
to furnish everybody proof of his manliness by drawing
blood beginning with his own household. Accordingly he
first had his paternal uncle, Constantius, put to death by
the soldiers, and next devised a similar plot against Dalmatius Caesar. Simultaneously he planned the murder of
Optatus as well, who had obtained from Constantine the
dignity of *patricius* (this honorific title Constantine had
invented, and had ordained by law that the holders of it

---

[1]The generally accepted view is that Minervina, Constantine's
concubine, was the mother of his eldest son, Crispus (for his death
see above, chapter 20), but that Fausta was indeed the mother of
Constantinus, Constantius, and Constans.

[2]Dalmatius and Hannibalianus were Constantine's nephews,
while Constantius was his brother.

should take precedence over the praetorian prefects). Then the praetorian prefect Ablabius was killed, Iustitia exacting the punishment he deserved: he had contrived the death of the philosopher Sopater because he envied Constantine's friendship with him.   And, as though to move against all his kin, Constantius added to the above Hannibalianus, having enjoined the soldiers to exclaim that they would suffer no rulers other than the sons of Constantine.   These, then, were the achievements of Constantius.

41. A dispute now arose between Constantinus and Constans over the part of Africa that extends to Carthage and over Italy as well. Constans, wishing to catch his brother off-guard, dissimulated his hostility for a continuous three-year period. The opportunity long awaited arrived when he entered a friendly province and dispatched soldiers supposedly to fight as Constantius' allies in the war against the Persians but in reality to set upon Constantinus, who anticipated no such attack. They carried out their orders and killed Constantinus.[1]

42. Constans, having gotten rid of his brother in this fashion, proceeded to treat his subjects quite cruelly, mounting a totally insufferable tyranny. For he purchased some good-looking barbarians and kept them by his side in the rôle of hostages, allowing them to commit all such deeds against his subjects as furnished him an occasion for lewdness; thus did he lead all the nations under his sway to extreme wickedness. The praetorians, displeased with this state of affairs, noted that he was devoted to the pleasures of the hunt. Thereupon they availed themselves of the leadership of Marcellinus, the treasury prefect. and of Magnentius, who had been entrusted with the command over the Jovians and the Herculians (these being

---

[1]Zosimus' account of Constantinus' death is in error: he was slain in battle at Aquileia in the act of invading Italy (340 A.D.).

the names of legions[1]), and hatched a plot against him as follows.   Marcellinus   spoke   of   celebrating   his   son's birthday and invited to a banquet many an eminent figure in the camp, including Magnentius.   When the party had been prolonged until midnight Magnentius, rising from the table as if nature called and absenting himself for a short   time   from   the   guests,   reappeared   as   though   on stage, clad in imperial robes.   Just as the company at the dinner had proclaimed him Emperor, so all the inhabitants of Augustodunum, where these things took place, were of like mind; and when the report of this matter spread even further   the rural multitude concurred with those inside the city.   At the very same time certain Illyrian cavalrymen who had been sent to reinforce the Celtic legions joined up with those assembled for this cause.   To make a long story short, all the leaders of the entire soldiery, coming into general agreement, when they observed the fathers of the conspiracy shouting, together cried aloud and called Magnentius Augustus even though they did not know exactly what was happening. Constans, learning of this, started to flee to a certain little town called Helene located near the Pyrenees, but he was apprehended by Gaiso, who had been dispatched with certain men selected for this purpose, and was killed, being destitute of any aid.

43. Magnentius, then, holding the sovereign power over the trans-Alpine nations and Italy itself, Vetranio, the general of the forces in Pannonia, when he heard that Magnentius had been promoted to the imperium, was smitten with the same desire. By vote of his legions he was hailed as Emperor while residing at Mursa, a Pannonian town. At this juncture the Persians were ravaging the cities of the East. especially of Mesopotamia.   Now Constantius, although he had been worsted in the war against the Per-

---

[1]The text is mutilated: cf. Book III. chapter 30.

sians, decided nonetheless to oppose the factions of Magnentius and of Vetranio. While he meditated upon and prepared for this, and while Magnentius delayed among the Celts, Nepotianus, the son of Constantine's sister Eutropia, collected a mob of lawless men who had abandoned t h e m s e l v e s to brigandage and vagrancy and approached Rome, sporting imperial garb. But Anicetus, who had been appointed praetorian prefect by Magnentius, armed some of the plebs and led them forth from the city to do battle with Nepotianus. A crisp battle ensued in which the Romans were routed without much trouble owing to their inexperience and disarray. The praetorian prefect, seeing them in flight and fearing for the city, closed the gates. Nepotianus' soldiers pursued and slaughtered all of them as they had no means of escape. However, a few days later Nepotianus was killed, Magnentius having dispatched a force against him led by Marcellinus, who held the post which the Romans called *magister officiorum*, that is, the command of the palatine orders.

44. Meanwhile Constantius, having set out from the East to do battle against Magnentius, thought it his first order of business to secure somehow the friendship of Vetranio, to the end that he might have a war with only one rather than with two pretenders. Magnentius likewise was eager to gain the friendship of Vetranio and to carry on with him the war against Constantius. When both had sent Vetranio envoys concerning this matter, he chose to side with Constantius rather than with Magnentius. Accordingly Magnentius' envoys departed with their mission unaccomplished, while Constantius bade his armies congregate in one place and hold a joint council concerning the war against Magnentius. Vetranio having been deceived by the words of Constantius, they both mounted a platform built for the occasion. Constantius had the privilege of speaking first owing to his illustrious ancestry.

In every part of his oration he reminded the soldiers of his father's liberality and of the oaths they had sworn to maintain kind feelings towards his sons. At the same time he demanded that they not allow to retreat scot-free Magnentius, the murderer of a son of Constantine, with whom they had toiled in many wars and by whom they had been favored with very great rewards. When the soldiers heard these things, having already been primed by means of rich gifts, they shouted out that the imperium must be kept clear of bastards. Simultaneously they stripped Vetranio of his apparel and led him down off the platform a private citizen. Constantius permitted him to suffer no further unpleasantness: he granted him enough to live on in Bithynia, where he survived, unemployed, for a while before dying.

45. When in this manner the trick against Vetranio had come off successfully, Constantius marched against Magnentius. He designated as Caesar his cousin Gallus (brother by the same father of the future Emperor Julian) and betrothed his sister Constantia to him. This he did, either that Gallus might withstand the Persians or that — which was the case — an excuse for his removal might be found. For he and his brother were, as it happened, the sole survivors of Constantius' family, all the others having been killed at his (Constantius') hands, as I have already narrated. Accordingly he put upon Gallus the garb of a Caesar and, having entrusted to Lucilianus the conduct of the war against the Persians, he proceeded in person against Magnentius, joining with his own forces Vetranio's army. Magnentius also was aware that he must make greater preparations for the encounter, and appointed as Caesar his kinsman Decentius to guard the trans-Alpine peoples. After the armies had come together in Pannonia and had approached each other near the town of Mursa, Magnentius laid an ambush in the valleys adjacent to the

Adrana[1] and sent a messenger to Constantius' generals
telling them 'to delay their journey so that the enemy may
reach Siscia; there, as it has expansive fields, Magnentius
will join battle.' When this news reached Constantius'
ears he was exceedingly glad that he, being superior in
number of cavalry, would be fighting in places suitable
for riding; and so he removed his army in the direction
of Siscia. But as his men proceeded without armor and
without array (for they were not at all expecting what
would happen), the troops that had been stationed in ambush
in the valleys fell upon them and nearly buried them under
a heap of stones, thus stopping them from advancing
further.

46. After much slaughter Magnentius, boasting greatly
about his huge success, would not allow the war to be
protracted longer, but moved his forces forward into Pannonia. When he had arrived at the plains in front of Po-
tovius that are intersected by the Dravus River (which
flows through Noricum and Pannonia and empties into the
Danube), intending to join battle near Sirmium he marched
into Pannonia. It is said that his mother tried to dissuade
him from this route, bidding him to cross over into Illyria,
but that he paid her no heed, despite the fact that by many
previous predictions she had proven herself to be a real
prophetess. Meanwhile, as Magnentius was deliberating
whether he should cross the Savus River by bridge or by a
chain of floating vessels (embarking his army thereon),
Constantius dispatched Philippus, a man of the highest
rank and of outstanding practical wisdom, supposedly to
confer about a peace treaty but really to meddle with
Magnentius' troops, ascertaining what were their thoughts
about the war and what roads they would take. When
Philippus came near the camp he encountered Marcellinus,
the man with the greatest influence over Magnentius, to

---

[1]Zosimus is in error, as the Adrana (Eder) River is in Germany.

whom they now went together. Then, having assembled
his army, Magnentius commanded Philippus to state the
cause of his coming. He replied in the soldiers' presence
that it was not fitting for them as Roman subjects to wage
war against Romans, especially against the Emperor, Constantine's son, with whom they had raised many a trophy
against the barbarians. He further told Magnentius that
he should hold in remembrance the benefits Constantine
rendered both him and his parents, 'for Constantine had
received him graciously and rewarded him with the greatest honors.'   And having recounted these he asked Magnentius to leave Italy and content himself with ruling over
all the trans-Alpine peoples.

47. These statements of Philippus stirred up the army
almost to a man and terrified Magnentius. The latter with
much labor calmed his soldiers down sufficiently to pay
attention to what he had to say, namely, that he too welcomed peace.   Then he ordered the assembly dismissed
until such time as he could survey what ought to be done,
saying that he would communicate his decision concerning
the matter on the following day. At this the meeting broke
up.   Marcellinus received Philippus as though to entertain him as a guest, but Magnentius deliberated with himself as to whether Philippus should be dismissed with his
mission unfulfilled or should be detained there in violation of the rule that treats of ambassadors. In the meantime it seemed best to invite the centurions and decurions, indeed, all his military officers, to dine with him
and at that dinner to pronounce his decision. Having done
so, at daybreak he again assembled the troops and recited
the many ways in which Constans had insulted them; he
told how they all, unable to endure that man's enormous
crimes against the State, had adopted a policy that was to
the public advantage, had liberated the cities from that

vile beast, and had bestowed the imperium upon himself, unwilling though he was.

48. While he was saying these things all arose for the purpose of waging war and immediately proceeded under arms to cross the Savus. Their onrush was reported by scouts, and those on guard in Siscia, a town situated alongside the Savus, pierced some of them as they endeavored to ascend the riverbank and thwarted others as they attempted to cross the bridge. Consequently many were slain, while still more plunged into the river, shoved by themselves as well as by the enemy. With one side in flight falling off the bridge into the river and the other side in highly strenuous pursuit, a great slaughter ensued. Now Magnentius as a last resort contrived the following stratagem, by which he was able to avert the present danger. He stuck his spear in the ground and with his right hand beckoned to the adversary that he wanted to talk peace terms. When he saw that they were lending their ears, he said that he was unwilling to cross the Savus without the Emperor's bidding. Thereupon Philippus told him he must, abandoning Italy and Noricum, enter Illyria, where the treaty should be discussed. Constantius, having heard these words, called off his men from the chase and allowed Magnentius to move his army into the plains between Noricum, Pannonia, Moesia, and Dacia, because he wished to be rid of rough ground and to fight the enemy in an area suitable for his cavalry, in which he was superior. His plan having been consummated, he considered Cibalis a likely spot for fulfilling his heart's desire: in this very place Constantine had engaged and forcibly conquered Licinius. The town occupied the site I described in my narrative of that event, [1] and there he quartered part of his army. Having readied a camp between the hill on which the town lies and the plain which extends

---

[1]Chapter 18, above.

to the Savus, he fortified with a deep ditch and a thick rampart all of it that was not surrounded by the river. On the
other hand, all of it that the river did surround he connected with a bridge of boats, a bridge which could be
severed whenever he wished and then joined together quite
easily. Here he pitched the ordinary soldiers' tents and
in the very center he set up his imperial headquarters,
which for size and elegance differed not one bit from the
towns round about. The Emperor then entertained at a
feast for all his military officers, all of whom attended
except Latinus and Thalassius. These favorites of the
Emperor were anxious about Philippus, whom Magnentius
was detaining though he had been sent to him upon an
embassy.

49. Now while they were taking counsel about this matter there arrived Titianus, one of the Roman Senators,
conveying haughty words from Magnentius. He had picked
up many absurd charges against Constantine and his prog-
eny, attributing to his negligence in government the
cities' destruction. He ordered Constantius to yield the
sovereignty to Magnentius and be content if the latter
should grant him a safe life. But Constantius, having
prayed God and Iustitia to avenge Constans' murder,
said that he with their succor would wage war. Titianus
was granted permission to return to Magnentius, despite
the fact that Philippus still remained with the latter.
Thereupon Magnentius led out his army, took Siscia on
the first assault and razed it to the ground. When he had
overrun all the regions around the Savus and captured
much booty, he marched to Sirmium, expecting to seize it
also without bloodshed. But he failed of this attempt (for
he was beaten back by the numerous inhabitants of the
city and the soldiers assigned to guard it) and removed
his entire force to Mursa. When that city's inhabitants
closed their gates before him and ascended to the parapets,

Magnentius was puzzled as to what should be done, having neither military engines nor any other means of approach to the wall. Indeed, he was being assailed with darts and stones hurled by the fighters on the parapets. Furthermore, when news of the siege was relayed to Constantius, he marched out with his whole army to come to the imperiled city's aid, passing by Cibalis and all the country through which the Dravus River flows.

50. Meanwhile Magnentius had moved nearer Mursa and set fire to the gates that he might consume the iron which covered the wood and thus make an open way for the army into the city. But this effort on his part did not succeed, as those on the wall quenched the fire with a great quantity of water. Learning that Constantius was heading for Mursa, he hit upon a different stratagem, as follows. There was in front of the city a certain stadium which at one time had been marked off for drilling exercises and contests but now was covered all over with woods. He hid therein four companies of Celts and gave the command that they, when Constantius should be close at hand and battle about to be joined before the city, attack the enemy unaware so as to intercept and utterly annihilate them. However, this was discovered by those who were standing upon the wall, and Constantius immediately dispatched the brigade-leaders Scudilo[1] and Manadus. They, having singled out according to merit both hoplites and bowmen for service under their command, blocked off all the gates of the stadium, occupied its upper tiers and, surrounding on all sides those inside it, shot down arrows upon them. When some of them put their shields over their heads and attempted to crash through the stadium gates, they fell upon these in like manner, continuing to pelt them with darts and to strike them with swords until all were destroyed. In this fashion Magnentius' scheme fell through; indeed,

---

[1]So Ammianus Marcellinus XIV.10.8; the textual reading is corrupt.

his trappers turned out to be the trapped. And now the two armies met and had at each other on the plain in front of Mursa; the battle which ensued was such as had scarcely taken place previously in this war, and many fell on both sides.

51. Constantius saw that, this being a civil war, victory would not result in his heart's desire and after much slaughter the Roman armies would be so weakened as to be unable to withstand the barbarians who were lying in wait on all sides. The thought occurred to him of terminating the war by means of certain treaty agreements. While he was considering these things, the armies continued to engage in close combat. Magnentius' men, roused to the higher pitch of fury, did not stop fighting even when night had fallen upon the combatants, and their leaders too persevered both in fulfilling their military functions in general and in encouraging each individual soldier to press heavily upon the adversary. Constantius' leaders likewise recalled the pristine courage and glory of the Romans. And now in the depth of night they were smiting one another with spear and sword and anything else that happened to be at hand. Neither darkness nor any other of the things which customarily cause a cessation of hostilities stopped the armies from their mutual slaughter. Indeed, they counted it the greatest good fortune to die all together side by side. Their generals displayed throughout the battle deeds of the greatest courage and valor, and among others there fell Arcadius, who commanded the ranks of the Abulci, and Menelaus, to whom had been given the leadership of the horse-archers from Armenia.

52. Now the things told of Menelaus should not be passed over in silence. They say that he simultaneously fitted three arrows to his bow and with a single discharge transfixed not one but three bodies. Using this mode of archery he shot down no small number of the foe, and was almost

singlehandedly the cause of the enemy's flight. Nevertheless, he was himself overthrown by the hand of the commander-in-chief of Magnentius' army, Romulus. The latter likewise fell, having been hit earlier by a missile hurled by Menelaus; after this blow he did not desist from the fray until he had killed the man who had struck it.

53. Constantius being the manifest victor in the light of the rout of Magnentius' troops, an immense slaughter of men and horses and other beasts of burden now took place. Bereft of all hope and fearful lest he be surrendered to Constantius by what men of his were still alive, Magnentius decided to leave the neighborhood of Pannonia and make a dash for Italy, thence to collect another force with which to renew the battle. But when he was informed that the people of Rome favored Constantius' cause he elected to cross over the Alps and to seek safety for his person from the peoples living on the far side. Then he learned that Constantius had by a great sum of money rendered the barbarians around the Rhine his enemies as well, and that the approaches to the Gallic nations had been closed off to him through the efforts of certain leaders who bore Constantius good will. Further, he was not able to proceed through western Spain to the Moors' country, for even there Constantius had drawn over to his side the allies of Rome. Thus without resource from any quarter, he preferred a voluntary death to a dishonorable deliverance and chose to depart this life by his own hand rather than the enemy's.

54. Magnentius died in this manner after a reign of three years plus six months. He was of barbarian extract, but settled down among the Leti, a Gallic tribe, and took instruction in Latin. He was bold when fortune smiled, cowardly when it frowned. He was clever at concealing his innate maliciousness and was held to be, by those who did not know his character, a sincerely good man. These

things it has pleased me to add concerning Magnentius (as some have thought him responsible for good things befalling the commonwealth at the time of his reign), so that the truth about him may be perceived, namely, that he did nothing with good intent.

Decentius, who had been summoned by Magnentius to bring help and was making his way to Italy, immediately upon learning what had happened to the latter fell foul of certain military divisions and squadrons and, seeing no hope of escape, died with his neck twisted in a noose.

55. Thereafter, with the entire Empire invested in Constantius alone, his arrogance increased because he could not stand prosperity. In addition there increased the rôle of the informers, who are wont to present themselves in such circumstances, plotting against the apparently well-to-do. For by toppling the latter from their good fortune they are hopeful that they will themselves attain their honors, and so naturally they resort to slandering them. These took as their associates in wickedness some of the court eunuchs and, standing round about Constantius, persuaded him that Gallus, his own first cousin, adorned with the rank of a Caesar, was not content with this honor but was attempting to envelop himself in the imperium. And, having convinced Constantius that such was the case, they drove him on to plotting the murder of Gallus, which was devised by Dynamius and Picentius, vile men, zealous to better their lot through evils of this kind. Furthermore, there joined them in this project Lampadius the praetorian prefect, a man always eager to be more powerful than the rest around the Emperor. Accordingly Constantius, lending an ear to such calumnies, summoned Gallus, who was ignorant of what had been designed against him. Upon his arrival Constantius stripped him of the dignity of a Caesar, reducing him to the rank of a private citizen, and then delivered him over to the ex-

ecutioners for slaughter. Nor was this the first abomination Constantius had committed against a blood relative, but it was added to several others.

BOOK III

Having perpetrated these things against Gallus Caesar, Constantius crossed from Pannonia into Italy. However, when he saw that all the territories subject to the Romans had been cut off by means of barbarian incursions; that the Franks, Alemanni, and Saxons had already taken and ravaged forty cities situated on the Rhine, abducting a countless number of their inhabitants along with a vast amount of spoils; that the Quadi and Sarmatae with utter abandon were overrunning Pannonia and upper Moesia; and that the Persians would not desist from molesting the East, albeit they had formerly been quiet for fear that Gallus Caesar might attack them — all this he bore in mind. And, being uncertain as to what he should do, he deemed himself incompetent in his own right to retrieve such painful situations; yet he did not dare choose a partner in Empire, not just because of his excessive fondness for ruling but also because of his suspicious feeling that absolutely no one would be altogether faithful to him. For these reasons he was in great distress indeed. With the Roman Empire thus exposed to the utmost danger Eusebia, Constantius' wife, who had attained a pinnacle of learning surpassing the female sex in wisdom, broached a suggestion to him, advising him to appoint Julian Caesar over the trans-Alpine peoples (he being Gallus' brother by the same father and also grandson of that Constantius whom Diocletian had made a Caesar). Now, since Eusebia knew that the Emperor Constantius was suspicious of all his kinsmen, she deceived her husband with the following mode of speech: "He's young and of artless character. His entire life he has devoted to the pursuits of knowledge and thus is totally unfamiliar with practical affairs — so much the better for our purposes hereafter. For in his administration of affairs he will either succeed or fail. In the former case the happy outcome will be publicly registered in the Emperor's name, while in the latter he'll perish and Constantius thereafter will have no one of the imperial family to be called to the imperium.''

2. Constantius accepted this advice and summoned Julian from Athens, where he was associating with philosophers and excelling his instructors in every species of learning. When in answer to his summons he had come from Greece to Italy, Constantius declared him Caesar, gave his sister Helena to him in marriage, and dispatched him to the trans-Alpine peoples. But being by nature distrustful, and not convinced that Julian would remain well-disposed and loyal to him, he sent along with him Marcellus and Salustius, entrusting to them rather than to the Caesar the administration of affairs there. Having disposed of Julian in this manner, Constantius himself proceeded to Pannonia and Moesia, where he settled matters with the Quadi and Sarmatae. Then he turned his direction towards the East, to which the Persian invasions were drawing his attention. Julian meanwhile had crossed over the Alps and reached the Gallic nations assigned to his sway. All the same the barbarians kept up their aggression with complete indemnity. Eusebia, employing the same arguments as before, persuaded Constantius to commit the management of affairs in those places to Julian. Now, the accomplishments of Julian thereafter until his life's end have been written up by historians and poets in lengthy books,[1] even

---

[1] The bibliography of Julian (beginning with his own works, which include addresses, epistles, encomia and satires) is an exceptionally long one, not only because of his personality and scholarly background but because of the controversy which his apostasy awakened among church historians. For modern works see A. Piganiol, *L' Empire*

if none of these writers has done justice to those deeds. One' who wishes may get an all-inclusive survey by reading Julian's speeches and letters: from these there is the likeliest possibility of comprehending the achievements of his administration over-all. Since it is not my business to fragment my history, I will speak briefly of individual events in their proper places, in particular, events which appear to have been omitted by others.

3. Constantius then, having permitted his Caesar to do whatever he thought would be advantageous for the nations under his sway, headed for the East to wage war against the Persians. But Julian, finding the Celtic military situation rotten for the most part, with the barbarians enjoying unrestricted passage on the Rhine even almost down to the towns hard by the sea, reviewed what armed forces were left. Noticing that the local people winced at the very sound of the name barbarians while the men Constantius had given him, just 360 in number, knew only how to say prayers (as he himself says somewhere), he enrolled as many as he could in the ranks and accepted many volunteers. He gave thought to weapons as well and, having uncovered in a certain town a store of old ones which he deemed fit for service, he distributed them to the soldiery. And as soon as he had heard his scouts' report that a vast horde of barbarians had crossed the Rhine in the vicinity of Argentoratum, which is situated on the river's bank, he advanced with his army on the spur of the moment. Having collided with the enemy, above and beyond all expression he it was who set up the trophy: 60,000 men perished in the battle proper and as many more plunged into the Rhine and were destroyed in its

---

Chrétien (Paris, 1947) 110 ff.; also W. E. Kaege Jr., "Research on Julian the Apostate, 1945-1964," *Classical World* 58 (1965), 229 ff. See in addition Edward Gibbon's masterful biography (Chapters 19, 22-24 in *The Decline and Fall of the Roman Empire*); also the recent (1964) and delightful novel by Gore Vidal entitled, simply, *Julian*.

current. Therefore, if any one should wish to compare this victory with the battle of Alexander against Darius, he would not find it inferior, to that.[1]

We should not pass over in s i l e n c e a d e e d of the Caesar's after the battle. He had a squad of 600 cavalry exceedingly well-drilled in military maneuvers. Confiding in their strength and experience, he had staked no small part of his hopes on them. When the battle was joined, all rushed against the adversary with a mighty display of zeal. While the Roman army easily came off the victor these cavalry alone were routed and deserted their ranks, so shamefully that, when Caesar in very person with a small group rode up and called them back, at the same time exhorting them to share in the victory, not even then did they want to be participants in the battle. Then Caesar, rightly indignant because, so far as in them lay, they had betrayed their own people to the barbarians, did not impose upon them the penalty constituted by law; instead he dressed them in women's clothing and paraded them en route to exportation, believing such punishment to be more severe for military men than death. Indeed, the end result was opportune both for himself and for them: for in a second war against the Germans they, almost alone and above all the rest, mindful of the ignominy inflicted upon them, conducted themselves bravely.

4. When Caesar had finished this chore, he collected a host of soldiers at leisure in preparation for his war against the entire German nation. As the barbarians lined up in opposition with a vast multitude, Caesar did not await their assault but crossed the Rhine himself. He preferred that the fighting take place on the barbar-

---

[1]Mendelssohn would change the MS reading from 60,000 to 6,000 on the strength of Ammianus Marcellinus XVI. 12, where it is reported that the Romans lost 243 soldiers and four officers vis-à-vis a German loss of 6,000 men in battle and of an untold number in the river.

ians' soil rather than on the Romans', in that the cities would not once again be oppressed by the barbarians' occupation. A very fierce battle occurred in which a countless throng of barbarians fell, Caesar pursuing the fugitives as far as the Hercynian Forest and wreaking much slaughter. Furthermore, he took alive Vadomarius, the son of the barbarians' leader. Then he led home his army which was raising the paean over their victories and praising in song their Caesar's skills. Julian shipped off Vadomarius to Constantius, to whose good fortune he attributed his victory. And the barbarians, having been driven to disaster's brink, and now fearful for their children and womenfolk lest Caesar might perchance advance all the way to those places where they were and exterminate the entire breed of them, sent envoys to talk of a peace in terms of which they would never again fight the Romans. But Caesar said that he would not confer with them concerning peace unless and until he should recover every one of the captives whom they had previously abducted from the cities they had seized. When they had agreed to do this also, that is, to return all that were still alive, Caesar worked up the following scheme to make sure that none of the captives would remain among the barbarians unbeknownst to him. He summoned the fugitives out of every town and village and asked them to name each and every one of the captives whom the barbarians had abducted from said towns and villages. When each had named the persons known to him either through consanguinity or neighborhood or friendship or some other circumstance, Caesar commanded the imperial secretaries to draw up a descriptive list of all these persons. This was done, and the envoys, who were ignorant of the design, he shipped across the Rhine with a commission to return with the captives. Not long after, when they had obeyed the injunction and reported that they had all the captives,

Caesar seated himself upon a lofty tribunal, behind which he stationed his secretaries. He then ordered the barbarians to present the captives as per the agreement. These filed past one by one stating their names, which the secretaries, standing by Caesar with their little books, looked up. Having collated those of whom they had made notes previously and those who appeared before Caesar, they discovered that the former group, that is, those who had been named by their fellow townsmen and villagers, was larger by far. They so informed Caesar from their post behind him, and he threatened the barbarians' envoys with war on the grounds that they had not made delivery of all the captives. Indeed, he then called off the names of the missing from each and every town and village as submitted by his secretaries. The barbarians imagined it was by some divine force that things so very cryptic and secret were revealed to Caesar. They agreed — indeed, they took their nation's oath on it — to return all, as many as they should find still alive.

5. This done, there was surrendered as great a host of captives as was likely to have been herded together from forty towns taken by storm. Caesar was now undecided what he should do, seeing that the towns had been completely destroyed, the land had remained untilled for no little stretch of time, and the people handed over by the barbarians needed lots of provisions (these could not be readily procured from the towns nearby because they too had experienced the barbarians' onset and did not have supplies in abundance). Therefore, not knowing how to handle the present situation, he devised the following scheme. The Rhine discharges itself into the Atlantic Ocean at the farthest limits of Germany. Here on the bank is a nation of Gauls, while 900 stades distant is the island of Britain. He gathered timber from the woods adjacent to the river and constructed 800 boats bigger

than skiffs. These he sent to Britain, whence he had grain fetched. He also invented a way for the grain to be carried up the Rhine River by boat. By doing this rather frequently (for the distance was short) he provided enough for those whom he had restored to their hometowns, so that they might live on part of the grain and sow part of it and have the necessities of life until harvesttime. These things he accomplished almost before attaining his twenty-fifth birthday.

Julian's soldiers were well-disposed towards him because of his plain style of living, his courage in warfare, his moderation in money matters, and his other virtuous qualities, in which he surpassed practically all the other men of his time. On account of these excellences Constantius was smitten with envy. Believing that the sagacity of Salustius (one of the advisers assigned to him) was responsible for his great reputation in military and other administrative matters, he summoned this man to place him in charge of affairs in the East. Julian readily dismissed him (for he had resolved to be obedient to Constantius in all things). Still, everything entrusted to Caesar's charge progressed no small amount day by day, so to speak, while the soldiers increased in number and military skill and the towns enjoyed peace and the blessings that come therefrom.

6. Now, when nearly all the barbarians dwelling round about had abandoned hope, as much as expecting that those who still survived would be destroyed en masse, the Saxons, who were held to be the staunchest of them in spirit and strength and endurance under combat, sent forth the Quadi, a part of their nation, into territory occupied by the Romans. Their neighbors, the Franks, however, prevented their passage, fearful that it would afford Caesar just cause for invading them again; so they built themselves boats and, passing by on the Rhine the land held by the Franks, they hastened toward Roman territory. They

landed on Batavia, an island formed by the splitting apart
of the Rhine, being bigger than any other river island.
Hence they tried to expel the Salii, a part of the Frankish
nation that had been driven out of their own country to the
island by the Saxons (this same island, which was at the
time occupied by the Salii, was formerly the Romans' altogether). Learning of this, Caesar rushed against the Quadi,
exhorting his army 'to fight them with might and main, yet
not to kill any of the Salii nor prohibit their crossing the
Roman borders, inasmuch as the latter were setting foot on
their land not as enemies but being forced to do so by the
Quadi.' This kindliness on Caesar's part being noticed,
some of the Salii crossed over with their king from the island onto Roman soil, while others betook themselves in
flight to the borders; but all came as suppliants to Caesar
and voluntarily made over to him themselves and their possessions. Now he observed that the barbarians no longer
dared to fight him but were intent on clandestine incursions
and forays, wreaking as a result extraordinary damages upon the region. In doubt as to what he should do, he avenged
this cunning of the barbarians with a shrewd stratagem.

7. There was a certain man whose body was bigger
than everyone else's and whose courage matched his bodily
size. Being a barbarian by race and accustomed to their
raiding parties, he saw fit to migrate from his ancestral
haunts to the Celts, subjects of the Romans. Then, having
lingered for some time at Treveri, which is the largest
city of the trans-Alpine nations, and having seen the barbarians on the far side of the Rhine overrunning the towns
opposite and plundering everybody's property without hindrance (Julian not yet having obtained the office of Caesar),
he thought of defending the towns. However, his hands
being tied inasmuch as no law allowed him to do any such
thing, at the outset he went into hiding by himself in the
densest part of the forests and awaited the barbarians'

incursions. He set upon them by night while they were
still exhausted and in a drunken stupor, and he cut off as
many of their heads as he could. These he carried into the
city and put on display. By doing this steadily he inspired
no little alarm in the barbarians, who did not know what
was happening but who were conscious of the fact that practically every day their ranks suffered loss. Moreover, when
other brigands had joined him, coming over one at a time
until they reached a considerable number, then indeed
Charietto — for such was the name of him who first hit
upon this plan against the barbarians — approached Caesar
and disclosed to him the matter, which was previously not
known to many. Caesar could not easily employ his army to
proceed against the barbarians' clandestine night raids (for
they spread themselves thin over a large area and practiced
their robbery; then at daybreak none was anywhere to be
found as they hid in the woods near the fields, living off
the produce of their brigandage). Having taken into consideration the difficulty involved in conquering the enemy, he
had no choice but to pursue the brigands not only with his
army, but with a robber band as well. Therefore he received Charietto and his men, and added to their numbers
many Salii. Skilled as they were in robbery he would send
them at night against the thieving Quadi, and in the daytime he would line up his soldiery out in the open and would
massacre as many as had been able to escape the robber
band. Caesar kept this up until the Quadi, reduced to the
direst strait (indeed, out of many there were few left),
along with their leader surrendered to him. He had already
obtained a host of prisoners during the early assaults,
including the king's son, who had been captured by Charietto.   When they held out the olive branch in pitiable
fashion he demanded as hostages certain of their distinguished men and together with these the king's son. At
that the barbarians' leader broke into most mournful

wails, avowing tearfully that he had lost among others his son also. Then and there Caesar took pity on a father's tears and showed him his son, who was living comfortably. Saying that he was holding him in the role of a hostage and taking other well-born hostages in addition, he generously acceded to peace on this condition, that they would never again raise a hand against a Roman.

8. These matters having been settled thus, Caesar enrolled Salii, part of the Quadi, and certain inhabitants of the island of Batavia alike, in ranks which even down to our own time apparently have been preserved. Meanwhile the Emperor Constantius in the East concentrated his thoughts upon Persia solely and persisted in his wars there. For the affairs in the trans-Alpine nations were going well for him thanks to Caesar's foresighted administration: and all Italy and Illyria were free of any danger because the barbarians above the Danube were restraining themselves within the bounds of moderation for fear that Caesar might set out through Gaul, cross the Danube and attack them. While Constantius, then, was occupied with these matters the Persians, whose king was Sapor, were plundering Mesopotamia. Having devastated everything in the vicinity of Nisibis they were now besieging the city itself with all their strength. But Lucilianus the commander was equipped to sustain the siege, and partly owing to the gifts of fortune which he used aright, partly owing to his generalship the city escaped disaster, although it had undergone extreme peril. How it did so I have felt it superfluous to recount, since Caesar himself has told all that was then done in his own writing; [1] if one take this in hand he may perceive the author's towering skill in oratory.

Now, when affairs in the East appeared to be calm and Caesar's successes were on everyone's tongue, Constantius

---

[1] This is Julian's "Panegyric in Honor of the Emperor Constantius." Oration I. 27ff.

was seized with violent envy. Bitter about the prosperous
state of the Celts and Spaniards both, he contrived preten-
ces through which he might be able gradually and imper-
ceptibly to reduce Caesar's forces and thus deprive him of
his rank. Accordingly he issued orders to him that his two
legions of Celtic soldiers be shipped out, alleging that he
needed these as auxiliaries. Julian immediately complied
with this injunction, because he did not know of Constantius'
purpose and at the same time in order that he might not afford him any occasion for anger. Still, he deemed Celtic
affairs worthy of every consideration and was continually
augmenting his army, keeping the barbarians settled on the
frontiers so cowed that not even in their dreams did they
contemplate war. Constantius, however, asked that other
military divisions as well be sent him by Caesar. Having
obtained this request, not long afterwards he commanded
that four squadrons be transferred to himself, and Caesar
instructed the soldiers to get ready to depart forthwith.

9. Julian was staying in Parisium (which is a little German town[1]) and the soldiers, preparing for traveling, were
dining late into the night near the Caesar's quarters, quite
unaware of the plots being laid for him. But some of the
tribunes, who had discovered that there was in very truth a
long-standing scheme against him, distributed secretly
amid the soldiery anonymous pamphlets signifying that
'Caesar, he who through his leadership ability had given
nearly everybody the opportunity to set up trophies taken
from the barbarians and who in actual combat differed in not
one particular from a private, would be exposed to extreme
danger shortly as the Emperor was surreptitiously stealing
his troops, unless they all hurriedly convened and prevented
the departure of the soldiers.' When certain of the soldiers
had read these handbills and reported to the multitude the

---

[1]Actually, this "little German town" was that Gallic town
Lutetia Parisiorum, now Paris.

machination, they aroused all to anger. And they rose up from their drinking-bout with much clatter, their cups still nested in their hands, and hastened to headquarters. Bursting through the doors with no semblance of order, they led Caesar into public view and, lifting him aloft upon a shield, they proclaimed him *Augustus Imperator;* then they forcibly placed the diadem upon his head.

Caesar was annoyed at what had happened, yet felt it unsafe to revoke what had been done. Though Constantius abided by neither oaths nor covenants and though he kept no other word of honor of those in use among men, nevertheless Caesar wanted to make trial of his intention. Therefore he sent envoys stating that the coronation had taken place against his own will and judgment and, begging pardon for the event, added that he was prepared to lay aside the diadem and hold the rank of Caesar. But Constantius got so carried away by anger and arrogance he told the envoys that 'Julian, in exchange for his life, should lay aside in addition to the imperium his Caesar's habit and, having made himself a private citizen, should wait upon the Emperor's pleasure; for he would not suffer anything terrible or what his temerity deserved.' When Julian had heard this from the envoys, he brought out into the open his deliberate choice regarding providence: he said directly within earshot of all that he would rather entrust himself and his life to the gods than to the words of Constantius.

Thereafter Constantius' hostility towards Julian was evident to everyone; indeed, Constantius was making preparations for civil war. Meanwhile, in addition to the things that had come to pass it vexed Julian that he would garner a reputation among the masses for ingratitude should he wage war against the man who had bestowed upon him the office of Caesar. While he was revolving all these matters in his mind and was exceedingly hesitant about undertaking the civil war, providence revealed to him in his sleep what was going to happen. He was at Vienna, and Sol appeared in a vision to show him the stars and speak the following verses:

"When Jove to Aquarius's wide bourne comes,
And Saturn walks on Virgo's twenty-fifth part,
A hateful, painful end will greet the dear life
Of Constantius, Emperor of Asia's land."

Relying on this dream, he applied himself diligently, as was his custom, to the public business. And, since it was still winter, he took such precautions as were deemed necessary concerning the barbarians' affairs, that, if he should have to take part in other matters as well, the status of the Celts might remain secure. At the same time, with Constantius lingering in the East, he was making plans to anticipate his attack.

10. Summer was now at its height. Julian had already disposed of matters having to do with the barbarians above the Rhine, having forced some of them into good behavior through fighting and having persuaded others to cherish peace rather than war through past experience. He began drawing up his army as though for a long journey abroad and, having placed civil and military leaders in charge of the towns and the frontiers, he proceeded toward the Alps with his troops. When he had come into Raetia (whence the Danube rises and passes by Noricum and both Pannonias and then Dacia and Moesia in Thrace and Scythia and so discharges itself into the Euxine Sea), having had river boats built he sailed down the Danube with 3,000 men, instructing the other 20,000 to take the overland route to Sirmium. And thanks to steady rowing coupled with the force of the current (since the etesian winds were a helpful factor) on the eleventh day he neared Sirmium. A report that the Emperor was close at hand having made the rounds, nearly everyone thought that Constantius was

meant. But having received Julian they were in a state of consternation altogether and likened what had happened to a prodigy.

Not long thereafter, when the Celtic force that was following had reached him, he wrote to the Roman Senate and the troops in Italy 'to keep the cities safe, for he was Emperor.' And because Taurus and Florentius, the consuls of that year,[1] who were on Constantius' side, upon learning that Julian had crossed the Alps and come into Pannonia had quit Rome in flight, he commanded that they be inscribed in the public records as fugitive consuls. But all the cities which he had happened to have gone through on the run already he cultivated, thus promoting in everyone high hopes. He wrote also to the Athenians and to the Lacedaemonians and to the Corinthians setting forth the reasons for his coming.

11. While he was at Sirmium there were envoys sent to him from almost all of Greece. Having made the appropriate replies to these and having bestowed upon them as much honor as was fair, he collected his Celtic army as well as another composed of divisions stationed in Sirmium proper and throughout Pannonia and Moesia. Marching forward he reached Naissus, where with the soothsayers he examined what he should do. The entrails signifying that he should stay put for a while, he did so, simultaneously watching closely the time revealed in his dream. When this appeared to coincide with the motions of the stars, while he was at Naissus a host of cavalry from Constantinople brought him the news that Constantius had died and that the armies had designated him, Julian, for the supreme command.

Having accepted this present from heaven he continued his forward progress. When he had approached Byzantium all welcomed him with songs of praise, hailing him their fellow citizen and foster child inasmuch as he

---

[1] A. D. 360.

had been born and reared in this city. In other respects
as well they made their obeisances as though he would
be the author of the greatest blessings for mankind.
Thereat he took charge of the city and the armies simultaneously. He granted the city the right to have a Senate
like the one at Rome and constructed for her a very large
harbor, a haven for vessels from the treacherous south
wind; a stoa, in the shape of a crescent rather than in a
straight line, running down to the harbor; finally, a library,
built inside the imperial stoa, in which were deposited
all the books he had. And now he made preparations to
wage war against the Persians. After having spent ten
months in Byzantium he appointed Hormisda and Victor
generals, handed over to them the tribunes and armies,
and set out for Antioch. Needless to say, the soldiers
carried out this long march with complete tranquility and
discretion, for it was unlikely that they would have made
any noise, drawn up as they were under Julian's command.
He sojourned at Antioch, where the people received him
cordially. However, they were by nature fond of spectacles and devoted more to luxurious living than to serious
business, and naturally resented the Emperor's good
sense and moderation in all things: he boycotted the theatre and rarely watched games, and then never throughout
an entire day. Voices of criticism accordingly were
raised, which distressed him. He made requital not in
deeds, by taking some vengeful action against them, but
in words, by addressing a most witty speech to them and
to their city alike.[1] It contains so much pungency as
well as irony that it served to disseminate throughout the
entire world the disgrace of the Antiochenes, who repented of their mistakes. But the Emperor came to the
city's aid when he could equitably and granted it a very

---

[1] This is the *Misopogon*, the "Beard-Hater," so named because
the Antiochenes had mocked his philosopher's beard.

large number of decurions, who would come by the office
in succession to their fathers, besides admitting as many
as were sons of decurions' daughters, which privilege,
we know, has been given few cities. Finally, having settled many other matters fairly and justly, he girded himself for his Persian war.

12. Winter had now ended. He assembled his army
and packed it off in good marching order. Then he himself went forth from Antioch even although the omens had
turned out unfavorable (I know why, but won't tell). On the
fifth day he reached Hierapolis, where all the boats, both
military and cargo, from Samosata and from the points
of navigation down the Euphrates, were to convene. He
placed in charge of these Hierius, one of his regular company commanders, and sent him ahead. He stayed on at
Hierapolis a mere three days, and then proceeded to
Batnae, a little town in Osrhoëne. There the people of
Edessa met him in a body, presented him with a crown,
and invited him into their city with acclamation. The
Emperor accepted, halted at the city, and transacted all
necessary business. Then he moved on to Carrhae,
whence there stretched two routes, one via the River
Tigris and the city of Nisibis as far as the satrapies of
Adiabene, the other via the Euphrates and Circesium
(this is a fortress around which the Aboras[1] and the
Euphrates itself flow, adjacent to the borders of Assyria).
While the Emperor was deliberating which of these passages he should use there was announced an incursion of
Persians, who were said to be overrunning places under
Roman jurisdiction. As a result of this announcement
the camp was thrown into utter confusion, but the Emperor
learned that they were robbers instead, who had departed
after plundering what was in their path. He decided that
an ample garrison should be left behind for the country

---

[1]More properly the Chaboras, the modern Khabour.

around the Tigris; otherwise, if his entire force should go with him to invade Persian territory by the one route, the Persians might secretly destroy Nisibis and all its environs, finding them destitute of help. Therefore it seemed best to leave there 18,000 heavy-armed soldiers under the command of Sebastianus and Procopius; while he himself along with his whole force should make his way via the Euphrates, his army being divided into two sections so that, if any of the enemy should appear, it would be ready to resist them on every side and not let them run riot over everything in their path.

13. Having settled these matters at Carrhae (which city separates the Romans from the Assyrians), he wanted to review the army from a certain eminence and admire the infantry legions and cavalry squadrons, a grand total of 65,000 men. He left Carrhae and passed quickly by the forts between there and Callinicum, whence he went to Circesium, about which there has been mention above. Having crossed the Aboras River, he sailed on board ship down the Euphrates. There followed the soldiers, bringing the provisions; as many of them as had been ordered to take shipping did so, for by now the fleet had arrived, consisting of 600 boats made of timber and 500 made of wood. Besides these there came along fifty military ships, as well as other flatboats, by means of which bridges could be formed, should the need anywhere arise, to give the infantry passage over the rivers. In addition there followed a great many other boats, some bearing victuals for the army, others wood for fabricating military engines, and still others siege machinery already constructed. Lucianus and Constantius were appointed admirals. Such being the order of the armed forces, the Emperor from a platform addressed them all together in proper fashion. Then, having given each of the soldiers a largesse of 130 silver coins, he made his move against

the Persians. He chose Victor general of the infantry, Hormisda of the horse, and with him Arintheus. Concerning Hormisda it has been previously[1] said that he was both a Persian and a king's son who, wronged by his brother, came as a refugee to the Emperor Constantine; furnishing proofs of good will, he was deemed worthy of the greatest honors and offices.

14. As therefore the Emperor penetrated the Persian frontier the cavalry held the left wing and part of the infantry, that was charging along the bank of the river, the right. The remainder of the army followed at a distance of seventy furlongs. The intervening space was taken up partly by the pack animals bearing loads of heavy armor and other matériel, partly by what sutlers there were, so that even these, protected by the army completely, could be secure. Having thus arranged his line of march, he decided to send ahead 1,500 men under Lucilianus' leadership to reconnoiter as to whether there was any enemy opposition either in the open or in ambush. After a march of sixty furlongs, he came to a place called Zautha, whence he went to Dura, by this time deserted although furnishing evidence (including the Emperor Gordian's tomb) that it had been a city once upon a time. There also a great herd of deer was spotted and shot by the soldiers, who feasted off the meat from these. Thence he advanced a four-days' journey to a spot named Phathusae, in the river opposite which there was an island with a fort containing very many settlers. Against this fort were sent Lucilianus and the 1,000 scouts under his command to besiege it. And as long as it was night the besiegers continued unobserved, but once daylight came they were seen by one of the fort's inhabitants, who had gone forth to fetch water. Those inside were thrown into a turmoil, all of them ascending the wall. Now the Em-

---

[1]Book II, chapter 27.

peror crossed over to the island with his engines of war and with other troops as well and pledged to those in the fort that, if they would surrender both themselves and it, they would escape obvious destruction. This they did, and their men, children and women alike were escorted under military guard into Roman territory. Their leader Pusaeus he found faithful, presented with a tribunate, and numbered among his intimate friends thereafter.

15. Advancing a certain distance the Emperor came upon another island in the river, on which was a very strong fort. Having attacked this and having found it impregnable on every side, he asked its defenders to give themselves up and not endure the danger of capture by storm. This, which they saw others also doing, they promised they'd do. Then the Emperor advanced past more forts, being satisfied with similar promises; for he thought he should not waste his time over trivia, but seek the very fountainhead of the war. After a march of some days he reached Dacira, a town lying on the right bank as one sails the Euphrates. When the soldiers found it deserted of its inhabitants they looted its great store of grain as well as no small supply of salt. And when they had slaughtered the women who had been left behind they destroyed the city so thoroughly that onlookers at the site don't believe it ever existed. On the opposite bank, along which the army was making its march, there was a spring that yielded bitumen. Afterwards he went in succession to Sitha, Megia, and the town of Zaragardia, where there was a lofty platform made of stone to which the inhabitants customarily referred as Trajan's. This town the soldiers very easily plundered and burned, and then rested both that day and the next.

The Emperor was surprised that the army had completed so much of its journey and yet not a single hostile Persian band had offered resistance either from ambuscade

or out in the open. He dispatched with a force to reconnoiter, as the man with the most accurate knowledge of
Persian affairs, Hormisda, who along with those with him
wasn't far from falling into extreme danger had not an
unexpected bit of luck rescued them. For a surenas
(this being the title of a magistracy among the Persians)
had set an ambush in a certain place and was lying in wait
for Hormisda and his soldiers, meaning to attack them
as they passed by all unsuspecting. And, indeed, the results hoped for would have come to pass had not a channel
in the middle of the Euphrates flooded beyond its wont
and prevented Hormisda and his soldiers from crossing.
For this reason was their crossing delayed. On the following day they uncovered the surenas and his fellow am-
bushers and, wheeling around, attacked them. Some they
killed, while some they routed and then mixed in with the
rest of the army.

16. Proceeding farther, they arrived at a certain channel
of the Euphrates which extended lengthwise as far as
Assyria and at the same time spread itself over the entire
countryside to the Tigris. Here the soldiers encountered
gluey mud and standing water and saw their horses in
particular afflicted by the rough going. Furthermore they
themselves were unable to wade across the channel with
their arms as its depth would not permit it, nor would the
mud yield such a passage. Situated in such a serious
predicament, they were faced with yet greater peril in that
the enemy was observed on the opposite bank, ready to
impede their crossing with arrows and stones shot from
slings. When no one could find a way out of the dangers
that beset them, the Emperor, who excelled in general
readiness of wit and in military skill, decided that the
1500 men under Lucinianus' command who were off on
a scouting expedition should be sent word to move against
the enemy's rear and divert their attacking force, thus

giving the Emperor's men clear sailing across the channel.
On this mission he dispatched with a goodly force his
general, Victor, who waited for nightfall lest his departure
from the army be noted by the Persians and, having advanced only so far as to give the enemy no chance to see
when day broke what was happening, he crossed the channel and sought out Lucilianus' company.

17. After further progress finding no foe whatsoever,
he called his countrymen again and again with a shout and
with the sound of trumpets signaled that they should come
to him.   When in accordance with his desire all had, for-
tunately, come together, Lucilianus formed a judgment:
mingling his troops with Victor's he attacked the enemy
from the rear unexpectedly.   Thus taken by surprise,
they either were killed or fled by whatever way was prac-
ticable.   And now the Emperor, for whom this stratagem
had turned out favorably, crossed the channel without any
opposition.   He embarked the cavalry on boats already at
hand, the infantry on ships which he found in various parts
of the channel.   Then he kept marching forward, the while
having no foe to dread.

He came to a city named Bersabora, the size of which
he surveyed, as well as the strength of its position; for
the city was encircled by two walls, and at its center
stood a citadel having its own wall, one that somewhat
resembled the segment of a circle.   To this citadel a road
with a by no means easy grade led from the city's inner
wall.   In addition, to the west and south of the town there
was a turning and twisting way out, while the side to the
north the inhabitants had protected with a wide channel
diverted from the river; through this channel, too, they
drew water for their private use.   Finally, the side to the
east was fenced around with a deep ditch and a palisade
made out of stout wooden pales; about the ditch there
stood tall towers built, from the ground up to their mid-

point, of bricks laid with asphalt and, beyond that point, of the same kind of bricks plus gypsum.

18. Having determined to take this city, the Emperor kept exhorting his soldiers to undertake the task. As they proceeded with great alacrity to carry out his commands, the town's residents asked to be received into the Emperor's favor, now begging that Hormisda be sent them to discuss peace terms, now hurling gross insults to the effect that he was a deserter, a fugitive, and a traitor to his country. At this the Emperor was, naturally, aroused to anger; he ordered everybody to keep working and to press the siege vigorously. As each of them pitched into his assigned job, those in the city, perceiving that they were not adequate for the task of garrisoning its walls, retreated in a body to the citadel. At sight of this the Emperor threw against the city, bereft as it was of its inhabitants, his forces, who demolished the walls and fired the houses; then upon the city's ruins they set their military engines, from which they shot with a steady discharge arrows and stones against those on the citadel. However, since the townspeople warded off the besieging party with a continuing round of the same weapons, a great loss was sustained on both sides.   Now the Emperor, whether from native wit in sizing up the situation of a locale or from much study of matters of this sort, constructed a special engine [1] as follows.   He fastened together four very large pieces of timber with iron and with these fashioned a square tower, which he placed opposite the wall of the citadel.   Then its height little by little was increased until it matched the walls'.   He mounted bowmen upon it, as well as men who could discharge stones and arrows from a machine.   Thereupon the

---

[1] This is the *helepolis*, or siege engine, invented by Demetrius Poliorcetes ('The Besieger').   A fuller description of the machine may be found in Ammianus Marcellinus XXIII. 4.

Persians were thrown into complete confusion, both by those besieging and those standing at the machine. Although they held out for a time, eventually they capitulated, promising to hand over the citadel if the Emperor would exercise moderation in dealing with them. And it was agreed that every one of the Persians within should have safe passage through the midst of the army, a fixed sum of money, and clothing, and that the citadel should be surrendered to the Emperor. This done, in the neighborhood of 5,000 men were freed, not to mention those who had managed to escape by small craft through the channel. Along with the rest there exited the crowd's leader, Momosirus. Now after the citadel had been captured in this manner the soldiers, making a search of the things left behind therein, found an immense store of grain, plus arms of every kind, engines, and no little amount of furniture and other household stuff. The greater portion of the grain was put on shipboard for the army's sustenance, while that portion which was held apart from the public provisions the soldiers divided up among themselves. As for the arms, all which seemed to the Romans useful for war were distributed to the army, but those suitable for Persian use alone and not theirs were either burnt or consigned to the river for removal by sinkage.

As a result no small credit accrued to the Romans' reputation because a large city, second only to Ctesiphon of those in Assyria and so well fortified, had been taken by storm in a bare two days. At this the Emperor in indulgent fashion praised the army with fitting words and presented each man with 100 silver coins.

19. Thus were these things accomplished. However, a surenas with a considerable force from a certain city in Assyria, having attacked the scouts of the Roman army, who were imprudently preceding the others, killed one of the three leaders together with some men under his com-

mand. Having scattered the rest, he got possession of the military standard bearing a dragon's figure in relief, such as the Romans were wont to carry in battle. When the Emperor learned this he took it hard: angrily, just as he was, he assaulted the surenas' men. As many of these as were able to get away he put to rout. Having recovered the standard that had been carried off by the enemy, he promptly approached the city wherein the surenas had hidden the ambuscade that attacked the scouts. This city he seized by force and set on fire. As for the scouts' leader that had forsaken the standard to the enemy and thus placed his safety ahead of the pride of Rome, he stripped him of his sword-belt and thereafter held him in disgrace along with those who were his partners in flight.

As he was making his way forward via the river he came to a certain fort near a town by the name of Phissenia, alongside whose wall there ran a very deep ditch. The Persians had filled this with water by diverting to it no small part of the nearby stream known as the King's River. After passing by this town (for nothing hostile was to be feared from it) they trekked through a place inundated by an artificial swamp; indeed, the Persians, having let loose upon the region channel and river alike, thought they had made it impossible for an army to cross. Nevertheless, with the Emperor running in front, the army followed in turn, although they sank up to their knees; for they felt ashamed not to do what they observed their Emperor doing. The sun having already set, the army bivouacked in this locale. The Emperor commanded a task force to attend him and cut down trees and timber, with which to bridge the sluices. He piled up dirt in the swampy places, filled up the ruts in the roads, and to some extent widened the narrow spots. Then, having returned, he led the army across with ease until he reached the town of Bithra, where there was a palace and dwellings sufficient to accommodate both the Emperor and his army.

20. Proceeding from there and being intent upon the same labors, he led the van and rendered the route more tolerable. And in this fashion he brought everybody through until he arrived at a place with no buildings but with a grove, planted with date palms in which vines also had sprung up, reaching with their shoots as high as the trees' foliage and presenting to view the fruit of the palm intertwined with grape clusters. He spent the ensuing night in this grove and on the morrow continued his advance. Having approached too close to a certain fortress, he was on the verge of receiving a lethal blow; for a Persian made a sally from the fortress and thrust his sword at the head of the Emperor. The latter, however, foresaw the blow and shook it off by putting his shield to his head. Then the soldiers fell upon the Persian and slaughtered him and all his men save for some who slipped away and took refuge in the fortress. The Emperor, indignant at this bold act, scanned the fortress, walking around it to see where it might be vulnerable. While he was engaged in this, the surenas showed himself unexpectedly before the soldiers who had remained in the palm grove. He hoped to get possession of the beasts of burden and the baggage, and at the same time to make the Emperor, upon learning this news, quit the siege of the fortress. But, although both these hopes he revolved in his mind, he was disappointed of both. Now the Emperor was placing much weight upon the storming of the fortress, for near it there was a populous city, Besuchis by name, plus a great many other fortified places deserted of their inhabitants, it so happened, as being too insecure; these had flocked together into the very one being besieged by the Emperor, except for those who had fled away to Ctesiphon or had hidden themselves where the grove was densest.

The Emperor therefore pressed the siege vigorously. Meanwhile, those who had been separated off from the army, for the purpose of exploration and of rescue should a hostile force appear anywhere, not only warded off attacks upon themselves but also rendered the Emperor's conduct of the siege safe by killing some men and chasing others with headlong speed. And when some of the fugitives got bogged down in the swamps underneath the grove not even these were let off scot-free by the scouts, who killed some and led others away captive. (21) But those who were being besieged inside the fortress repelled their adversaries by hurling all sorts of missiles; since they had no rocks within they flung clods of earth ignited with bitumen. Their throws easily hit their marks inasmuch as they were sent both from vantage ground and against throngs. Yet still the Roman soldiers, even though at a disadvantage as a result of the enemy's high position, did not remit their display of manliness and military know-how; for they kept heaving rocks as large as the hand can hold, and discharging arrows not only from bows but also from machines. The latter had been constructed in such a way as to strike not one mere body but rather two or three or more. But because the fortress was situated on a hill, and fortified with two walls and sixteen lofty towers, and completely surrounded by a deep moat which at a certain point fed water suitable for drinking to the inhabitants, the Emperor ordered his soldiers to pour earth into the moat and, furthermore, to erect a second earthwork that would be equal in height to one of the towers. At another place he decided to tunnel through under the wall towards the center of the inner enclosure, thinking that by such laborious tunneling he could approach the enemy. Now, as the enemy impeded those who were raising the earthwork with unintermitting throws, the Emperor undertook to do battle out in the open, employing

various means of defense against the shooting both of bolts
and of firebrands. To Nevitta and Dagalaiphus he handed
over the tunneling and the raising of the earthworks. To
Victor he assigned both hoplites and horse, and gave
instructions to explore the countryside as far as Ctesiphon
itself so that, if anything hostile should appear anywhere
with intent to divert the Emperor from the siege, he
(Victor) could cut short such an attempt through the soldiers
under his command, and simultaneously could make easier
for the Emperor and the army the way to Ctesiphon, ninety
stades distant, by constructing bridges and booms.

22.   These charges having been laid upon the several
commanders, the Emperor had his soldiers drive a battering ram to one of the gates, which was not only shaken
but actually broken down.   Now, when he saw that those
assigned the task of tunneling were working carelessly, he
superseded them with other men, bringing this disgrace
upon them for their want of diligence. After he had brought
a second ram to bear against a second gate, which did not
withstand the impact, there came some one with the news
that those appointed to tunnel through from the moat into
the town had already completed their work and stood ready
to surface, all three cohorts of them — *mattiarii, lancinarii,
victores*.   But the Emperor stemmed this impetus of theirs
for the time being while he ordered a machine to be moved
to another gate; there he stationed his entire force, to
persuade the foe that on the morrow he would bring on the
machine and become master of the fortress.   This he did
with the purpose of removing any idea on the Persians'
part of an attack via the tunnel.   Thus all in the fortress
applied themselves to the business of knocking out the
machine.   Meanwhile those who had been instructed to dig
their way through underground emerged inside a house
where a woman miller happened (even though it was still
dead of night) to be grinding wheat flour.   As she was about

to cry aloud she was killed by a blow from the man who had surfaced first, Superantius, a worthy from the cohort of the *victores*. After him came Magnus, while third came Jovianus, the tribune of the notarial order, and then came more. The exit being gradually widened, all stood in the center, whence they made for the wall. Totally unexpected they set upon the Persians, who were chanting native lays, hymning the valor of their own King and traducing as unattainable the assault of the Romans' Emperor, "who," they said, "would more easily get possession of Jupiter's palace than of the fortress." In the attack they struck some down in hand to hand combat and then destroyed them by shoving them off the wall, while others they pursued and removed by various modes of death, sparing not even women and children save only for some whom they saw fit to hold as captives. Anabdates, supreme commander of the garrison, was caught in the act of running about the fortress together with his companions, eighty in number; he was led to the Emperor with hands tied behind his back. Thus was the fortress taken by storm, and its inhabitants of all ages were wiped out except for a few who, remarkably, came through safely. The soldiers proceeded to loot the wealth stored up in it. When everyone had carried off his windfall, a great many machines were brought to bear against the wall, which was razed to the ground. Further, the buildings were destroyed so completely, both by fire and by the soldiers' own hands, that after the event they seemed never to have existed.

23. As he marched forward the Emperor passed by other fortresses not worthy of mention until he arrived at an enclosure called the King's Preserve. There there was a wall sealing off a large area within that was planted with manifold trees. Also there were confined therein all kinds of wild beasts. These did not want for nourishment, which, indeed, was catered for them, and they afforded the King

facility for hunting whenever he wished. Having noticed this, Julian commanded that the wall be rent in many places, whereupon the wild beasts in their flight were shot down by the soldiers. Somewhere near there he saw a palace magnificently gotten up in the Roman fashion and learned that it had been constructed by Romans. He left it alone, not allowing his brigade commanders to mutilate anything inside, out of respect for the tradition that Romans were its builders.

Thence the army rushed past certain forts en route to a town named Meinas Sabatha, which is thirty stades distant from the former Zochasa, now called Seleucia. While the Emperor encamped nearby with the majority of the soldiery, scouts moved on ahead and took the town by storm. The next day, when the Emperor was making the rounds of its walls, he spied bodies fastened to pales in front of the gates. The natives told him they were the bodies of relatives of a certain man accused of betraying a town which the Emperor Carus had snatched out from under Persian suzerainty. Thereupon Anabdates the garrison commander was brought to trial. For a long time he had been leading the Roman army astray, as if about to assist it in its war on Persia. Now he was charged with having reviled Hormisda in the presence of very many people by calling him a traitor and instigator of the campaign against Persia. And on these grounds he was convicted and dispatched.

24. As the army advanced farther Arintheus searched throughout the swamps and took captive many men found in them. At this point the Persians rallied themselves for the first time and assaulted the scouts who were preceding the army, but they were quickly routed and gladly fled together to the town hard by. However, on the opposite bank of the river the Persians attacked the sutlers that had been assigned to guard the draft animals, as well as all the other men with these; some they killed, others they led

away alive. This loss, the first sustained by the Romans, indeed disheartened the army.

Thence they moved on to a very large channel which the men of the region said had been cut through by Trajan during his Persian campaign. Into this the Narmalaches River discharges itself en route to the Tigris. The Emperor decided to dredge it and at the same time explore it, in order to furnish passage for his boats to the Tigris and, if at all feasible, to prepare bridges for the crossing of much of his army. (25) While these things were being done there, a host of Persians on the bank opposite gathered together, cavalry and infantry both, and endeavored to prevent anyone's attempting to cross. The Emperor, looking at this scheme of the enemy's, was provoked into sailing against them and impulsively commanded his generals to board the boats. But when they observed that the opposite bank was steeper and simultaneously that there extended along it a kind of fence, originally constructed to enclose a royal park but now doing service as a wall, they said they were afraid of missiles and torches being thrown from above. At the Emperor's insistence two ships filled with hoplites made the crossing; these the Persians immediately set on fire with a rain of flaming arrows. With the army frightened all the more, the Emperor counteracted by stratagem his calamitous mistake. "They have succeeded in their crossing," said he, "and have obtained possession of the bank; for that fire which attaches to their boats signifies the very thing I myself enjoined the soldiers on board to do as token of their victory." Thereupon all, just as they were, boarded the boats and crossed over. And wherever the water was fordable they jumped in and engaged the Persians at close quarters. Not only did they gain the bank, but also they recovered the two boats that had crossed first and been half-burnt and they rescued those of the hoplites on board them that were still alive. Henceforth the armies fell upon one another, the battle lasting continuously from midnight until midday. Finally the Persians gave way in a headlong flight led by their generals: Pigraxes, who outstripped all except their King in birth and character, Anareus, and the surenas himself. Both the Romans and the Goths together took out after the runaways, many of whom they destroyed. They secured possession of much gold and silver, plus all kinds of ornaments for men and horses alike, and whatever silver couches and tables the generals of the fortified camp had abandoned therein. Furthermore, there fell in the battle 2,500 Persians, but not more than seventy-five Romans. However, the army's victory paean seemed muffled because Victor, their leader, had been wounded by a catapult shot.

26. The following day the Emperor conveyed the army over the Tigris River in complete security, and the third day after the battle he himself went across with his entire bodyguard. Having come to a certain fort which the Persians call Abuzatha, he tarried there five days. Meditating upon the march ahead he believed it better not to lead the army along the bank of the river any longer but to withdraw inland, as now there remained for them no need of boats. Having conceived this plan, he introduced it to his army, giving orders that the boats be burned; indeed, all of them were consumed by fire, with the exception of eighteen Roman and four Persian ones which were carried along on wagons, likely for use in emergencies.[1] The remainder of the journey was now to be made a little above the river. When they reached a place called Noorda they halted; there on every side many Persians were captured and slaughtered. Then, having come to the Durus River, they threw a bridge across it and stepped over.

---

[1]According to the conjecture of Ammianus Marcellinus (XXIV. 7), Julian planned to move upland into Armenia, and burning the boats would mean freeing 20,000 men for the army.

Since they observed that the Persians had burned to the ground all the fodder so that the Romans' draft animals might be hard pressed for aliment; and since they further observed that the Persians had formed into several companies and had now assembled at one place to await the Romans, as if believing them to be not very numerous; they retreated to the bank of the river. When the scouts who preceded the army had joined battle with a certain Persian division, one Macamaeus in his zeal rushed unarmed against the enemy, killing four of them. Many men at once turning upon him, he was struck down. But his brother Maurus both snatched up his body, having seen it lying in the Persians' midst, and killed the man who had inflicted the first blow. And, although shot at, he did not stop until he had delivered his brother, still breathing, to the Roman army.

27. Having come to the town of Barsaphthae, they found that the fodder had been burned by the barbarians. Now a band of Persians and Saracens together appeared but did not abide even the sight of the Roman army, vanishing immediately. Then the Persians, coming together in small numbers until they were assembled en masse, furnished grounds for suspicion that they would attack the beasts of burden. Thereupon the Emperor was the first to don his cuirass and personally outran his entire army. The Persians did not wait, but decided to disperse into places known to themselves. And the Emperor proceeded to a village, Symbra, which lies between two towns named Nisbara and Nischanadalbe. The Tigris separates these towns, and there was a bridge, affording the inhabitants of both free and steady commerce, which the Persians burned so that the Romans might not by means of it harry both at will. Hereabout some Persian cohorts were espied and routed by the scouts who were out foraging. Simultaneously the army found quite bounteous provisions stored in the village

and, having taken as much as sufficed for its own use, destroyed the entire residue. While the army was marching between the towns of Danabe and Synca the Persians, falling upon the rear guard, killed many but lost even more and turned tail, having gotten altogether the worse of it; for in this battle there was killed one of the nobility, a satrap by the name of Daces,[1] who had once been sent on an embassy to the Emperor Constantius to discuss peace and dissolving hostilities.

28. When the enemy saw the Romans nearing the town of Acceta they set fire to the fruits of the earth. The Romans ran over to these fruits and, having extinguished the fire, saved what remained for their own use. Advancing farther they arrived at the village of Maronsa, where squads of Persians attacked and encountered the army's rear guard. Among the soldiers they destroyed was Vetranio, who had the command of the company[2]... and had fought manfully. In addition there were taken ships which, being far behind the army, fell into the enemy's hands. The Romans now passed by certain villages in haste and came to Tummara, where they all repented of having burned the ships; for the draft animals, weary as they were from so long a journey (all of it, too, through enemy territory), were not equal to the task of conveying the necessary supplies, while the Persians gathered up as much produce as they could and stashed it away in the most secure places, thus depriving the Roman army of the use of it. Nonetheless the Romans, although in this condition when the Persian divisions put in an appearance and a conflict occurred, won out in superior fashion, simultaneously killing many of the Persians. But on the day after this, around high noon, the Persians, marshalled en masse,

---

[1] Adaces, according to Ammianus Marcellinus XXV.1.

[2] Here Mendelssohn marks a lacuna; Ammianus Marcellinus, loc. cit., states that Vetranio "legionem Ziannorum regebat."

unexpectedly fell upon those in the rear of the Roman army. Although they were at the time in disarray and were confounded by the sudden assault, they still met it gamely, the Emperor making his accustomed rounds and arousing the legions to courageous action. (29) When all had come to close quarters, he met his brigadiers and tribunes and mingled with his soldiery. In the very heat of the battle he was struck by a sword, placed on a shield, and carried aloft to his tent. He lasted until midnight and then died, having nearly reduced the Persian power to utter destruction.

Meanwhile, the Emperor's death being kept a secret, the Roman army had conquered to such an extent that fifty of the most powerful satraps fell, in addition to a countless host of ordinary Persians. However, when the Emperor's death became known, the majority of the Romans withdrew to the tent where the corpse lay, although some continued to fight and conquer the enemy. Certain bands made an attack on Hormisda's ranks from a Persian fortress and engaged them hand to hand. In the fierce battle that ensued there fell Anatolius, the leader of the palatine orders (called by the Romans *magister*). Furthermore, Salustius, the praetorian prefect, tumbled from his horse and was almost slaughtered as the enemy pressed upon him, except that one of his servants dismounted from his horse, which furnished him a ready means of escape. There withdrew along with him the two divisions that attend the Emperor and go by the name of *scutarii*. But out of those who took to flight sixty men only, remembering their own dignity and that of Rome, exposed themselves to a violent death and gained possession of the fort from which the Persians had attacked the Romans and apparently gotten the advantage. And although the enemy encamped there for three days straight the Romans were rescued by no inconsiderable force which assailed the

besiegers. (30)   Thereupon all those in authority came
together with the army, and deliberations were held regarding who should be granted the imperium, as it was not
possible for them to escape the perils that lie in the midst
of enemy territory without a supreme commander. And
in a communal vote Jovian, son of Varronianus the tribune
of the household troops, was elected Emperor.

   In this manner, then, occurred the events up until Julian's death. Jovian, having put on the purple and assumed
the diadem, held fast to the march homeward. When he
had come to the fortress of Suma the Persian cavalry
attacked his men.   Quite a few elephants were brought in
and molested the right wing, on which were stationed the
Jovians and Herculians (these are names of legions established by Diocletian and Maximian, whose cognomens they
bear: for the former took the name of Jupiter and the latter
that of Hercules). Now at first they were overpowered by
the elephants' might, and many fell while fleeing. But when
the Persians drove the elephants alongside the horse in a
combined assault, all reached a certain place where the
Romans' sutlers happened to be located; these, having
now a share in the common danger, hurled javelins at the
Persians from high above. Some of the elephants were
wounded and fled in pain with a roar, as per their habit,
that disrupted the entire cavalry. Consequently the elephants were butchered in the act of fleeing at the hands of
the soldiers, and many of the enemy fell in the actual
combat. There also perished on the Roman side three centurions who had fought nobly, Julianus, Maximianus, and
Macrobius. Their men, in searching thoroughly for their
wherabouts, found among them the corpse of Anatolius, to
which they gave as honorable a burial as considerations of
time permitted, with the enemy pressing them in every way.

   The Romans then advanced for four days, harassed on
all sides by the foe, who pursued whenever they saw the

Romans on the move and fled whenever the Romans stood their ground against them. Having opened up some space apart from them the Romans decided to cross the Tigris. Accordingly they tied together bottles, through which they had somehow strung bands, and riding upon these they made the crossing. After they had gained the opposite bank, then their leaders also in addition to the rest passed over safely. Yet not even so did the Persians withdraw but along every piece of the way kept threatening them with a large number of men. The Romans were in constant danger, oppressed both by the ills that ringed them and by their lack of provisions besides.

31. Although this was the army's condition the Persians still were making overtures concerning peace, having dispatched the surenas and others of those who held authority among them.   Jovian received their talk of peace favorably and sent Salustius the praetorian prefect together with Arintheus to confer on the matter. A bilateral thirty-year treaty was concluded whereby the Romans agreed to cede to the Persians the nation of the Zabdiceni, as well as the Cardueni, the Rhemeni,[1] and the Zaleni,[2] plus all the forts (fifteen in number) around these, with their inhabitants, properties, animals, and all paraphernalia; and to hand over Nisibis, but without its inhabitants (for these, it was agreed, were to migrate to whatever place should seem best to the Romans). The Persians took over besides the greater part of Armenia, allowing the Romans to keep only a little bit of it. On these terms the treaty was made and was ratified by both parties' written instruments. The Romans were granted a visa to journey back home in such fashion that, doing no damage inside the Persians' territory, they in turn were set upon by no Persian ambuscade.

32.   When I had reached this point in the history it oc-

---

[1] The district is called Rehimena in Ammianus Marcellinus XXV. 7.

[2] The district is called Arzanena in Ammianus Marcellinus, loc. cit.

curred to me to revert to former times and to ascertain
whether the Romans had ever consented to delivering over
to the other side any acquisition of theirs, or, generally
speaking, had permitted the other side to hold anything
whatever of theirs, once it had come under their sovereignty. Indeed, after Lucius Lucullus had subdued Tigranes
and Mithridates and first brought under the Roman sphere
of influence their territories as far as the heart of Armenia
and, in addition, Nisibis and the forts bordering it, Pompey the Great confirmed the possession of these for the
Romans through a peace established by himself, thereby
capping Lucullus' successful ventures. Again, when the
Persians bestirred themselves the Senate selected Crassus
general with supreme power; he came to blows with the
Persians and, having been captured in the battle and killed
by them, bequeathed the Romans ignominy that has lasted
to this day. Next, Antony assumed the command and,
captivated by love for Cleopatra, handled his military
affairs in a casual, indifferent manner; and he, too, departed this life having committed deeds unworthy of the
Roman name. Still and all, despite these calamitous
reverses, the Romans lost not a one of those regions.
Even after their form of government had been changed
into a monarchy and Augustus had set as boundaries for
the Romans' Empire the Tigris and Euphrates, they still
did not withdraw from this country. A great while later,
the Emperor Gordian attacked the Persians and fell in the
middle of enemy territory, yet not even following this
victory did the Persians sunder anything that was subject to Roman jurisdiction (no, not even following the
imperial successor Philip's settling for a most disgraceful
peace with the Persians[1]). Not long thereafter, when the
Persian fire had swept over the East, the Persian forces
having overcome the great city of Antioch and penetrated

---

[1]Cf. Book I, chapter 20.

even the Cilician Gates, the Emperor Valerian took the
field against them, only to come into their hands; but not
even then did he grant the Persians freedom to appropriate these regions, for the loss of which the Emperor Julian's death alone sufficed. And, indeed, until this day the
Roman Emperors have been unable to recover any of them,
but have gradually lost even more peoples besides, some
becoming autonomous, others surrendering to barbarians,
while yet others being reduced to utter desolation. As our
history progresses these matters will be pointed out in
course.

33. After peace had been established with the Persians
in the manner described, the Emperor Jovian was making
a safe return with his army, having traversed many rough
and waterless places and having lost many of his soldiers
in the passage through enemy soil. He ordered Mauricius,
one of the tribunes, to bring the army supplies from Nisibis and to come as far as possible to meet him with
these.   He dispatched others into Italy to announce the
death of Julian and the designation of himself as Emperor.
With much difficulty and distress he neared Nisibis, which
city he was unwilling to enter because it had been surrendered to the enemy.   Having bivouacked in a spot in
front of the gate, on the following day he received crowns
and supplications combined, all the townspeople beseeching him 'not to desert them nor make them experience
barbarian customs, they who for so many hundreds [1] of
years had grown up under the laws of Rome. Besides,
it was particularly disgraceful that Constantius had undertaken three Persian Wars and, although unsuccessful in
all of them, had protected Nisibis; when it had been besieged and brought into extreme danger he had been exceptionally zealous about keeping it safe, while he (Jovian),
with no such necessity pressing him, was ceding the city

---

[1]The text is mutilated.

to the enemy and showing the Romans a day which they
had not seen before, in that they were being constrained
to ignore the abject surrender of so great a city and
region.'   When the Emperor upon hearing these things
offered in excuse the agreements that had been made,
Sabinus the chief decurion added to the items presented
by the people by way of supplication, stating that 'for bat-
tling the Persians there would be no need of either expense
or imported help, but they could themselves with their
own bodies and contributions fend off the war brought
against them.   And if victorious they would again be the
Romans' subjects, fulfilling their commands in the very
same manner as before.'   As the Emperor said he absolutely could not violate the agreements the townsfolk
begged him importunately that the Roman Empire not be
deprived of their protection.   (34)   But they were none
the more successful.   The Emperor departed angrily and
the Persians wanted, in accordance with the treaty, to
take possession of the peoples, the forts, and the city.
Some of the peoples and the inhabitants of the forts, provided they could not slip off secretly, allowed the Persians
to do whatever they wished with them.   However, the people of Nisibis obtained an armistice for the purpose of
moving.   The majority, indeed almost all, of them emi-
grated to Amida, although a few settled in other cities.
Everywhere weeping and wailing were replete, each city
supposing that it lay exposed to the attack of the Persians
now that Nisibis had been surrendered to them. The people
of Carrhae were so afflicted by the news of Julian's de-
mise that they stoned to death its announcer and then
raised a very tall heap of blocks over him.   Thus the de-
cease of one man was able to effect a great change in
public affairs.

Jovian passed through the towns in haste inasmuch as
they were steeped in sorrow and gloom and their commons

had none of their customary joyousness or kindness to offer. In company with as many soldiers as formed his bodyguard the Emperor arrived at Antioch, while the entire army followed in attendance upon Julian's corpse, which was conveyed into Cilicia and consigned to a regal burial place in a suburb of Tarsus. The following inscription was engraved on the tomb:

"Here lies Julian, leaving swift-flowing Tigris,
Good Emperor and stout warrior alike."

(35) Jovian, intent upon imperial affairs, having disposed of other matters, sent to the armies in Pannonia Lucilianus, his father-in-law, and Procopius and Valentinian (who after these events was made Emperor) to announce that Julian had died and that he, Jovian, had been named his successor. But at Sirmium the Batavi, who had been left to guard that city, upon hearing the news slew Lucilianus as though he were a reporter of great evils, holding in no regard his relationship to the Emperor. Procopius, on the other hand, they dismissed unharmed, out of respect for his kinship with Julian.[1] Finally, Valentinian by running away escaped being killed at their hands.

Jovian, having departed from Antioch and being en route to Constantinople, was overtaken by a sudden illness at Dadastana in Bithynia. His life was brought to its end after a reign of eight months, without his having the opportunity to accomplish anything useful in public affairs. (36) A council was now called to decide who should head the government. There was much discussion about many candidates by the army and by its leaders, but finally one man was accorded everybody's vote, Salustius the praetorian prefect. However, he pleaded old age, saying that on this account he would not be equal to the toil of handling

---

[1]Cf. below, Book IV, chapter 4; according to Ammianus Marcellinus XXIII. 3 Procopius was a cousin of Julian's on his mother's side.

affairs. They then asked that his son, at any rate, accede to the supreme power; but Salustius replied that he was young and, besides, not cut out for the burden of so great an Empire. They thus failed of choosing the man who was better than any one else of that particular period of time, and transferred their vote to Valentinian, who had been born at Cibalis (which is a Pannonian town) and had taken part in many a war but was innocent of any erudition. Although he was not at hand they still summoned him, and there passed an interval of a few days during which the state was without a ruler. Having met the army at Nicaea, a Bithynian city, he there entered upon the imperium and continued his march forward.

BOOK IV

The history of the Roman Empire up to the death of the
Emperor Jovian, who was succeeded by Valentinian,
has been recounted in the preceding book. Sickness having
overtaken Valentinian on the march and having roused
the man, who was by nature prone to anger, to even
greater severity and utter derangement, an erroneous
suspicion entered his mind that he was ill thanks to some
witch's brew prepared by Julian's friends. Charges were
laid against certain i l l u s t r i o u s men, charges which
Salustius, who was still the praetorian prefect, quashed
by shrewd thinking. When his illness had abated Valentinian
departed from Nicaea and came to Constantinople. His
army and the rest of his followers exhorted him to choose
a partner in empire in order that, should any accident befall
him, there might not be lacking a vicar and they might not
suffer what they had suffered at Julian's death. He took
their advice and, having turned the matter over in his mind,
he selected his brother Valens, in the belief that he, out of
all the men he considered, would be the most loyal to him.
And so he proclaimed Valens his imperial colleague.

2. While they both were in Constantinople, certain men
who were plotting against Julian's friends kept spreading
the rumor in the Emperors' presence that these friends
were laying traps for them; in turn they provoked the
unthinking herd to outcries such as this. The Emperors,
who on other grounds were inimical to Julian's friends,
were now aroused to even greater hatred against them,
concocting charges that had no basis in fact whatsoever.
Valentinian remembered old injuries on the part of Maximus
the philosopher in particular, recalling some slander that

he happened to have uttered against him during Julian's reign to the effect that he had committed impiety against the sacred rites owing to his espousal of the Christian religion. But at this point in time civil and military affairs diverted the Emperors' attention. Accordingly they devoted themselves to the allocation of provinces among the magistrates and to the selection of officers for the palace guard. Thus all to whom Julian had granted provincial appointments or other offices were detached from them— all (including the praetorian prefect, Salustius) except the generals Arintheus and Victor, who retained their former military commands. The remaining magistracies were assumed by men who sought them, in order; this one matter, indeed, seems to have been done reasonably, for if any applicant stood convicted on just complaints, he was punished, securing no indulgence.

3. These matters having been managed thus, Valentinian decided to divide up the Empire with his brother and to hand over to him the East as far as Egypt and Bithynia and Thrace. Having assigned himself the cities in Illyria, he crossed over to Italy and reserved for his own jurisdiction the cities there, together with the trans-Alpine nations, Spain, Britain, and the whole of Africa. Following this distribution Valentinian, becoming more and more strict, kept his magistrates in line. He was most scrupulous about the exactions of tribute and the provisions furnished the soldiers therefrom. Having decreed that laws be promulgated, he prohibited the performance of nocturnal sacrifices, beginning with his own household (as they say); by this law he meant to impede mystical rites. But when Praetextatus, the proconsul of Greece, a man outstanding in every virtue, maintained that this law would make life for the Greeks not worth living, since it would put a stop to the most sacred mysteries ever to bind together humankind, the Emperor remitted the law and

allowed the mysteries to be duly performed, provided that all was done in exact accordance with ancestral custom.

Now the barbarians across the Rhine who, as long as Julian was alive, dreaded the Roman name and were content if no one disturbed the peace in their own territory, when Julian's death was announced, straightway left their abodes and made preparations for war against the Romans. Hearing of this, Valentinian began to dispose his forces in fitting fashion, infantry and cavalry and light-armed, and to fortify the towns situated along the Rhine with the requisite garrisons. Thus did Valentinian, not altogether a novice in the art of war, arrange these matters.

4. Meanwhile disturbances surrounded Valens on every side. He had been accustomed to a life of ease and, when of a sudden he received his realm, he could not sustain the burden of administration. The Persians, who were fired with greed owing to the favorable armistice made with Jovian, were making forays fearlessly. They brought Nisibis under their control and, disturbing other Eastern cities, they attracted to themselves the attention of the Emperor, who set forth from Constantinople. At this point the rebellion instigated by Procopius broke out. To this man Julian, on the grounds of blood-relationship, had entrusted a certain portion of his forces and had given instructions that he march with Sebastianus through Adiabene, and join him as he was going by another route to meet the enemy. To this same man Julian had granted the right to wear the imperial purple, for a reason that no one else could figure out. But afterwards, when fate decreed otherwise and Jovian assumed the throne following Julian's death, Procopius hastily handed over his imperial vestment, telling Jovian the reason why he had accepted it. He besought the Emperor earnestly to release him from military duty and to let him retire and devote himself to agriculture and his household. Having gained his request, he moved with wife and children

to Caesarea in Cappadocia, where he had determined upon settling because he had a valuable estate there. (5) While he tarried there, Valentinian and Valens, having been made Emperors, even before they had any grounds for suspicion hurriedly sent men to arrest him. He surrendered himself to them and bade them lead him wherever they might wish, as long as he might first be permitted to speak to his wife and see his children. Permission granted, he had a feast prepared for them and, seeing them overcome with wine, he ran down with his entire household to the Euxine Sea. Boarding ship, he made passage to the Tauric Chersonesus. There he delayed for some time but, observing that the natives were untrustworthy, he grew fearful lest some day he be handed over to people coming and inquiring about him. When he spied a freighter sailing in he committed himself, together with his household, to it and arrived at Constantinople by night. He took up quarters at the home of a friend of long standing. Observing the state of affairs in the city at the Emperor's departure he decided to seize power. Such was the start of his insurrection.

There was a certain eunuch, Eugenius by name, recently ejected from the imperial court and not well-disposed towards the Emperors. Procopius cultivated his friendship after finding out about his exceedingly great wealth. Procopius then informed Eugenius who he was, for what purpose he had come, and how the insurrection ought to be carried out. Eugenius assured him that he would be his ally in any such venture and would even furnish the money for it when the occasion demanded. They began their undertaking by bribing the watch that was stationed in the city, consisting of two divisions of soldiers. Besides these they armed slaves and with little effort collected no small body of men, inasmuch as many offered their services of their own accord. In the dead of night they sent the forces into the city and caused universal commotion. Everyone, upon being routed from his house, observed Procopius playing the role of Emperor. (6) A very great tumult possessed the entire city, no one of whose inhabitants could conceive what should be done on account of the unexpectedness of the enterprise. Procopius believed that he was as yet unobserved by most men and supposed that he would secure the power for himself as long as he kept quiet for a while. Having apprehended Caesarius, whom the Emperors happened to have set up as city prefect, as well as Nebridius, whom they had appointed praetorian prefect to succeed Salustius, he forced them to put in writing his decrees to their subjects. He kept each under separate guard, to prevent their plotting together against him. When he had taken these precautions he paraded in splendor to the palace, the tribunal in front of which he mounted. Having filled one and all with hopes and grandiose promises, he entered the palace to attend to the remaining business.

The Emperors had just divided between themselves the armies, which were not as yet drawn up, being in process of reassignment. Procopius felt certain men should be dispatched to bring over to his side whomsoever they could. This was easily accomplished by distributing largesse among the soldiers and their leaders. There came over to him a force not to be despised, and he was openly making preparations for an assault. Accordingly he dispatched Marcellus with an army into Bithynia for the purpose of arresting Serenianus and the imperial cavalry he had with him, expecting to wipe them out. When they fled to Cyzicus, Marcellus after a naval battle seized that town, being superior with his land force as well. He caught up with Serenianus, who had slipped away and taken refuge in Lydia, and killed him.

(7). Procopius, jubilant over this success, little by little kept winning over troops to himself until, in the opinion of the majority, he was a match for the Emperors in fighting strength. For not only Roman legions but also barbarian forces were flocking to his standard. In addition, the glory of his being related to the former Emperor Julian, plus the fact that in all the wars which that great man had waged he had been his partner in the field, drew men to his side. Moreover, he dispatched certain illustrious men to the chief of the Scythians above the Danube, who sent him 10,000 robust allies. Other barbarian peoples likewise betook themselves to him to participate in the expedition. Judging that he must not fight both Emperors at once, he thought it best to war against the nearer one first and then to see what further would have to be done.

While Procopius was in the midst of these preparations, in Phrygian Galatia the Emperor Valens learned of his rebellion. He was terrified by the news and full of consternation, but when Arbitio bade him take courage he drew up for battle what troops he had to hand. At the same time he sent messengers to his brother announcing Procopius' large undertakings, but Valentinian resolved not to send aid to one who was not strong enough to defend the portion of the Empire allotted to him. Valens prepared to do battle against Procopius, appointing Arbitio commander for the war. Before the armies could come to hand to hand combat, Arbitio countered Procopius' reckless haste by wheedling as many of the latter's soldiers as he could over to himself and from them learning in advance his adversary's plan of action. (8) Then the Emperor and Procopius marched against each other and opposite Thyatira, as it happened, their forces clashed. Procopius' side had almost won victory and tipped the scale in his favor, the Persian Hormisda (his father's namesake) apparently having gained the upper hand in the battle. But Procopius' other general, Gomarius, a partner in the plot of all those who, though fighting for Procopius, favored the Emperor's cause, during the battle itself pronounced in a loud voice the name Augustus and, the watchword having been sounded brought it about that all his soldiers uttered the same cry. When this happened, Procopius' entire soldiery went over to Valens.

Following his victory Valens sojourned in Sardis and thence marched into Phrygia. Having discovered Procopius in the town of Nacolia, Valens (because Agilo, Procopius' general, had disposed matters to the Emperor's advantage) gained so forceful a victory that he took the tyrant under his power; not much later he caught up with Marcellus as well, and had them both put to death. Having found in Marcellus' quarters an imperial cloak, given him by Procopius, and having become greatly upset thereby, he raged against one and all bitterly, investigating not alone those who had backed the tyranny openly but also those who had been privy to the plot and even those who had gotten wind of something and had not at once given information on what was afoot. And he kept raving furiously against one and all, for no just cause, with the result that there were destroyed both those who participated in the insurrection and those who, wholly innocent themselves, were relatives or friends of the guilty.

9. While these incidents were occurring in the realm allotted to Valens, the Emperor Valentinian, living among the peoples across the Alps, was experiencing difficulties equally great and unexpected. For the entire German nation, recalling their sufferings of the period when Julian had been Caesar, as soon as they learned of his death shook off the terror he had implanted in their spirits and resumed their innate audacity. They invaded all together in a body places subject to Roman sway. The Emperor went forth to encounter them, and a fierce battle ensued in which

the barbarians were victorious, pursuing the Roman army headlong. Valentinian determined not to turn aside in flight from danger but, bearing up under misfortune, he made inquiries concerning those who had been responsible for the defeat, that is, those who had been the first to flee. Having probed with acumen and having uncovered the culprit in the Batavian legion, he ordered his entire army to convene in panoply, as if all the soldiers were to hear such words as would be to their common advantage. Instead he employed words which inflicted lifelong shame upon those who began the flight: he commanded that the Batavians lay aside their arms and be sold at public auction, just like runaway household slaves, to those who could produce spot cash. Thereupon all the soldiers fell flat upon the ground and besought him to free the army from so great a disgrace, promising that they would hereafter acquit themselves like men worthy of the Roman name. When he ordered that this be proven in very deed, they rose from the ground, armed themselves in due fashion, and renewed the battle. Having gone forth beyond the rampart, they displayed such great zeal in fighting that, out of an infinite number of barbarians, few returned home safely. Thus ended the war against the entire German nation.

10. The Emperor Valens, having killed many men after the death of Procopius and having confiscated the property of even more, was stopped short in his expedition against the Persians because a group of Scythians above the Danube were disturbing the Roman border. Having sent off a sufficient force against them, he checked their forward progress; and, having forcibly extorted their weapons, he distributed them among his towns hard by the Danube, with the mandate that they be held in custody free of chains. Now these, as it happened, were the men whom the chief of the Scythians had dis-

patched as allies to Procopius. When, therefore, the chief
begged Valens that they be released (they whom, he said,
he had sent off at the request of envoys from the one who
at the time had been ruling), the Emperor in no wise complied with his entreaty. He insisted that they had been
captured by him as enemies, not sent to him as friends.
For this reason the Scythian War was set in motion. When
the Emperor sensed that the enemy was planning to invade the Roman boundaries and for this purpose was now
with all speed mustering its entire fighting force, he spread
out his army along the bank of the Danube while he himself
quartered at Marcianopolis, the largest of the Thracian
cities. He saw to it that his soldiers exercised under arms
and, above all, that they did not lack victuals. He appointed Auxonius praetorian prefect, Salustius being retired
of age from this office after having twice served therein.[1]
And Auxonius, although so great a war was imminent, was
nonetheless fair in his exactions of tribute, not allowing
anyone to be saddled with more than his bounden duty.
The soldiers' provisions he consigned to a fleet of mer-
chant vessels which sailed through the Euxine Sea to the
mouth of the Danube; thence the provisions were transferred to river barges and transported to the towns along
the bank, so that the soldiery had ready supplies.

11. These matters were taken care of while it was yet
winter. At the beginning of spring the Emperor quitted
Marcianapolis and, proceeding together with the Danube
guard, attacked the barbarians. They did not dare to stand
and slug it out, but hid themselves in the marshes and
from these made secret forays. Valens ordered his soldiers
to hold their ground and, having collected as large a
throng of sutlers as he could, plus those to whom the
custody of the baggage was entrusted, he promised to

---

[1]Apparently Salustius had been restored to the office after Nebridius' tenure; cf. chapters 2 and 6 above.

give a fixed sum of gold for every head of a barbarian they brought in. Straightway then they all, excited at the prospect of lucre, dashed off to the woods and marshes and throttled every man they came upon. As they produced the heads they were paid the stipulated price. When a multitude had been killed in this fashion the survivors sued the Emperor for peace. He did not reject their plea, and a treaty was effected that entailed no disgrace to the majesty of Rome. For it was settled that the Romans were to hold in complete security all that they formerly held, while the barbarians were forbidden to cross the river or ever again to set foot inside the Roman borders. Having made this peace, Valens went to Constantinople. Since his praetorian prefect had died, he handed this office over to Modestus and, having done so, set out quickly for the war against the Persians.

12. While Valens was occupied with preparations for war, the Emperor Valentinian, having righted the German situation, thought he should make provision for the future security of the Celtic people also. Accordingly he collected a very great band of youth from the barbarian dwellers near the Rhine and from the husbandmen of the nations subject to Roman sway. Having enlisted them in his military ranks, he drilled them in the arts of war, so successfully that, out of respect for their training and practice, not one of the people across the Rhine troubled the cities subject to the Romans for nine whole years. At this point a certain Valentinianus, who had been relegated to Britain for certain delicts, attempted a tyranny and lost his life in the attempt. Moreover, the Emperor Valentinian was stricken with an illness which almost proved fatal. When he had shaken it off his courtiers convened and exhorted him to designate an imperial successor, that the affairs of state might not suffer loss if anything should happen to him. Persuaded by their words, the Emperor named his

son Gratian Emperor and partner in empire (he was still a youth, not having attained the age of puberty).

13. While this was the status of affairs in the West the Emperor Valens in the East was proceeding at a leisurely pace with his initial plan of attack against the Persians. He came to the aid, where necessary, of cities which sent embassies to him, and duly administered many other matters, readily acceding to reasonable requests. Arriving at Antioch, he attended to military affairs with every precaution and, having spent the winter in his palace there, he set out in the springtime for Hierapolis, whence he led forth his forces against the Persians; but with the return of winter he went back to Antioch. In this way was the war with the Persians protracted.

While the Emperor was at Antioch occasion for action arose unexpectedly, as follows. There was, numbered among the imperial secretaries, a certain Theodorus. Well-born and well-educated, he was nonetheless still a boy and in the fervor of youth easily led astray by the adulation of hangers-on. Some men of this sort approached him and persuaded him that they were steeped in culture and experts at making out the future by a kind of divination clearly perceived by themselves. 'Making inquiry as to who would reign after Valens,' they said, 'they had set up their tripod, which through a certain arcane ritual pointed out to them what was to come. On the tripod there appeared the written letters Θ and E and O and after these Λ — which letters [1] fairly shouted aloud the indication that Theodorus would succeed to power after Valens.' Elated by this nonsense, in his excessive zeal he frequented mountebanks and wizards, telling them what had happened. He was betrayed to the Emperor, and received a punishment worthy of his enterprise.

---

[1] The Greek equivalent of Theod..

14. After this incident still another took place. Fortunatianus, prefect of the imperial fisc, trying the case of a soldier under his command who had been accused of sorcery, put him to the torture. When the soldier under duress implicated others by name as his confederates, the conduct of the case was transferred to the praetorian prefect, Modestus, since personages had been introduced who were not under the jurisdiction of him who had been judge at the outset (i. e., Fortunatianus); indeed, the trial was now processed against one and all. The Emperor, provoked to uncontrollable anger, suspected everyone who was then known as a philosopher or was cultured in other respects, as well as some of those upon whom court honors had been conferred (for even these were announced to the Emperor as intriguers). On all sides there was emitted a common howl of lamentation, as the prisons were full of people who had been incarcerated unjustly while on the roads there wandered greater numbers than were the numbers left in the cities. Moreover, the cohorts to whom had been committed the safekeeping of all those who were jailed without cause owned that they were not numerous enough for the job and that they were afraid lest the prisoners by sheer weight of numbers might force their way out. The informers withdrew without any risk, being forced to make accusations only. Some of the accused were now sentenced to death without due process of law while others lost their estates, abandoning to their fate children, wives, and other relatives. The intention was that the fisc collect a great horde of money by various nefarious means.

15. The first of the well-known philosophers to be killed was Maximus, and after him Hilarius of Phrygia (on the grounds that he had interpreted all too clearly a certain ambiguous oracle), and then Simonides and Patricius the Lydian and Andronicus of Caria. These had all reached the pinnacle of learning, and were condemned

more out of spite than by just verdict. Everywhere was confusion, so great that the sycophants, together with crowds of passers-by, unrestrainedly broke into homes, seized whomever they encountered and handed them over to those who had been instructed to put to death anyone and everyone without a trial. Now, of these scoundrels the *ne plus ultra,* as it were, was Festus, who, ready for every form of savagery, had been sent to Asia as proconsul by the Emperor, that no gifted man of learning might remain alive. And the Emperor's design was carried out in very fact. For Festus, having tracked down all he could find, put them to death without a trial; the rest he forced to inflict upon themselves voluntary exile. Thus ended the calamity that befell the cities as a result of Theodorus' guilt.

16. Valentinian, though he had appeared moderate in his conduct of the war against the Germans, was very hard on his own subjects, pressing exactions of tribute quite severely, and dunning for more money than was the customary practice. As his pretext he used the great cost of the soldiery, which had obliged him to spend the treasury's reserves. Therefore, having aroused against himself general hatred, he became more bitter than ever. He was unwilling to cross-examine his officers to see whether they were abstaining from profiteering, he begrudged those who led a blameless life their reputation, and (to speak plainly) his character was different from that which he had displayed at the beginning of his reign. For this reason indeed the Africans, who could not abide the rapacity of Romanus, the military commander in Mauretania, granted the purple to Firmus and proclaimed him Emperor. Naturally, the announcement of this action perturbed Valentinian, and right away he ordered certain divisions of soldiers to abandon their garrison duties in Pannonia and upper Moesia and to sail off to Africa. When they

did, the Sarmates and Quadi, who had ere this been hostile to the man in charge of the guard of those regions (his name was Caelestius), invaded Pannonia and Moesia. Indeed, Caelestius had deceived their chief with a pledge confirmed by oath and then had killed him fraudulently right at the dinner table. Needless to say, the barbarians used this as their excuse for their incursion against, and plundering of, the people along the Danube. They snatched everything that was outside the towns. And so the Pannonians were exposed to the rapine of the barbarians, while the soldiers defended the towns slackly and harassed the places located this side of the river no less than did the barbarians. Moesia, on the other hand, suffered no ill because the military commander Theodosius played the man in resisting the invaders and chasing them away. As a result of the glory obtained from this victory he subsequently became Emperor — but these matters will be set forth in their own proper time.[1]

17. Valentinian could not bear to hear what was announced to him. He crossed over from the Celts to Illyria, planning to make war upon the Quadi and Sarmatae. He placed in charge of the entire army Merobaudes, who seemed to possess greater military experience than his other men. Winter lasting longer than usual, the Quadi kept sending him envoys who used immoderate language, at which Valentinian grew so angry that he was beside himself. The blood rushed forth into his mouth and blocked his power of speech. He died going into the twelfth year of his reign, having spent nine months, less a few days, in Illyria.

18. Following his death a thunderbolt fell upon Sirmium, burning up the palace and the forum; it seemed to those who are keen at judging such things a portent that boded

---

[1]Chapter 21 below.

ill for the commonweal. Further, earthquakes occurred
in some places: Crete was shaken rather violently, as
were the Peloponnesus and the rest of Greece, where
several cities tottered outside of Athens and Attica; these
last according to report were spared as follows. Nestorius,
who was at the time hierophant, had a dream prescribing
that the hero Achilles should be honored with public
honors, which would prove the salvation of the city. When
he imparted this dream to the magistrates, they thought
him delirious (he was already a decrepit old man) and
accounted as nothing what he had told them. He then deliberated with himself, schooled as he was in divine doctrine, as to what should be done. Having fashioned in his
tiny house an image of the hero, he placed it below the
cult-statue of Athena Parthenos. And, as often as he performed the customary rites sacred to the goddess, at one
and the same time he performed those which, he knew,
had been ordained for the hero. Thus did he fulfill the
counsel of his dream and, when the earthquake hit, the
Athenians alone, as it happened, were saved, all Attica
as well sharing in the hero's benefactions. That this story
is true may be learned from the memoirs of the philosopher
Syrianus, who composed a hymn in the hero's honor, and
I have inserted it here as being not irrelevant to the subject at hand.

19. With Valentinian dead the legionary tribunes, Merobaudes and Equitius, seeing that Valens and Gratian were
far away (for Valens was still in the East, while Gratian
had been left behind by his father in western Gaul) and suspecting that the barbarians above the Danube might just
pounce upon a state of anarchy, summoned Valentinian's
young son, born to him of the spouse who had been Magnentius' wife previously; the son was living with his mother
not far away. They escorted him, clad in purple, barely
four years old, into the palace. The Empire was divided

between Gratian and the infant Valentinian II as seemed best to those who were administering affairs in their name (the Emperors themselves were not *sui juris* on account of their youth): to Gratian were allotted the Celtic tribes, all of Spain, and Britain, while it was decided that Valentinian should hold Italy, the Illyrian people, and all of Africa.

20. Valens meanwhile was beset by enemy raids from several different directions. In the first place, the Isauri (whom some call Pisidians, others Solymi, and still others Cilician mountaineers — we shall speak with more accuracy about this matter when we come to its proper place[1]) were sacking the cities of Lycia and Pamphylia. They were unable to master walls, but they plundered everything that was out in the open. When the Emperor, who was still at Antioch, sent against them what he supposed was a sufficient force, the Isauri with all their loot took refuge in the roughest tracts of the mountains; and the soldiers, being out of condition, were unable either to give chase or to minister in any other way to the cities' distress.

At this juncture a certain barbarian nation attacked the Scythian peoples above the Danube — a nation hitherto unknown but now of a sudden revealed. They called themselves "Huns": either they should be styled "royal Scythians" or (as Herodotus says[2]) "snub-nosed and unwarlike men dwelling alongside the Danube." Or perhaps they crossed over from Asia into Europe, for this also I have found recorded, that out of the slime carried down by the Tanais the Cimmerian Bosporus was formed, which furnished them a means of crossing by foot from Asia to Europe. In any event, having set forth with their horses, wives, children, and belongings, they moved in upon the Scythians living above the Danube, neither being

---

[1] Book V, chapter 25.   [2] V.9.

at all able nor knowing how to fight a pitched battle (how would they, they who could not plant their feet firmly upon the ground, living, even sleeping, as they did on horseback?). They rode around the Scythians with timely sallies and retreats, shooting down at them from their horses, and wrought untold slaughter. Operating ceaselessly in this manner they brought the Scythian nation to such a pass that the survivors abandoned their houses, leaving them for the Huns to occupy, crossed over in flight to the opposite bank of the Danube, and with outstretched hands supplicated that they be received by the Emperor, promising that they would fill the role of allies faithful and true to him. The guard assigned to the cities on the Danube deferring the decision on this matter to the Emperor's judgment, Valens suffered them to be received, on condition that they first lay down their arms. The tribunes and leaders of the soldiers, crossing over for the purpose of escorting the barbarians, unarmed, into Roman territory, instead picked up good-looking women and chased comely young men for lewd purposes, or got hold of slaves and husbandmen; intent solely on these acquisitions, they neglected what things pertain to the commonweal. And owing to this neglect it came about that a great many of the enemy escaped notice being convoyed across with their arms. These, as soon as they set foot on Roman soil, remembered neither their entreaties nor their oaths: all Thrace and Pannonia and the countryside as far as Macedonia and Thessaly were filled with barbarians plundering everything in their path.

21. While the greatest peril hung over these regions messengers sped to the Emperor to announce what had happened. He, having settled Persian affairs as best he could, came on the run from Antioch to Constantinople, whence he proceeded towards Thrace, bent on waging war against the Scythian renegades. To the army on the march

and to the Emperor himself a portent appeared, as follows. The body of a man was seen lying on the road, like one who had been lashed from top to toe, altogether immobile save that his eyes were open and looked out upon those who approached him. They inquired who he was and whence, and at whose hands he had suffered so; he answered not at all. Regarding him as a prodigy, they pointed at him as the Emperor passed by. When the Emperor put the same questions to him he was no less silent. He was reckoned neither as alive (because his entire body was motionless) nor yet as wholly dead (because his sight appeared unimpaired). And then of a sudden the portent vanished. Those who were standing about were in a quandary as to what should be done. The men who were clever in explaining such things conjectured that the portent bespoke the condition of the State, which would continue to suffer beatings and lashings, like a person breathing out his last, until it was completely destroyed by the wickedness of its magistrates and rulers. And indeed it will appear, as we survey events one by one, that this prediction was true.

22. The Emperor Valens, discerning that the Scythians were pillaging the whole of Thrace, decided to send ahead against their cavalry the Saracens whom he had brought with him from the East and who were very experienced in fighting on horseback. These, a small band, at the Emperor's signal moved in single file outside the gates of Constantinople and, transfixing the Scythians from a distance with their pikes, each day kept bringing back many heads. Since the speed of their horses and the thrust of their pikes seemed to be unconquerable, the Scythians determined to outmaneuver the Saracen tribe: their resolve was that three Scythians, lying ambushed in the hollows, would attack each Saracen. But this endeavor did not succeed, for the Saracens escaped at will whenever they saw a group making for them, owing to the speed

and agility of their horses, while they would attack the laggards and cut them down with their pikes. So great was the slaughter that in despair the Scythians preferred to cross the Danube and surrender themselves to the Huns rather than be wiped out utterly by the Saracens. When they had left the vicinity of Constantinople and moved quite far away, the Emperor had plenty of space in which to move his troops forward.

Valens took counsel with himself as to how the war against so great a number of barbarians should be waged. At the same time he was bothered by the wickedness of his officers, whom, however, he was reluctant to deprive of office owing to the tempest in which current affairs were tossed. While he was in a state of perplexity as to what men he should grant positions of leadership, no one of them appearing worthy of consideration, Sebastianus (who had quit the West because the Emperors there owing to their youth could not run things by themselves but submitted completely to the calumnies of the eunuch-chamberlains) came to Constantinople. (23) Valens, learning this fact and knowing of the man's prowess in battle and statecraft alike, selected him general with plenipotentiary power to conduct the war. Noting that the tribunes and the soldiers were soft and altogether indolent, trained only for taking to their heels and making weak, womanish pleas, Sebastianus asked that there be given him 2,000 men of his own choosing. For he judged it difficult to lead a host of soldiers who had been laxly governed, but not too difficult to train a few and bring them around from effeminate to manly ways; furthermore, he thought it more advantageous to take a chance on a small number than on a great throng. Speaking thus he persuaded the Emperor, and in his selection he sought, not those who were nurtured in fright and practiced in flight, but those who, recently enlisted in the army, were endowed by nature with outstanding physique and who besides appeared to his experienced eye to be capable of any deed they might be called upon to perform. On the spot, then, he made trial of their temper and made up what was lacking through continuous exercise, lauding the obedient and plying them with gifts while appearing to the disobedient severe and inexorable. Having drilled his men in every warlike discipline he removed them to walled cities, where, he reasoned, his army would be most safe. With thick ambushes he lay in wait for barbarians who would come out to forage. Now finding some weighted down with spoils, he butchered them and became master of the loot; now finding others drunk or yet others bathing in the river, he throttled them.

When he had wiped out a majority of the barbarians with stratagems like these, the survivors refraining from foraging out of fear of his generalship, there arose very great resentment against him. Resentment bred hatred, and from both sprang up accusations in the Emperor's presence, those whose powers had been abrogated putting the court eunuchs up to this. To the Emperor, who was led astray thus to irrational suspicion, Sebastianus made it clear that he should remain where he was and not proceed farther, that it was by no means easy to conduct open warfare against so great a host, and that he must pass the time in circlings and clandestine assaults until the enemy, worn out from want of provisions, would either surrender or depart from Roman territory, committing themselves to the Huns sooner than to the customarily very miserable consequences of hunger. (24) However, while he was advising thus, those of the opposition party were urging the Emperor to march forth to battle with his entire force, as if, since the barbarians were already to a great extent destroyed, he could without effort complete the victory. The worse judgment prevailed owing to fortune: the Emperor led out to action all his forces in disarray. The barbarians encountered them in battle fair and square and, easily victorious, wiped out almost all of them. The Emperor, however, escaped with a handful of men and took refuge in a village that was unwalled. The barbarians placed kindling all around the village, lit it, and cremated those who had taken refuge there, together with the inhabitants. As a result, no one could even identify the Emperor's body.

With matters reduced to the slimmest hope the leader of the Roman cavalry, Victor, escaped the danger along with some of his horses and headed for Macedonia and Thessaly, thence for the Moesians and Pannonians, on the run. To Gratian, who was staying in those regions, he announced what had happened, including the destruction of the army and of the Emperor. Gratian bore the news of his uncle's death fairly calmly (a certain suspicion existed between them) but he realized that he was incapable of ruling the Empire by himself: Thrace was occupied by the barbarians who had invaded it, parts of Moesia and Pannonia were being harassed by barbarians resident there, the people beyond the Rhine were infesting cities unrestrainedly. He chose as his fellow ruler Theodosius, a native of a town in Portugal called Cauca, a warlike man by no means inexperienced in military command. Having put him in charge of affairs in Thrace and the East, Gratian himself headed for western Gaul to deal with matters there as he could.

25. While the Emperor Theodosius remained at Thessalonica, many men, coming to him from all sides on account of public and private necessities, went away having secured from him what was fitting. A great host of the Scythians above the Danube, that is to say, the Goths and Taifali and the other peoples who were living with them, crossed the river and harried the cities under Roman jurisdiction perforce because a multitude of Huns

had seized their former habitations. The Emperor Theodosius prepared for all-out war. Indeed, the whole of
Thrace was already occupied by the aforesaid peoples,
and those on garrison duty in the towns and forts there
did not dare go forth from their walls even a short distance, much less fight at close quarters in the open.
Modares, scion of the royal clan of the Scythians, who a
short time earlier had gone over to the Romans and through
the good faith he had displayed had been designated a military commander, led his soldiers up a certain hill which
was as smooth as a ploughed field on top and which, in
itself long, also overlooked extensive plains below. He
accomplished this without the barbarians' notice. When he
had learned through his scouts that the enemy as a body
were lying in the plains below drunk, having completely
consumed the provisions they had come upon in the fields
and unwalled villages, he bade his soldiers quietly to
attack them in their current wanton condition, carrying
no large or heavy arms, not even their customary inter-
locking shields, but swords and bucklers only. As a result
the soldiers set upon the barbarians and in one brief part
of a day slaughtered them all; they struck some who felt
no pain at all, others who were just barely sentient, and in
divers ways put them to death. When not a man survived
they stripped the corpses and then, making for the wives
and children, they seized 4,000 wagons together with as
many captives as were likely to be riding thereon, not to
mention those who were following on foot (their wont was
to take turns at resting on the wagons). Thus did the army
leader make use of the good fortune that had come his
way, and Thracian affairs, which had been at an extremely
fateful juncture, were now peaceful, the barbarians having
been destroyed contrary to all expectation.

26. However, the situation in the East was not far
removed from total loss, for the following cause. The Huns

having attacked the peoples above the Danube in the manner described,[1] the Scythians, unable to withstand their assaults, begged the Emperor Valens (who was then still alive) to receive them in Thrace, saying that they would be dutiful subject allies and would do everything he demanded of them. Won over by their words Valens received them and, supposing that he would have sufficient security of their good faith if he saw to it that their children who had not yet arrived at maturity were brought up in another country, he sent a huge band of the very young to the East, placing in charge of their education and custody Julius, who he thought could discharge both duties owing to his readiness of mind. Julius distributed the barbarian youth among the cities, that they might not, collected in such great numbers and far removed from their own people, have any opportunity to mount a conspiratorial revolution. To these, scattered among the cities and now in the full bloom of manhood, came the news of what had befallen their fellow tribesmen in Thrace. They took it in bad grace, and as many as were in the same city huddled with one another and secretly passed on to their comrades elsewhere the word that they intended to avenge their parents and fellow tribesmen by attacks upon each individual city. Julius' attention was called to the barbarians' scheme. He didn't know what to do, afraid as he was of the turn the barbarians' endeavors might take. He decided that he should not disclose what he contemplated to the Emperor Theodosius, partly because the latter was staying in and around Macedonia and partly because he had received his charge from Valens, not from the present Emperor, with whom he was as yet barely acquainted. He wrote a confidential letter to the Senate in Constantinople and received from it instructions to do whatever

---

[1]Chapter 20 above.

he thought advantageous. In the following way he warded off the danger that threatened the cities. Having summoned all the military leaders and having exacted oaths from them, he communicated to them his intentions. When they had learned what was to be done, they spread rumors among the barbarians in each and every city that the Emperor wished to bestow upon them some very handsome gifts, not money only but also land, in order that he might bring them over to friendship with himself and with the Roman people. To this end they were ordered to convene within the metropolises at a certain fixed date. The barbarians, inflated with expectations, abated their anger somewhat and dropped the idea of destroying the cities. On the long-awaited day on which they had been instructed, each and all, to come, they flocked together. Now, the soldiers who at a given signal had occupied the roofs of the houses facing the marketplace assaulted the barbarians as they entered with stones and missiles until they had wiped them all out in one mass destruction. Thus did they free the cities of the East from the fear that hung over them.

27. The catastrophic losses which had occurred in the East and in Thrace were thus ended thanks to the shrewdness of the generals. Moreover, the Emperor Theodosius, tarrying in Thessalonica, appeared affable to all who approached him but, after beginning his reign in a pleasure-loving, easygoing fashion, he shook up all the established offices and constituted more military leaders than there had been before. Whereas there had been one master of horse and one of infantry, he distributed these magistracies among more than five men, and by this act he burdened the fisc with higher maintenance costs (for whatever formerly only two leaders had individually had was now furnished to five or even more). At the same time he exposed the soldiery to the avarice of a great number of

officers each one of whom wanted, from the huckstering of military provisions, to amass not just a petty profit but a fortune as large as if there were still only two of them. Not only this — he increased also the cavalry-wing prefects and squadron leaders and tribunes to a number double that which he had inherited; meanwhile the soldiers received no similar windfalls from the fisc.

28. Thus matters stood, owing to the negligence and the enormous covetousness of the Emperor. He introduced such extravagances to the imperial table that, because of the multitude and costliness of the dishes, the population of cooks and cupbearers and the like could not be totaled up without many entries in a notebook. Concerning the host of eunuchs in the Emperor's service — and the majority of these, especially the ones of conspicuously youthful bloom, called to account such officers as they willed and held the control of the entire Empire, diverting the Emperor's mind whithersoever they pleased — concerning these, I say, what need is there to make a longer speech, when I should be recounting the causes of the Empire's destruction consequent therefrom? For, since he poured out the public funds at random to unworthy persons, he naturally needed more money. He put up for sale the provincial magistracies to any chance takers, paying no heed at all to a man's reputation or earnestness but judging as suitable anyone who could produce a goodly sum of gold or silver. And so it was possible to observe money changers and brokers and partners in the most sordid businesses in the marketplace wearing the insignia of offices and handing over their provinces to those who had more wealth.

29. Such was the turn for the worse in the State's affairs: within a short period of time the military forces were lessened in importance and in number alike while the cities were destitute of money, some being exhausted

by immoderate levies of tribute, others by the avarice of magistrates who overwhelmed with slander those that did not cater to their insatiable desires, all but shouting aloud that they must of necessity recover everything they had paid out for their magistracies. Hence the inhabitants of the cities, afflicted with both penury and magisterial wickedness, led a most unfortunate and pitiable existence, supplicating and begging providence to find a way out of all their problems. For it was still possible for them to frequent the temples fearlessly and to propitiate the gods according to their ancestral rites.

30. The Emperor Theodosius, having observed the considerable diminution of his fighting force, invited whosoever wished among the barbarians above the Danube to desert to him, promising he would enroll them in the ranks of his soldiers. Having accepted this agreement they came to him and joined his soldiery, being of the opinion that, if their number should increase, they would easily gain complete control of the Empire. The Emperor, seeing that the ranks of the deserters already exceeded those of his own soldiers, and simultaneously pondering how impossible it would be to check them if they contemplated anything contrary to their agreement, thought it best to mix some of them in with the forces stationed in Egypt and in turn to call to himself some of the men filling up the legions there. When this was done at the Emperor's bidding, the barbarians proceeding thither and the Emperor hither, the latter went quietly from town to town, buying up necessary supplies at fair prices, while the former, traveling in disorderly fashion, dealt as they pleased with the wares in the markets. In time their paths crossed, at Philadelphia in Lydia, the Egyptians, far fewer in number, observing military order, the barbarians far superior in number, usurping more than their fair share. Now, when one of the dealers in the market-

place demanded payment of a barbarian for what he had
handed over to him, the latter struck him with his sword.
At the dealer's scream, still another man as he was
about to offer help was wounded. The Egyptians, feeling
sorry about the incident, politely asked the barbarians
to refrain from such untoward acts, 'for these do not
become men who have opted to live in accordance with
Roman law.' But the barbarians kept brandishing their
swords at the Egyptians until the latter gave way to anger, fell upon the former and did away with more than
two hundred of them, killing some outright and forcing
others to flee to the sewers and drown themselves therein. The Egyptians, having done these things to the barbarians in Philadelphia, convinced them of the need for
self-control, 'for there would not be lacking those who
could stand up against them'. Then they continued on
their way, and the barbarians proceeded as instructed
to Egypt, under the command of the Persian Hormisda,
son of that Hormisda who had taken part in the Emperor
Julian's war against the Persians.[1]

31. The Egyptians having arrived in Macedonia and
having been attached to the legions there, no order existed
in the camp, no distinction between Roman and barbarian: all lived intermingled, nor were any records kept
of those enrolled among the soldiery. Nay more, permission was granted deserters who had already enlisted
in the legions to return to their homeland and send others
in their stead and then, whenever they so wished, to
serve again under Roman standards. When the barbarians saw such confusion reigning in the soldiers' ranks
(for the deserters, enjoying the opportunity for mutual
intercourse, pointed everything out to them), they considered the time to be ripe for moving in on a situation so

---

[1] Book III, chapters 11-29 passim.

badly bungled. Without strain they crossed the river and
reached Macedonia, for no one hindered them, the deserters in particular allowing them free passage whithersoever they wanted to go. It was now dead of night when they
sensed that the Emperor was going to oppose them. Observing a big fire, they guessed that it was burning for
the Emperor and his attendants and, as soon as they
learned from deserters who came over to them that
such was the case, they went on the run to the Emperor's
tent, the fire pointing the way for them. The deserters
joining forces with them, only the Romans, plus as many
of the Egyptians as were present, stood in their way.
These few did not suffice against so many, but they did
allow the Emperor opportunity to escape; then, after fighting manfully and slaughtering countless hordes of barbarians, they were cut down one and all. Had the barbarians now followed up on their victory and given chase to
the fleeing Emperor and his retinue, they would have conquered everything without opposition. But they were content with their conquest of Macedonia and Thessaly, which
were left undefended, and they even let the cities alone,
doing not one thing to them in the hope of gaining thereby a certain measure of tribute money.

32. The Emperor, when he had learned that they had
for these reasons called retreat back to their homeland,
fortified the strongholds and walled cities with garrisons
and proceeded himself to Constantinople. Then he drew
up a letter to the Emperor Gratian in which he indicated
clearly what had happened and pointed out the necessity
of succoring with all speed affairs which had arrived at
a stage of crisis. Having dispatched the couriers to
Gratian, he instructed the tribute exactors to enforce
payments with all rigidity, just as if nothing untoward
had befallen the Macedonian and Thessalian cities. Then
one could see expropriated all that had been left thanks

to the barbarians' philanthropy. For not alone money, but also women's jewelry and every article of clothing right down almost to underwear, were listed in the tribute assessments; and each town and farmstead was full of wailing and lamentation, all alike calling upon the barbarians to come to their aid.

33. While the affairs of the Thessalians and Macedonians were in this state the Emperor Theodosius entered Constantinople in splendor as if in celebration of a glorious victory, taking no notice of the public misfortunes but indulging his wantonness throughout the length and breadth of that great city. The Emperor Gratian, upset no end by the reports, dispatched a considerable force, giving the command to Bauto, with whom he sent along Arbogastes as well. Both men were Franks by birth, exceedingly well-disposed to the Romans, completely immune to bribes, and outstanding as regards warfare in brain and brawn. After these men had come with their army into Macedonia and Thessaly, the Scythians who were dwelling there knew as soon as they arrived their intent and purpose, left those regions on the run, and removed to Thrace, which they had previously sacked. Then, in a quandary as to what to do, they resorted to their quondam trickery and strove to cheat the Emperor anew. For they sent to him deserters of the worst possible sort, who promised to do in good faith and friendship whatsoever he should command. And he took them at their word trustingly, apparently not having profited at all from his past experience with them. Others likewise followed hard upon these, all of whom he received, and once again the deserters had the situation in hand, thanks to the Emperor's folly bred of riotous living. For all things that contribute to the corruption of life and morals increased at the Emperor's bidding to such an extent that practically everyone who emulated his pursuits defined

human happiness in these terms. Ludicrous comedians, dancers totally depraved, plus everything connected with obscenity of the most salacious sort and with dissolute music, were rehearsed both in his time and then...[1] The State plunged headlong into destruction because of those who imitated such madness. Furthermore, the abodes of the gods were assaulted throughout cities and countryside, and danger threatened all who believed in deities or who looked to heaven and venerated its phenomena at all.

34. While Theodosius was involved in these things the Emperor Gratian sent off to command the legions stationed in Illyria Vitalianus, a man who could in no wise handle toilsome matters. During his administration two sections of the German tribes above the Rhine, one commanded by Fritigernus, the other by Allotheus and Saphrax, pressed the Celtic peoples hard. They compelled Gratian to grant them the right, provided they gave up their Celtic holdings, to cross the Danube and settle throughout Pannonia and upper Moesia; as a matter of fact, he was anxious to be rid of their constant irruptions. When accordingly they were sailing down the Danube, minded to go through Pannonia into Epirus and then to cross the Achelous and invade the Greek cities, they thought that they should first secure provisions for themselves by getting out of the way the head of the entire royal household of the Scythians, Athanarichus, lest they have at their rear a man who might impede their plans. And so, having set upon him, they effortlessly drove him out of his regions. He betook himself quickly to Theodosius, who was just then rid of a disease that had held his life in the balance. Theodosius received him amicably, together with his barbarian company, going forth some little distance from Constantinople to greet him, and, when he died forthwith, commanded that he be given

---

[1]The passage is mutilated.

royal burial. Such great magnificence marked the funeral
that all the barbarians were struck dumb. The Scythians
went back home and stopped molesting the Romans, marveling at the Emperor's kindness. Moreover, as many as
had attended the dying king stationed themselves on the
river bank and for a long time prevented anyone from
mustering an attack against the Romans.

At this same time certain other strokes of good luck
came Theodosius' way. For he drove off the Scyri and
Carpodacae, among whose ranks there were Huns, and
having conquered them in battle he hurled them across
the Danube and forced them to take up again their former
abodes. As a result his soldiers were filled with fresh
courage and seemed to recover a bit from the losses sustained earlier...[1] and let both the farmers tend the land
and the draught cattle and herds graze without fear.
(35) Thus did the Emperor Theodosius appear to repair
his losses. Moreover, Promotus, the leader of the infantry
in Thrace, with his soldiers and with riverboats met
Oedotheus, who had collected a very great force not only
from the settlers along the Danube but also from tribes
quite remote and unknown and, having come with this host
to the river, was trying to cross it. Promotus wrought
such slaughter that the very river was filled with corpses,
while those who lay dead on the ground were not easily
counted.

This being the situation in Thrace, Gratian meantime
was surrounded with problems neither inconsiderable nor
capable of easy solution. For listening to courtiers, who
are wont to corrupt the manners of autocrats, he received
certain Alan deserters, enrolled them in his ranks, bestowed largesse upon them, and considered them worthy
of trust in affairs of the greatest moment, the while slight-

---

[1]The passage is mutilated.

ing his own soldiery. Such treatment begot hatred of him among his troops, which little by little was fanned and increased until it stirred to a desire for revolution not only the other soldiers but above all those stationed in Britain, who were preeminent in rashness and hot temper. They were provoked to this the more by Maximus, a Spaniard by birth, who had campaigned with the Emperor Theodosius in Britain. This man was indignant that Theodosius had been esteemed worthy of the throne while he himself had not been advanced even to an honorific magistracy, and so he roused his soldiers to greater hatred of the Emperor. They readily revolted and proclaimed Maximus Emperor, endowing him with the purple and the diadem, and promptly sailed across the sea to the mouth of the Rhine. The armies in Germany and thereabouts most warmly endorsing Maximus' appointment, Gratian stood in his path to do battle, having no small part of the troops still by his side. The forces had been skirmishing a mere five days when Gratian descried that first the Moorish cavalry to a man had deserted, hailing Maximus Augustus, and that now all the rest were gradually going over to Maximus' side. Giving up hope, he took 300 cavalry and with them fled headlong into the Alps; finding these ungarrisoned, he made his way to Raetia, Noricum, Pannonia, and upper Moesia. Maximus, not indifferent to his flight, dispatched in pursuit his cavalry-commander Andragathius, a native of the Euxine Sea region who appeared to be well-disposed, with his stoutest horses. He pursued Gratian without stopping, caught up with him as he was about to cross the bridge at Sigidunum, and killed him. Thus he made Maximus' reign the more secure.

36. Worthy of recording as not irrelevant to the instant event is the following. In Roman religious ceremonies the chief place was held by the Pontifices, whose name, if translated into the Greek language, would turn

out to be "Gephyraioi." [1]   They got this appellation for
the following reason.   At a time when mankind did not
yet understand veneration by means of cult-statues, the
first representations of gods were fashioned in Thessaly.
There being no shrines (for their usage was likewise unknown), the effigies were set up on a bridge over the
Peneus River, and those who were appointed to minister
to the gods were called "Gephyraioi" from the images'
first location.   The Romans took over this designation
from the Greeks and styled those who first held priestly
offices in their midst Pontifices, amongst whom they
ordained that the Kings be numbered, as a mark of their
superior dignity.   Numa Pompilius was the first to take
the title, followed by all those who were called Kings and
then later by Octavian himself and those who succeeded
to the Principate.   Indeed, at the same time as each received the highest position the sacerdotal robe was offered
him by the Pontifices, and straightway the title of Pontifex
Maximus (signifying the chief priesthood) was ascribed to
him.   Now, all previous Emperors appear to have welcomed the honor and to have borne the title most gladly,
even Constantine when he came to power (although in
religion he turned from the right way and embraced the
Christian faith) and likewise after him the others in order,
including Valentinian and Valens.   But when the Pontifices,
in accordance with custom, offered Gratian the robe he
rejected it, on the grounds that it was not lawful for a
Christian to wear such garb.   When the robe had been returned to the priests, he who was foremost amongst them
in rank reportedly said: "If the Emperor does not wish to
be called Pontifex, soon enough there will be a Pontifex
Maximus."

37. Thus Gratian's reign came to an end.   Now Maxi-

---

[1] The Greek word for "bridge" was *gephyra*, while the Latin word
was *pons*.

mus, believing that he had a secure hold on the Empire, sent to the Emperor Theodosius an embassy that proffered no excuses for what he had done to Gratian but, on the contrary, was almost overweening. The head of this embassy was the keeper of the royal bedchamber, though he was not a eunuch (for Maximus could not abide eunuchs in his praetorian guard) but rather an elderly man, one of those who had attended Maximus from youth up. The embassy demanded of Theodosius a pledge of concord and alliance against any and every enemy of the Romans or, failing that, it proclaimed open warfare against him. Theodosius conceded that Maximus was Emperor and pronounced him worthy of sharing with himself the imperial insignia and title, but secretly he was making plans to fight him and cozen him with every kind of flattery and adulation. To this end he even sent Cynegius, his praetorian prefect, to Egypt with explicit instructions to forbid all worship of the gods, to put bolts on the shrines and to display before the Alexandrians the icon of Maximus set up in public, proclaiming to the people that Maximus had been made coruler. Cynegius thereupon followed the instructions, closed the doors of the temples throughout the East and all Egypt and Alexandria itself, and prohibited age-old sacrifices and every ancestral holy ritual. (38) What befell the Roman Empire as a result from that time until this will be shown subsequently, item by item, in my narrative of events.

About this same time there appeared above the Danube a certain nation of the Scythians unknown to all those dwelling there, but the barbarians called them Grothingi. These, being many and being armed with the necessary weapons besides excelling in strength, most easily ran over the barbarians in their way as they made for the very bank of the Danube, and then demanded the right to cross the river. Promotus, who was in command of the soldiers there, having stretched out his troops as far as he could along the river bank, prevented the barbarians from crossing. And in accomplishing this he came upon another modus operandi as well, to wit: having convened certain men who were conversant with these barbarians' language and whom he had come to trust in such matters, he sent them forth to spread words of treason among them. They asked a huge reward for handing over the Roman commander and his army to the barbarians. When the latter maintained that they could not afford so large a reward, those in turn who had been sent by their general, in order to instill confidence by their words, kept insisting on their original proposal, not allowing one whit to be lopped off their profit. After both sides had agreed upon a set sum they made a secret compact of treason, to the effect that the traitors should receive a part of their pay at once, the balance being reserved until the time of victory. When now it had been decided how the signals were to be given and at what hour the traitors were to go to work, they reported this agreement to their general, namely, that when night came on the barbarians were to engage in the enterprise of crossing against the Roman army.

Accordingly the barbarians gave orders that the stoutest portion of their army should embark on a number of rafts, be the first to cross, and attack the soldiers while they were still asleep; that then others who were of average strength should follow bringing aid to those who had already begun the assault; and that finally there should come all the rest of non-fighting age, timing their arrival to coincide with the successful completion of the affair. (39) Promotus the general, having learned in advance all these plans of the barbarians from the men whom he had dispatched in the guise of traitors, made ready to encounter them. He stationed his ships prow to prow three deep, taking special care that his line extended over two and a half miles of the river bank. By this means he prevented his adversaries' crossing and, as for the ones who already were endeavoring to row over on the rafts, he drowned these upon contact with them. The night being moonless, the rest of the barbarians went ahead with their attempt in ignorance of the Romans' preparations. In deep silence they boarded their rafts, imagining that their plans were altogether unknown to the Romans. The signals having been given (those who had contrived the plot, having forewarned the general of each detail and forearmed themselves conformably to the enemy's preparation) with their heavy ships and very powerful crews sailed against them and sank all they met, while not one of those who fell overboard could be rescued owing to the weight of their armor. Moreover, those rafts which had avoided the Roman sailors ran into the boats that were spread out along the river bank and, being hit with all kinds of weapons, were destroyed along with their passengers, not one of them being able to get past the wall of Roman boats.

The slaughter was enormous, greater than any that had ever before taken place in a naval engagement. The river was strewn with corpses and as many weapons as by nature remain afloat. If there were any persons who did manage to swim across, these died at the hands of the foot soldiers on the river bank. In this manner the entire flower of the barbarian soldiery perished. The Romans took to plundering, carrying off the children and women and gaining control of the barbarians' paraphernalia. Then, to be sure, the general Promotus summoned the Emperor Theodosius, who was not far off, to witness at first hand his success. The latter, having observed the number of captives and the heap of spoils, loosed those captives from their bonds and plied them with gifts, by this gracious act persuading them to desert of their own accord (besides, they would prove of use in the war he intended to wage against Maximus). Promotus remained in Thrace as prefect of the guard, in secret readiness for said war.

40. At this same time there occurred something very similar which needs must be recorded. There is a city in Scythian Thrace called Tomi. The leader of the soldiers stationed there was Gerontius, a man of trained bodily strength, fit for any wartime emergency. Now, there were outside this city certain barbarians settled in accordance with their merit by the Emperor, men endowed with fine physique and highly superior courage. Though the Emperor had granted them more provisions and other donatives than he had granted the ordinary soldiers, they did not intend to repay these honors with good will but rather with arrogance toward Gerontius and with contempt for his men. When he perceived their mind, and their intentions of molesting the city and upsetting the status quo, he communicated with his most intelligent soldiers his desire to punish their petulance and insolence. Noting that they hesitated out of cowardly dread that the barbarians might make a move, he took up arms and lined up a very small number of his attendants to fight the entire host of barbarians. He strode forth through the opened gates while his soldiers were either still asleep, bound and fettered with fear, or were running to the walls to watch the action. The barbarians started to laugh at Gerontius' dementia and, thinking that the man wanted to die, sent against him their bravest warriors. Gerontius grappled with the one who rushed at him first and, having handily grabbed his shield, fought courageously until one of his attendants, observing the two men locked in mortal combat, slashed the barbarian's shoulder and toppled him from his horse. The barbarians were dumfounded by Gerontius' bravery and daring alike, as well

as by the fact that he was going after others of his opponents; while those who were looking on from the walls at
their general's deeds recalled to mind the Roman name,
came out against the barbarians to their amazement, and
felled them. The ones who escaped death took refuge in
a building held in honor by Christians and considered as
an asylum.

Now Gerontius. having freed Scythia from imminent
peril and having won over the barbarians who had been in
rebellion there by his fortitude and greatness of spirit,
was expecting a reward from his Emperor. But Theodosius
was terribly upset that the barbarians whom he had held
in such high honor should have been destroyed, regardless
of the fact that their actions had been outrageous; he
forthwith arrested Gerontius and demanded of him an explanation for his exploits in Rome's behalf. When the
latter argued that his opponents had rebelled against
Rome, at the same time telling of their rapine and destruction of the inhabitants, the Emperor paid no need.
He persisted in the charge that Gerontius had not acted
for the common good but had coveted the imperial grants
made over to the barbarians and, in order that he might
not be convicted of such covetousness, had wanted to get
the holders of the grants out of the way. Gerontius. having
retorted that after slaughtering them he had sent their
grants on to the treasury (including the gold necklaces
given the barbarians by the Emperor for their personal
adornment). barely was able to snatch himself from imminent danger by distributing what resources he had to the
eunuchs. paying over the wages of his labor earned in
faithfulness to the Roman cause.

41. Thus things went from bad to worse under Theodosius' rule: nothing excellent and exemplary was applaud-
ed. but every form of luxury and wantonness day by day
increased a cubit in stature. as the saying goes. The

citizens of Antioch-the-Great in Syria, intolerant of the
piling on of public taxes which were being dreamed up
daily by the assessors, revolted and, defiantly tearing
down the statues of the Emperor and his wife, they raised
howls worthy of the injustices done them, yet mixed with
banter and their customary urbanity. When the Emperor,
provoked at this, threatened to inflict the penalty due such
a trespass, the city council, fearful of the Emperor's
anger, decided to send a delegation to make apologies.
They selected Libanius, the professor whose glory is
proclaimed by speeches that are still extant, and Hilarius,
outstanding in splendor of family and in every form of
erudition. The professor, in fact, delivering the oration
"On the Sedition" before the Emperor and the Senate,
was able to deflect the Emperor's wrath away from the
Antiochenes (incidentally, the Emperor, laying aside completely his bitter feelings towards their city, enjoined him
to make still another oration, "On the Reconciliation").
Moreover, Hilarius was praised for his great virtue and
appointed prefect of all Palestine by the Emperor.

42. While this was the situation in the East and Thrace
and Illyria, Maximus, opining that to rule over only those
nations which formerly had belonged to Gratian was not
good enough for him, gave thought to deposing the young
Valentinian from his realm — all of it, if possible, but,
failing this, as much of it at any rate as he could manage.
Having made up his mind he was preparing to cross the
Alps and reach Italy. But, having noted that he would
have to make his way by a narrow path over very rough
and difficult mountains, followed by lakes and marshes
through which there lies an exit for the traveler proceeding at a leisurely pace but not for a tremendous army, he
laid hold upon a better plan of action. Since Valentinian
wanted to send an embassy from Aquileia to treat of a

more secure peace for himself, Maximus agreed to his
request, pretending that he himself would welcome it
most cordially.   Valentinian thereupon sent Domninus,
who, though a Syrian by birth, was a familiar of his of the
better sort. Endowed with power second only to Valentinian's, Domninus appeared to surpass others in trustworthiness and practical experience; moreover, whatever
the Emperor wished to do without anyone else's knowledge
he knew could be entrusted to this man especially. And
so Domninus came to Maximus and set forth all the chief
points of the embassy. He was received with every mark
of courtesy. Indeed, Maximus treated him with exceptional
honor and loaded him down with so many gifts that Domninus believed no man could be a better friend of the Emperor Valentinian. Maximus succeeded in deceiving Domninus the more by sending back with him part of his army
to help the Emperor out against the barbarians who were
threatening the Pannonians subject to his sway. Thereupon
Domninus departed, pluming himself on the number and
size of the gifts he had received and on the escort of
allies he had been given, and unsuspectingly made the
route from the Alps to Italy the simpler for Maximus.
All of this Maximus had foreseen and prepared for. He
followed behind him with his entire army, quietly sending
ahead scouts along the road, who took every precaution
that no one should break forth on the run and announce
to Domninus and his company the passage of Maximus
into Italy. And the guarding of this secret was ludicrously
easy, as it was not possible for people proceeding through
the narrowest part of the Alps to escape notice. When
accordingly Maximus knew that Domninus and company
had gone through the pathless narrows of the Alps to
those marshy places beyond the mountains which posed
difficulties for a host of soldiers, expecting that he would
come upon no line of battle to oppose him on such slippery

ground he made for Italy with all speed, no one interfering, and then led his forces to Aquileia.

43. Valentinian was paralyzed by this sudden arrival which was contrary to every expectation. His courtiers began to fear that Maximus would take him alive and kill him. Therefore he took ship and made for Thessalonica, with his mother Justina as fellow passenger. She, as I have related,[1] had first been married to Magnentius and after his death was joined in wedlock to the Emperor Valentinian because of her extraordinary beauty. She brought along with her her daughter Galla. Having sailed the seas and anchored off Thessalonica, they dispatched an embassy to the Emperor Theodosius, begging that he avenge right away the outrage perpetrated against Valentinian's entire family. He was struck dumb at the news and forgot a little about his excessively riotous living, laying aside his mad dash after pleasure. Having held a council, he decided to go in person to Thessalonica with certain members of the Senate. Thereafter a fresh consultation took place to discuss what ought to be done about Maximus, and it was decided by common decree that the crimes committed by him should be punished with death: there should be allowed to live no longer himself the man who had taken away Gratian's life and usurped his kingdom and who had followed up this success by proceeding to strip his brother of the kingdom bequeathed to him. (44) Theodosius took exception to this decree, being hesitant about going to war owing to his innate effeminacy and the softness of his past life. He referred to the evils that result from civil wars, how of necessity the State must undergo mortal blows from both sides: 'wherefore,' he said, 'heralds should first be sent and, if Maximus should choose to restore Valentinian to his

---

[1]Chapter 19 above.

kingdom and pursue peace, then the Empire should be divided among all in accordance with the former setup, but if Maximus should be overcome by avarice then war should be undertaken with no further evasion.' Against these sentiments no one of the Senate dared to speak, as they somehow seemed conducive to the commonweal.

Justina, however, who was· neither inexperienced in practical affairs nor at a loss for hitting upon clever solutions, knowing Theodosius' erotic proclivities set before him her extremely good-looking daughter Galla, grasped him by the knees, and besought him not to let go unavenged the death of Gratian, who had bestowed upon him his Empire, nor to leave the two of them lying there abject and devoid of any hope (while saying this she pointed to the maiden, who was tearfully bewailing her fate). Theodosius as he listened was smitten at the sight of the girl's beauty, and betrayed the fact clearly by his glance; however, he postponed action, simply intimating that they should cheer up. Yet, smoldering more and more with desire for the girl, he approached Justina and asked for her daughter's hand inasmuch as his former wife Placilla had died. She insisted that she would give her to him only on condition that he make war on Maximus, avenge Gratian's death, and restore Valentinian to his father's Empire. Upon these terms he obtained the girl's hand, and then devoted himself wholly to preparations for war. Indeed, goaded by the woman, he gratified his soldiery with increased rations and, prodded by necessity, he corrected his sluggishness in other respects, even deciding to take care in advance of matters which would require attention after his departure. (45) Accordingly. when Cynegius the praetorian prefect died on his way back from Egypt, Theodosius busied himself about a successor for him and. having considered many men over and over again, at last found just the one for the job — Tatianus. who had already filled other posts under Valens and was in every regard a worthy person. Having summoned him from Lycia, he declared him praetorian prefect with headquarters in his native land; and, having delivered to him the symbols of office, he appointed the same man's son, Proculus, urban prefect. In fact, he conducted himself well in entrusting the most important magistracies to men of this caliber, men who could administer brilliantly the affairs of the Emperor's subjects even in his absence. As regards generalships, he put Promotus in command of the cavalry and Timasius in charge of the infantry.

Just when nothing further appeared to need doing prior to departure a rumor reached the Emperor's ears that the barbarians mixed in with the Roman legionaries had been seduced into committing treason by a promise of huge gifts on Maximus' part. They, perceiving that the rumor had already spread far and wide, were taking flight toward the marshes and recesses of Macedonia to hide themselves in the thickets. Having been chased and rooted up out of there by every contrivance, they perished in such great part that the Emperor was freed from any fear from this quarter and with great zeal proceeded together with his entire force against Maximus. Having embarked Justina and her son and daughter upon ships and having put them in the safekeeping of a convoy, he dispatched them to Rome, persuaded that the people there, whose affections were alienated from Maximus, would receive them most joyfully. He himself was speeding his army through upper Pannonia and the Apennines to Aquileia, intending to come upon the enemy unprepared.

46. While Theodosius was holding to this route, Maximus heard that Valentinian's mother together with her children was about to cross the Ionian Gulf. He collected some fast-sailing ships, delivered them to Andragathius, and sent him off on the chase. Andragathius sailed around

hither and yon but missed his quarry (for they had fer-
ried across the Ionian Strait unnoticed). Then, having
gotten together a sufficient force, he kept sailing around
everywhere in those regions, thinking that Theodosius
would engage in a naval battle.

With Andragathius intent upon these matters Theodosius, having proceeded through Pannonia and the Apennine
passes, attacked the troops of Maximus unaware and off
their guard. After a portion of the army with very swift
impetus had fallen upon the walls of Aquileia and had
forced an entrance through the gates (where the guards
were too few to put up a defense), Maximus was deposed
from the imperial throne just as he was starting to dis-
tribute money to his own soldiers. He was led stripped
of his royal clothing into the presence of Theodosius, who
by way of reproach recited a few of the man's crimes
against the State and handed him over to the public execu-
tioner to pay the deserved penalty. Thus ended the life
and the tyranny of Maximus, who after his clever success
against Valentinian dreamed that he would gain control,
effortlessly, over the entire Roman Empire.

47. The Emperor Theodosius, having heard that Maximus in crossing the Alps had left his son Victor there
dignified with the rank of a Caesar, immediately dispatched
the general Arbogastes, who deposed the stripling from
his realm and slew him. When these things had been
announced to Andragathius (who was still scanning the
regions around the Ionian Strait), since he knew that he
would undergo untold suffering he did not await the advent
of the enemy but inflicted punishment upon himself, pitch-
ing his body into the sea, to which he preferred to commit
it rather than to very hostile adversaries. Then Theodosius handed over to Valentinian his Empire as intact
as his father before him had held it — which act seemed
to be performed courteously. But of the men who had

fought under Maximus he selected the cream for his own army. He allowed Valentinian to administer the Italian, the Celtic, and whatsoever other affairs belonged to his realm. Also, his mother attended him and supplied what was lacking to her son in the way of judgment on account of his youth, insofar as a woman can.

48. Theodosius returned to Thessalonica only to find no slight disturbance in the affairs of Macedonia. For what barbarians, hidden in the marshes and forests around the lakes, had survived the previous onslaught of the Romans, taking advantage of Theodosius' preoccupation with the civil war, were pillaging the regions of Macedonia and Thessaly without hindrance. When the news of the Emperor's victory and return home reached them they again hid themselves in the marshes, whence they would secretly sally forth to harry and plunder everything in their path; then at daybreak they would go back to their habitats. As a consequence, the Emperor thought that the aggressors might be phantoms rather than men. In his perplexity he shared with no one his plan of action, but he took with him five cavalrymen, bidding them draw three or four horses apiece with a trace so that when the horse bearing its rider became winded the rider might change and in this way the horses might endure any labor involved in the undertaking he contemplated. The Emperor was going about the countryside incognito, furnishing to no one who saw him any cause for suspicion, and if at any time he or his companions were in need of food they sought it from rustics. One day he came to a humble lodging inhabited by an old woman; he asked her to receive him beneath her roof and give him a drink. She admitted him hospitably, sharing with him what wine and other things she had and, as night approached, he asked to sleep there. When this request also had been granted by the old woman the Emperor, upon lying down in a

corner of the hovel, spied a man who spoke not a word but looked as if he wanted to stay hidden. Marveling at this, he called the old woman to him and inquired who and whence the man was. She replied that she neither knew him nor knew why he had come, but this she did know: ever since it had been reported that the Emperor Theodosius and his army had returned this man had been staying with her and had been giving her pay daily for his keep; he was gone all day, roaming wherever he pleased, but at night's approach he came back as if from work, took supper, and lay down just as observed at present. Having heard these things the Emperor, conjecturing that he ought not to leave the old woman's story unexamined, grabbed the man and commanded him to identify himself. When he refused to give any answers an inquisition was instituted with whips applied, but even under duress he would not yield. Theodosius then ordered his horsemen to lacerate his body with their swords, adding that he was the Emperor. At this the man revealed that he was a scout for the barbarians hidden in the marshes, who reported to them where the army was, what places ought to be raided, and which men ought to be attacked. Immediately thereafter the man's head was cut off.

The Emperor set out for his army, which was encamped not far off, and then led his soldiers to the places where he had learned the barbarians were. He made a rush upon them and killed them, youths and all, leading out the ones who lay hidden in the marshes but murdering the others right in the water. The slaughter of the barbarians was indeed great. (49) And now the general Timasius, though admiring the Emperor's fortitude, asked permission for his troops, who were without food and who could no longer endure the hard going through the marshes, to victual. Permission granted, the trumpet called retreat and the soldiers ceased from their labor of pursuing the barbarians.   They took to feasting and then, having had their fill and being overcome with wine and fatigue, they fell into a very deep sleep. The remnant of the barbarians, noticing this, resumed arms and, falling upon the soldiers exhausted with sleepiness and drunkenness, they pierced them with spear, sword, and every other weapon suitable for slaughter.   The Emperor himself would have been slain along with all his troops had not some of those who had not yet dined run to his tent and announced what had happened.   Thereupon the Emperor and his company became perturbed and decided to flee the impending danger by taking to their heels.   And Promotus met them in their flight (he, as it happened, had been summoned by the Emperor) and begged Theodosius to save himself and his attendants from death; 'for,' he said, 'the barbarians would be his concern and he would inflict upon them a punishment worthy of their contumacy.' As soon as he had said this, with the greatest dispatch he attacked those whom he discovered troubling the Roman soldiers that were still asleep.   He cut down so many that no one, or at most a very few, escaped unharmed to the marshes.

50. These, then, are the things that befell the Emperor Theodosius upon his return from destroying Maximus. Having come back to Constantinople, he was in high spirits because of his victory over the tyrant but in low spirits because of what had happened to himself and his whole army at the hands of the barbarians in the marshes. He determined to renounce wars and battles and, having entrusted Promotus with the charge over these, he returned to his former way of living, busily staging magnificent banquets and reveling in the vanity and pleasures of the theater and of chariot racing.   It is a wonder to me how this man could go from one extreme of life to the other. For, being by nature indolent, devoted to every creature comfort and to the vices already mentioned, so long as no

sorrow or fear afflicted him he succumbed to this nature;
but, when some urgent matter which threatened to upend
the status quo called, he laid aside his knavery, bade
farewell to luxury, and went back to a more manly spirit,
patient of toil and suffering. At the present time, when he
was free of all worry, he showed his true colors, becoming
a slave to the practices that befit a slothful nature.

51. Of the men to whom the magistries had been committed Rufinus was held in the place of highest honor; a
Celt by race, he was master of the palatine orders. The
Emperor confided in him completely, to the neglect of
his other courtiers. It stung Timasius and Promotus
that after their great efforts in the State's behalf they
should remain in the second rank. Moreover, Rufinus
was stuck on himself: one day at a public council meeting
he exultantly hurled a rather nasty insult at Promotus,
who did not take it lying down but struck him across the
face. Rufinus went to the Emperor, showed him his face,
and roused him to such anger that he said, ''Unless they
lay aside their jealousy of Rufinus they will soon see him
ruling.'' Now when Rufinus heard this, being in other
respects hateful to all on account of his exceeding zeal for
primacy, he persuaded the Emperor to bid Promotus live
somewhere outside the palace and there train his soldiers.
And having accomplished this he laid an ambush of barbarians to attack Promotus on his journey into Thrace.
These, acting under orders, caught Promotus unaware
and slaughtered him, a man who had disdained wealth and
had always acted honorably towards the State and the
Emperors; on the other hand, having subserved those
who administered public affairs in a thoroughly careless
and impious manner, he was paid the wages due his deliberate choice.

52. Word of this outrage was noised abroad and was
on the lips of all, every right-thinking man taking it hard.

But Rufinus, as if he had performed an honorable act, was designated consul. Then Tatianus and his son Proculus (who were offensive to Rufinus for no other reasons than that in their tenure of the chief prefectures, the former the praetorian, the latter the urban, they were absolutely incorruptible and administered their offices in highly dutiful fashion) were retired for no just cause. And, in order that the plots laid against them could be carried into execution, even before Tatianus stepped down from his magistracy and was brought to trial Rufinus was designated his successor as praetorian prefect. Other men also were appointed to share with Rufinus in the conduct of the trial for the sake of appearances, but in reality he had sole jurisdiction of the case. When Proculus, sniffing the plot, went into hiding Rufinus looked askance at the man's activity. Fearing lest Proculus might be contemplating a revolution whereby he would upset the whole affair, Rufinus wooed his father Tatianus fraudulently under oath; he even convinced the Emperor to hold out before father and son alike the brightest hopes. In this way, winning over Tatianus from his correct misgivings to idle fancies, he induced him to write a letter to his son calling him back. As soon as Proculus appeared he was arrested and taken to prison, while Tatianus was consigned to his native land.[1] Frequent hearings having been held in connection with Proculus' trial, the judges finally, according to their agreement with Rufinus, ordered him led off to the suburb of Sycae, there to be put to death. When the Emperor heard the sentence he dispatched a man to call off the execution, of course, but the man was under orders from Rufinus to go in leisurely fashion and arrived on the scene too late, Proculus' head already having been lopped off by the sword.

---

[1]Lycia; cf. chapter 45 above.

53. At this juncture the news of the death of the Emperor Valentinian was announced. The manner of his death was as follows. Arbogastes the Frank, whom the previous Emperor, Gratian, had appointed second in command to Bauto, at the latter's death had taken for himself the office of general, acting on his own initiative, not on the Emperor's authority. To the soldiers under his command he seemed like a suitable successor, for he was brave and experienced in warfare and contemptuous of money. And so he came to great power, such that even in the Emperor's presence he spoke quite freely, and he vetoed those actions which he thought were wrong or unbecoming. Valentinian was vexed at this and frequently opposed him, but to no avail, for Arbogastes was supported by the good will of all the soldiers. At last Valentinian could stand this state of subjection no longer: seated upon his imperial throne, when he saw Arbogastes approach he gave him a withering look and held out to him a rescript deposing him from his command. Arbogastes read the rescript and said, "You have neither given me my command nor will you be able to take it away." Having said this he tore up the rescript, hurled it on the floor, and walked out. From that time forward, suspicions were no longer entertained furtively: the enmity between the two was out in the open for all to see. Valentinian, indeed, wrote frequent letters to the Emperor Theodosius in which he informed him of Arbogastes' arrogance towards the imperial majesty and at the same time begged him to come to his aid, swearing that he would flee to him unless he acted just as soon as possible. Now, Arbogastes, pondering what he should do, hit upon the following scheme:

54. There was a certain man living at court named Eugenius, an outstandingly brilliant professor and head of a school of rhetoric. This man his intimate, Richomer, commended to Arbogastes as being quite charming and

witty, with the request that he be counted among Arbogastes' friends and companions, on the ground that he
would be of use if ever any business arose that required
true friendship. Accordingly, after Richomer had gone
off to Theodosius' court, frequent contact rendered Eugenius most friendly to Arbogastes, to the point where
there was no important matter that Arbogastes did not
confide to Eugenius. At this juncture, then, Eugenius
came to mind and Arbogastes shared with him his
thoughts, to the effect that, owing to his vast erudition
and the solemnity of his life in other respects, he would
be best fitted to rule well. But, seeing that Eugenius
was offended at this proposal, Arbogastes proceeded to
flatter him, beseeching him not to refuse the gifts of
fortune. Having convinced him, he thought it better first
to get Valentinian out of the way and then hand over the
monarchy to Eugenius. The Emperor was at the time at
Vienna, a city in Gaul, and while he was outside its wall
engrossed in games with some of his soldiers Arbogastes
caught him totally unaware, dealt him a lethal blow, and
cut him down. Since all who saw the deed committed
kept silence owing to the doer's rank and bravery in war
(furthermore, the soldiers respected the man highly because of his complete indifference to money), he proclaimed Eugenius Emperor and asked all to place their
highest hopes in him because of his eminently humane
talents.

55. When these things were announced to the Emperor
Theodosius his wife Galla, bewailing her brother's death,
upset the whole court. The Emperor likewise was smitten
with grief and anxiety — with grief because he had lost
a partner in empire who was both youthful and related
to him by marriage, with anxiety because he had fallen
in with men who were estranged from him and were in
other respects invincible owing to Arbogastes' courage

mixed with daring and Eugenius' virtues conjoined with learning. Although he kept muttering these things and turning them over in his thoughts, nonetheless he decided to cast the die concerning the supreme power and started making battle preparations of every sort. And he was planning to commit the cavalry squads to Richomer's charge, having already tested the man's courage in many wars, and to assign various commanders to the other posts; however, during the period of the Emperor's deliberations on these matters Richomer died of a disease, and so of course he had to shift to choosing other leaders. While the Emperor's thoughts were still absorbed in this problem an embassy from Eugenius was now announced: it inquired whether he wished to accept Eugenius as co-Emperor or whether he rejected the appointment as invalid. The head of this embassy was Rufinus of Athens, who carried with him no letters of Arbogastes nor made any other reference to him. As the Emperor procrastinated, giving the ambassadors no suitable reply, still another episode was taking place, as follows:

56. At the time when Theodosius had first obtained the Empire he had admitted certain barbarians into his friendship and alliance, bestowing upon them hopes and gifts to boot. In like manner he continued to court with great zeal the leaders of every nation, and invited them to share his table with him. Among these a division of opinion had arisen leading to a quarrel. For some insisted it was better to make light of the oaths which they happened to have taken when they gave themselves over to the Romans; others, on the contrary, said they would in no wise go against their pacts. And there was one man, Eriulphus, who wished to trample on his pledged word and was exhorting his fellow tribesmen to do the same, while another, Fravitta, contended that one must stand on one's oath. Now for a long time it had not been clear that this

argument existed between the two men, but when they presented themselves at the Emperor's table, the drinking
period being protracted, they got carried away and showed
clearly their angry feeling towards each other. The Emperor, perceiving the willfulness of each, dismissed the
banqueters. When they had departed from the palace they
were still so hot under the collar that Fravitta impa-
tiently drew his sword and smote Eriulphus, killing him.
Then, when the latter's soldiers purposed to set upon
Fravitta, the Emperor's spear-bearers interfered and prevented the tumult from proceeding further.

57. When the Emperor learned of these things he
bore it with equanimity and suffered the disputants to
become exhausted fighting amongst themselves. And
now he sent back home the ambassadors, having hoaxed
them with gifts and specious words; following their departure he busied himself with preparations for war.
Supposing, correctly, that the key matter herein was the
selection of the generals, the Emperor appointed Timasius
leader of the Roman forces and Stilicho second-in-command (this latter was married to Serena, Theodosius'
niece). His barbarian allies he placed under Gainas and
Saul; also sharing the command with these was Bacurius,
an Armenian but a man entirely above reproach and with
fine military training besides. He had made this selection
of leaders and was already hastening to set out when, as
it happened, his wife, Galla, died in childbirth together
with the infant. Her death the Emperor mourned for days,
in Homeric fashion. Thereafter he marched his army
forth to war, leaving behind his son Arcadius, who had
already been proclaimed an Emperor. And because
Arcadius was still a youth he left behind with him, to
make up what was lacking to him in judgment, Rufinus,
who at the same time was praetorian prefect and had

extraordinary powers to do in the name of the imperial
majesty whatsoever else he judged should be done.

58. Having made these arrangements he took with him
Honorius, the younger of his two sons, and coursed rap-
idly through all the nations in his line of march. He gained
easy access through the Alps and, completely unexpected,
attacked the enemy. Eugenius was terrified by his sudden
appearance. But Theodosius, thinking it better to array
the barbarians against the enemy and let them run the
first risk, ordered to the attack Gainas with the peoples
under his command; the other leaders were then to follow,
that is to say, the other leaders of barbarian forces,
cavalry (including mounted bowmen) and infantry. Against
these Eugenius led out his entire army, and there was a
mighty clash.   Now at the very moment of battle there
occurred an eclipse of the sun; as a result for more than
half the time the participants thought it was night rather
than day.   The armies accordingly adopted a style of
night-fighting which produced such great slaughter that
on that day the majority of Theodosius' confederates
were slain, including one of their generals, Bacurius,
who most bravely exposed himself to danger at the head
of his men (the other generals unaccountably got away
together with the remnant that survived).   At nightfall
the armies regrouped themselves.   Eugenius, revived by
the victory, distributed rewards to those who had distinguished themselves in battle and then gave his troops
an opportunity to eat, as if there would be no further
fighting after so stunning a defeat.   However, when the
men had turned to feasting, the Emperor Theodosius,
noting the approach of dawn, with all his troops rushed
upon them as they still lay on the ground, and throttled
them as they felt no pain whatsoever.   He proceeded
right up to Eugenius' tent and, attacking his attendants,
killed the greater part of them.   Others were captured

while, roused to terror, they were undertaking flight; among these was Eugenius himself. After his arrest his head was cut off, stuck on an extra long pole, and paraded throughout the entire camp, to show those who were still on his side that it befitted true Romans to render allegiance to their Emperor, especially now that the tyrant was removed from their midst. Thereupon nearly all who survived the defeat ran to the Emperor, hailing him Augustus, and sought forgiveness for their wrongs; this the Emperor granted affably. But Arbogastes, who did not care to test Theodosius' clemency, fled to the roughest tracts of the mountains and, sensing that every place was crawling with people who were after him, killed himself with the sword, preferring suicide to capture by the enemy.

59. Theodosius' success having reached this point, he journeyed to Rome and declared his son Honorius Emperor, at the same time creating Stilicho general of the legions there and leaving him in charge as his son's guardian. Then, having convened the Senators, who adhered to their long-standing ancestral rites and would not be moved to assent to those who contemned the gods. he delivered a speech in which he exhorted them to recant their ''error'' (as he called it) and to embrace the Christian faith because it promised forgiveness of every sin and every impiety. None was persuaded by this exhortation or was willing to give up the rites, which had been passed on from generation to generation since the City's founding. in favor of an absurd belief ('for,' they said, 'by preserving the former. they had inhabited a city unconquered for almost 1.200 years. while they didn't know what would happen if they exchanged them for something different'). In turn Theodosius said that the treasury was burdened by the expense of the rites and the sacrifices, that he wanted to abolish them, that he did not

approve of them and, furthermore, that military necessities called   for additional funds. The Senators replied
that the ceremonies could not be performed duly except
at public expense. Notwithstanding a law abolishing them
was laid down, and, as other things which had been handed
down from ancestral times lay neglected, the Empire of
the Romans was gradually diminished and became a domi-
cile of barbarians — or, rather, having lost its former
inhabitants, it was ultimately reduced to a shape in which
not even the places where the cities lay situate were
recognizable. That matters were brought to such a pass
my narrative of individual events will clearly show. And
the Emperor Theodosius, having handed over to his son
Honorius the peoples of Italy and Spain and Gaul, and all
Africa besides, while returning to Constantinople died of
a disease.   His body was embalmed and borne to the imperial burial grounds in Constantinople.

BOOK V

The Empire had been committed to Arcadius and Honorius, but they had authority in name only: the supreme power was held by Rufinus in the East and by Stilicho
in the West. These latter decided all cases at will, and the
successful party was he who purchased the decision with
cash or otherwise gained the good will of the judge by
friendship. Estates which had made their owners by common report acclaimed happy found their way into the
hands of Rufinus and Stilicho. Some flattered them with
gifts and thereby evaded slanders; others gave up their
possessions of their own free will and thereby attained a
magistracy or procured some other ruination of the
cities. Indeed, every manner of wickedness flourished in
the cities. Wealth from all sides flowed into the households of Rufinus and Stilicho, while everywhere poverty
was inflicted upon the households of those who had formerly been rich. The Emperors were aware of none of these
happenings, but simply signed anything Rufinus and Stilicho instructed them to sign. When they had heaped up
untold wealth, Rufinus started to dream of obtaining the
Empire for himself. He envisioned handing over his nubile
daughter in matrimony to the Emperor, using this marriage as his entree. He slyly broached the matter to the
Emperor via certain men attendant upon the latter's service, he himself supposing that no one knew anything
about his scheme; but the rumor about what he was contemplating spread even to the plebs. For all men guessed,
from the very swell of his haughtiness and the daily increase of his arrogance, what he had in mind, and the
general hatred of him grew. Yet he, just as if he wanted

to hide his lesser faults carefully beneath greater crimes, dared another deed, as follows:

2. Florentius, who was praetorian prefect among the trans-Alpine peoples when Julian the Great held the title of Caesar, had a son, Lucianus, who enjoyed the patronage of Rufinus since he had yielded up to him the choicest of his possessions. In return Rufinus continually acknowledged his gratitude to the young man, singing his praises in the presence of Theodosius, [1] who made him *comes Orientis*, an office which empowers its holder to oversee all the governors of the Oriental provinces and to amend whatever is being done improperly. Lucianus then exhibited every fine quality of leadership towards his subjects and became celebrated for his justice, moderation and other virtues that beseem a magistrate. He made no distinction of persons, nor had any intention other than what the law prescribed. Thus when Eucherius, the uncle of Arcadius himself, approached him on something beyond the bounds of decorum, he rejected it out of hand, angering him so much that he slandered him before the Emperor. The Emperor placing the responsibility upon Rufinus for having so high an office conferred upon such a man, Rufinus grasped the opportunity and, seeming to be aggrieved at the Emperor's reprimand and confiding in no one his plan, went with a mere handful of men to Antioch. Having entered the city at dead of night he arrested Lucianus and brought him to account, no charge whatsoever being stated. He ordered him to be whipped on the neck with lead bullets and, when he died, had him carried away forthwith in a covered litter, giving everyone the impression that he was not dead and would receive completely humane treatment. When the city bore this insolent deed very ill Rufinus cajoled the populace by constructing a royal

---

[1] Other authorities read "Arcadius."

portico, a handsomer building than any other the city possesses.

3. After these acts he returned to Constantinople and busied himself about his relationship to the Emperor, being more than ever anxious to marry off his daughter to him. But a certain fate dealt him a blow contrary to his expectations. Rufinus' hopes were dashed for the following reason. Promotus had two sons who, while Theodosius was still alive, were brought up with the latter's children. One of them had in his household an exceedingly good-looking maiden whom Eutropius, a eunuch in the imperial service, was urging the Emperor to marry, praising all aspects of her beauty. Observing that his words were received cordially, he produced a portrait bust of the girl and, thereby arousing Arcadius' desire all the more, persuaded him to marry her. Rufinus was completely ignorant of these transactions, but imagined that his own daughter would be married to the Emperor very soon and that shortly thereafter he himself would be his consort in empire. Now the eunuch, seeing that he had successfully completed negotiations for the marriage, bade the people dance and wear garlands, as is customary at imperial weddings. He took from the palace a robe and adornment befitting royalty and handed it over to the Emperor's attendants to carry. Then he paraded through the center of the city, the people leading the way. Everyone supposing that the nuptial gifts were to be given to Rufinus' daughter and running along beside the attendants, when they on their line of march neared, then entered, the house of Promotus' son and handed the gifts over to the maiden who had been brought up there, the identity of the future wife of the Emperor stood revealed. And so Rufinus was thwarted in his hope. Since he had seen another girl married to the Emperor, he was reduced to planning how he might do away with Eutropius.

4. This was the situation in Arcadius' realm. But Stilicho, who was guardian of the Western realm, gave in marriage to the Emperor Honorius the daughter born to him of Serena. This Serena was the daughter of that Honorius who was the brother of Theodosius, the father of the Emperors. Having made secure his power through this connection by marriage with the Emperor, Stilicho besides was holding in his sway almost all the forces of the Romans. For when, after the overthrow of Eugenius, Theodosius had died in Italy Stilicho, being general of the entire army, kept for himself the healthiest and most war-like men while dispatching to the East the run-down and worn-out. Having arranged things in this way, he was incensed at Rufinus' desire to have power throughout the East equal to his own. He planned to go to Arcadius, wishing to dispose the latter's affairs also according to his own pleasure. Indeed, he repeatedly said that Theodosius on his deathbed had given him instructions to take especial care of the affairs of both Emperors. (5) Cognizant of these things, Rufinus was desirous of preventing Stilicho's departure for the East by every conceivable device while still dissipating and rendering more feeble the existing military forces of Arcadius. Busy with all these projects, he found for their accomplishment men even more base than he wanted, by employing whom he turned out to be the author of great woes for the Roman Empire. How this came to pass I shall explain.

Musonius, a Greek of the highest education, had three sons: Musonius, Antiochus, Axiochus. Musonius and Axiochus were eager to surpass their father's virtues in erudition and integrity, but Antiochus was enamored of every contrary pursuit, being the epitome of wickedness. Rufinus, having discovered in him a man suited to his plans, appointed him proconsul of Greece, as he desired to set up the destruction of that country by barbarian

assault; at the same time he handed over the garrison
at Thermopylae to Gerontius, who himself would comply
with his plans against the State. Having accomplished
these base deeds, Rufinus observed that Alaric was up in
arms against legal authority (now, Alaric was mad because he was not in charge of a force of soldiers but had
only those barbarians whom Theodosius had delivered
over to him at the time when, with his help, he had over-
turned the tyranny of Eugenius). Rufinus therefore made
secret overtures to Alaric to lead out further the barbarians, both those he already had and those he could
collect from other nations, that all might be in readiness
for conquest. Thereupon Alaric departed from Thrace
and proceeded to Macedonia and Thessaly, overthrowing
everything en route. When he neared Thermopylae he
covertly sent to the proconsul Antiochus and to the prefect
of the guard there, Gerontius, messengers to announce
his approach. Gerontius moved his garrison away, leaving
the barbarians free and untrammeled access into Greece.
They in turn proceeded to plunder the countryside and to
destroy the cities utterly, killing all males from youth up
and herding together the women and children as booty,
along with all the wealth. Next all Boeotia and whatever
other peoples of Greece the barbarians passed on their
descent from Thermopylae were laid low, and from that
day to this have shown the marks of that devastation for
every eye to behold; only the Thebans were spared, partly
because of their city's fortification, partly because Alaric,
in his zeal to capture Athens, did not want to take the
time to besiege them. And so the Thebans avoided the
crisis as Alaric made for Athens, supposing he would
take the city very readily because its great interior size
made it impossible to guard and, besides, because the
Piraeus was short of supplies and would surrender to the
besieging party after a little while. These were the hopes

Alaric cherished. But the city by virtue of its venerability was destined to invoke in its behalf a certain divine providence, even in such impious times, and to survive unsacked.

6. The reason why the city was saved ought not to be passed over in silence, being somehow a work of the gods that should restore its hearers to piety. While Alaric with his entire force was approaching the city he spied Athena Promachos patrolling the wall just as she can be seen in statue form, armed and looking capable of withstanding the invaders: she appeared to stand exactly like the heroic Achilles that Homer portrayed opposed to the Trojans when in his wrath he waged a war of revenge for the death of Patroclus. Alaric could not bear the sight of her, but put a stop to any attempt against the city and offered terms of peace through heralds. [The Athenians] received these favorably, and exchanged oaths, whereupon Alaric with a small escort entered Athens. He encountered an altogether cordial welcome and, having bathed, dined with the city's notables, and received gifts besides, he departed leaving the city and all Attica unharmed. Thus Athens, which during the reign of Valens alone came off unscathed from the earthquake that shook the whole of Greece (in the manner described in the preceding book[1]), now once again, having been led to the brink of disaster, escaped.

Alaric, having left all Attica unravaged out of fear of the specters that had appeared to him, moved on to Megara; taking the city on the first assault, he headed towards the Peloponnesus. He met no resistance, Gerontius permitting him to cross the Isthmus, and thereafter all the rest was his for the taking without toil or struggle, as nearly every city was unwalled on account of the security the Isthmus

---

[1]Chapter 18.

provided. Accordingly Corinth (together with its neighboring towns) was the first to be captured, quickly and
forcibly, and thereafter Argos and the places that lie between it and Lacedaemon. Then there was added to the
ranks of captive Greece Sparta, no longer defended by
either arms or valorous men: thanks to Roman avarice
it had been handed over to magistrates who treasonably
and eagerly subserved the pleasure of the conquerors
in everything that looked to the common destruction.

7. When Greece's suffering was announced to Rufinus
his lust for the throne increased the more, for he supposed
that, with the commonwealth thrown into utter confusion,
no roadblock would appear against his enterprise. But
Stilicho embarked his soldiery on ships and sailed forth
hurriedly to succor Achaea in her misfortunes. Landing in
the Peloponnesus he forced the barbarians to flee to Mount
Pholoë, and would very easily have wiped them out owing
to their lack of provisions had he not devoted himself to
riotous living, ludicrous mimes and utterly shameless
women. He granted to his soldiers license to loot whatever the barbarians had abandoned, and to his enemies
opportunity to withdraw from the Peloponnesus with all
their booty and to cross over to Epirus, whose cities
they ravaged. When Stilicho saw what they had done he
sailed to Italy, his mission unaccomplished, having saddled
Greece with even greater and harsher woes because of the
soldiers he had brought with him.

Upon reaching Italy he straighway plotted Rufinus'
murder, in the following way. He told the Emperor Honorius that he ought to send some military cohorts to his
brother Arcadius to assist the nations under his sway
that were in sorry case. Having been instructed to carry
out this mission, Stilicho appointed soldiers to be sent
out thereon; he placed Gainas in charge of them, and explained to him his design against Rufinus. Now when the

soldiers were nearing Constantinople, Gainas went in advance of them and announced to the Emperor Arcadius their presence, saying that they had come bent on helping him to restore his tottering fortunes. The Emperor agreed, and met them in front of the city; Rufinus also went along, in his capacity of praetorian prefect. The soldiers, when they had bowed the knee and been received in turn with appropriate cordiality by the Emperor, at a given signal from Gainas all at once surrounded Rufinus and struck at him with their swords. One man clipped off his right hand, another his left, while yet another separated his head from his neck and went away singing paeans of victory. To such extent did they make sport of the deceased that they carried his hand around everywhere throughout the city, begging passers-by to feed it money because it was insatiable.

8. And so Rufinus, who had been the cause of intolerable ills for many individuals and of detriment for the whole body politic, paid the penalty befitting his crimes. Eutropius, on the other hand, who had cooperated with Stilicho in all aspects of the plot against Rufinus, was now master of affairs at court. He appropriated for himself the greater part of Rufinus' net worth, though he did allow other men to pick up out of the residue whatever they deemed worthy of their possession. To Rufinus' wife and daughter, who had fled to the Christian church for fear of perishing with him, Eutropius gave a pledge, permitting them to sail to Jerusalem (which formerly had been a Jewish settlement but ever since Constantine's reign had been adorned with Christian edifices). There those women spent the rest of their lives. But Eutropius, wanting to remove from his path everyone of any authority so that no one except himself might govern alongside the Emperor, for no just cause laid a snare even against Timasius, who had been master of soldiery ever since the

time of Valens and had taken part in many campaigns. The slander was as follows:

9. Bargus, a native of Laodicea in Syria who sold sausages in the agora, having been caught in certain unnatural acts fled from Laodicea to Sardis, where, having shown what species of man he was, he was bruited abroad for his wickedness. Timasius, who had come to Sardis, seeing that the man was both garrulous and clever at winning over by flattery whomsoever he met, made him his friend and forthwith put him in charge of a cohort of soldiers. What's more, he even took the man back with him to Constantinople. Those in authority did not approve of this act (for as it happened Bargus had already been forbidden to sojourn in Constantinople on account of certain base acts). But Eutropius, having found ready to hand just the instrument, as it were, to use in his intrigue against Timasius, set this man up as his accuser, producing false pamphlets which charged Timasius with coveting the throne. The Emperor presided as judge for the case; at his side was Eutropius who, since he was, among other things, head chamberlain, held the power of pronouncing sentence. When everyone bore it ill that a sausage-seller was pressing charges against a man distinguished by so many offices and honors, the Emperor withdrew from the case and turned it over to Saturninus and Procopius. Of these two men the former was of quite advanced age and had been decorated with great honors; still he was not above flattery, having grown accustomed in lawsuits to subserve the interests and intentions of those who had the Emperor's ear. On the other hand, Procopius had been related by marriage to the Emperor Valens, and was a gauche and indomitable man who seemed in some matters to speak the truth frankly. Consequently, when the time came to pronounce sentence, Procopius objected to Saturninus that it was not fitting for Timasius, a man distinguished by so many

offices and honors, to be prosecuted by the calumnies of
Bargus, a cheap, lewd fellow or (what was even more
absurd) for a benefactor to suffer at the hands of the re-
cipient of his benefits. Nonetheless, Procopius' boldness
of speech availed nothing, the judgment of Saturninus,
praised to excess, prevailing: Timasius was condemned to
exile in the Great Oasis, whither a public convoy escorted
him. This was a most depressing place, whence no one
once deported escaped. For the route to the Oasis (which
was sandy, altogether deserted and uninhabitable) destroyed
every trace of those who travelled it, because, first, the
wind blew sand over their tracks and, second, there was
neither tree nor house to serve as any kind of landmark.
Nevertheless a story received wide currency to the effect
that Timasius had been rescued by his son, Syagrius, who
had given those sent to fetch him the slip and had snatched
away his father with the aid of some robbers. Whether this
story is true or whether it was sown amongst the populace
by men seeking to gratify Eutropius no one knew for certain, but in any event neither Timasius nor Syagrius was
ever heard from thereafter.

10. Bargus, having freed from all fear of danger
Eutropius, who no longer had to suspect Timasius' ill will,
was granted a source of easy money, the prefecture of a
military division. He departed duped in his hopes of
greater rewards, for (what he did not realize) Eutropius
anticipated that one who had dealt thus with his benefactor
Timasius might likewise deal in similar fashion with himself. Accordingly, when Bargus had gone abroad to fill
his post, Eutropius persuaded his wife, who was for some
reason mad at him, to produce before the Emperor a
petition which contained a great many complaints leading
to the gravest of charges against Bargus. When the petition
had been heard, Eutropius immediately ordered the fellow
to be brought to justice, convicted, and punished as he

deserved. Thereafter one and all assiduously admired and praised in song the eye of Nemesis, whose notice it is impossible for anybody who perpetrates a nefarious deed to escape.

Eutropius was now drunk with riches and fancied himself to be wafted above the clouds. Among almost all the nations he had spies watching what was going on and how every man was faring. There was not a single enterprise of his which was not a source of profit. And so his jealousy, together with his greed, roused him against Abundantius, a native of Thracian Scythia. Abundantius had been campaigning ever since Gratian's reign, had come by the highest honors under Theodosius, and recently had been made general and consul-designate. When Eutropius desired that he be shorn of his entire substance as well as of his rank, the Emperor wrote a mandate to that effect. Thus Abundantius was expelled from the court and assigned residence at Sidon in Phoenicia, where he lived out the remainder of his days.

11. Eutropius now had no one whatsoever in Constantinople who dared cross him, and only Stilicho, master of affairs in the West, to be concerned about. He meant to prevent Stilicho's coming to Constantinople. He persuaded the Emperor to convene the Senate and have Stilicho declared an enemy of the crown by public decree. This done, he soon allied with himself Gildo, the general of Carthaginian Africa in its entirety, and through this man's agency he removed the province from Honorius' realm and added it to Arcadius'. At this Stilicho was mad and quite perplexed until there came his way a stroke of luck. Gildo had a brother, Masceldel by name, against whom he in his barbaric frenzy was plotting. He had reduced him to the necessity of sailing to Italy and announcing to Stilicho his sufferings at a brother's hands. Stilicho, handing over to him some stout forces and supplying him with a sufficient

number of ships, sent him off to make war upon Gildo. When he had disembarked at the spot where he had heard his brother was and had fallen upon him unexpectedly with his army, after a brisk clash he conquered to such an extent that he caused Gildo to commit suicide by hanging (this course he preferred to being taken alive by the enemy). Then Masceldel, having restored Africa to Honorius' dominion, returned victorious to Italy. There Stilicho, vexed at his success, nevertheless pretended to cultivate him and build up his highest hopes. One day taking a walk to a suburb he was standing upon a bridge overlooking a river, and Masceldel and others were following behind. At a given signal from him his henchmen obediently shoved Masceldel into the river, and Stilicho laughed as the current caught up the man and drowned him.

12. Thenceforth the enmity between Eutropius and Stilicho was unmasked and was on everyone's tongue. Through their mutual antagonism they reveled licentiously in the woes of their subjects (Stilicho had already given his daughter Maria in marriage to the Emperor Honorius, while Eutropius lorded it over Arcadius as over a head of cattle). If some subject had a noteworthy estate, its title would be handed over to one or the other of them; in like manner all coined wealth flowed from former possessors into their hands. On every side there was a great swarm of sycophants, to whom instruction had been laid down to inform on such matters.

13. This being the state of Empire both East and West, all members of the senatorial order were discontented with the mismanagement of affairs, especially Gainas, who demanded honors unbecoming a general and whose barbaric lust could not be satisfied by gifts. He was all the more irritated by the money that kept pouring into Eutropius' household. Chafed for these reasons, he made Tribigildus privy to his plans. The latter was a venturesome man,

very ripe for any foolhardy undertaking. He commanded some cavalry troops stationed in Phrygia (barbarian troops, not Roman), having been given this command by the Emperor. Putting on that he wanted to inspect the barbarians serving under him, he left Constantinople for Phrygia. Having picked up his barbarians he attacked everything on his line of march, abstaining from the murder of neither men nor women nor children and pillaging all the property he could get his hands on. Within a short time he had collected so great a crowd of menials and other vile persons that he brought all Asia to the brink of disaster. For Lydia was completely filled with tumult, almost all men fleeing with their entire households to the ports and sailing to the islands or elsewhere, while the coast of Asia expected a danger to descend upon it the like of which no other place had ever seen. (14) Yet, when this news had been announced to the Emperor, he took no account of the common disaster (utterly silly man that he was, he could not comprehend what had taken place), but handed over the entire administration of his Empire to Eutropius. Eutropius chose Gainas and Leo as generals, intending to send the latter off into Asia to attack the barbarians and men recruited helter-skelter that were overrunning that province, while sending Gainas off through Thrace and the straits of the Hellespont to deal with any hostile forces he might find harassing those regions.

Now Leo, who had been appointed to relieve the situation in Asia, had had no previous experience whatsoever as a commander, nor did he possess any other credential worthy of a promotion to so privileged a position, outside of the fact that he was Eutropius' friend. Gainas was being sent to Thrace to prevent Tribigildus' troops from crossing the Hellespont and to offer them battle at sea should occasion demand this. Arrayed in this fashion the generals led out their forces in their respective assigned directions. Gainas, bearing in mind his agreements with Tribigildus, since the time was at hand for him to undertake the enterprise, bade Tribigildus lead his forces to the Hellespont. Indeed, if he had managed his plot against the State well and departed from Constantinople with his barbarians quietly, his design would have been carried through to completion: all Asia would have been occupied and nothing could possibly have prevented the simultaneous destruction of the Eastern Empire. But fortune willed that those cities still remain under the dominion of the Romans. Gainas got carried away by the maniacal hotheadedness natural to barbarians. He left Constantinople with almost complete power to wage war. Hardly had he arrived at Heraclea when he signaled to Tribigildus what must be done. But the latter decided not to make a move, fearful lest he might come up against the troops stationed at the Hellespont. Instead he devastated Phrygia and made an attack upon the Pisidians; no one hindering his attempts, he departed having sacked everything. When news of these events reached Gainas he took no notice of those who were being attacked, mindful only of his agreements with Tribigildus.

15. Meanwhile, Leo was lingering around the Hellespont, not daring to join battle with Tribigildus and at the same time expressing fears that Tribigildus might send off a part of his army by another route and make a sneak attack upon the Hellespontine countryside. Consequently, Tribigildus was storming cities willy-nilly without hindrance, and killing all the inhabitants including the soldiery. Not one barbarian sided with the Roman cause, for in actual combat the barbarians would attach themselves to their fellow tribesmen and march against those who were Roman subjects.

Gainas, appearing to be indignant about the Roman disasters, at the same time feigned to marvel at Tribigildus' stratagems, saying that he was all-conquering because of his shrewdness and sagacity rather than his strength. Having crossed into Asia, Gainas attacked no one and ignored the destruction of the cities and the countryside, but only tailed along and observed how matters were progressing. While watching expectantly for the transit of Tribigildus to the East he furtively sent him forces, future auxiliaries for his plot; he did not yet expose his hand concerning this business. If then Tribigildus, having come to Phrygia, had made straight for Lydia rather than veering into Pisidia, nothing would have prevented his capturing and destroying Ionia as well as Lydia with ease; and thence he could have proceeded on shipboard to the islands, procured as large a fleet as he wanted, overrun the entire East, and laid waste everything as far as Egypt without encountering any battle-worthy forces. But none of these things occurred to him. Instead he decided to lead his forces into Pamphylia, which borders upon Pisidia. There he came upon difficult roads, altogether inaccessible for cavalry. Although no organized force opposed him, a certain Valentinus, a resident of Selge, (which is a hillside hamlet of Pamphylia), a man of some education and not altogether inexperienced in warfare, having collected a large group of slaves and farmers, all of them conditioned through constant collisions with their marauding neighbors, took his stand on the slopes overlooking the approach-roads; there his men could observe all who passed without being observed themselves even if their enemy should march by in the daytime.

16. Tribigildus had by now ridden with his barbarians up the more level route into the lower regions of Pamphylia. It was dusk when he arrived at the country below Selge. His barbarians were pelted thick and fast with slings that discharged rocks the size of a man's hand or even larger (which, indeed, it was easy for the enemy to hurl down

from their vantage points). There was no escaping them — on one side of the road stood a deep pool and marshes, on the other a narrow upward path which barely afforded passage two abreast (this path the inhabitants call the cochlea as being circular and resembling somewhat the form of a snail). Here a certain Florentius was standing guard, having enough comrades with him to forestall any attempts at passage. In these places the barbarians were intercepted, overwhelmed by the quantity and size of the rocks, and in great part killed; for owing to the cramped quarters the descending rocks did not miss their targets. Accordingly, several in their hopeless straits dashed on horseback to the pool, and escaped death from the rocks only to die in the marshes. Tribigildus, however, with 300 men made it up the cochlea and, having won over Florentius and his fellow guards with enormous bribes, secured transit. Having escaped in this manner, he let all the rest be utterly wiped out.

Thus Tribigildus supposed that he was rid of the danger brought on by Valentinus, but he was plunged headlong into others no less perilous than the earlier. For nearly all the townsfolk, having snatched up what arms they had to hand, hemmed him, together with his 300 companions in flight, in between the Melas and the Eurymedon Rivers, the former of which runs above Side, the latter of which flows through Aspendus. Not knowing what to do in these straits, he sent emissaries to Gainas. Now, the latter was chagrined about what had happened, but still did not reveal how he felt about the uprising. He dispatched Leo, the second in command, to bring aid to the Pamphylians and, along with Valentinus, to attack Tribigildus' forces and prevent their crossing either river. And Leo, although by nature wanton and luxury-loving, nevertheless carried out the order.

17. Gainas, however, fearful lest Tribigildus might be beset on every side and, with no fighting force worth the

telling, might be utterly destroyed, sent wave after wave
of the barbarians who were with him against the Roman
camps, that these might be wiped out in short order and
that Tribigildus might be granted an opportunity to flee.
Thereupon the barbarian auxiliaries whom Gainas had
given to Leo made irruptions this way and that against the
Romans, devasted the countryside, and killed the soldiery;
nor did they desist from their wholesale assaults until
they had destroyed Leo's army completely together with
its leader and had laid waste and bare almost the entire
region.   And so there came to pass that which Gainas
devoutly wished.   For Tribigildus in his escape from
Pamphylia inflicted disasters upon the cities of Phrygia
graver than their former ones.   The man's successes
Gainas praised to the skies in the Emperor's presence, and
instilled great apprehension in the Senate and the entire
court as he kept threatening that the enemy would come
even as far as the Hellespont and would turn everything
topsy-turvy that had not yet been turned topsy-turvy unless
the Emperor should see fit to respect his demands.

Gainas was contriving these things in the hopes that
his own intentions would escape the Emperor's notice and
that he might accomplish what he had in mind through the
charges brought to bear against Tribigildus. Indeed, the
fact that he had been overlooked himself did not nettle him
so much as the fact that Eutropius had already arrived at
the pinnacle of power, whereby he was even proclaimed a
consul, having borne this title for a period of time, and
had attained patrician dignity. These things in particular
motivated Gainas to rise up against the commonwealth.
With his mind set upon this purpose he decided first to
compass Eutropius' death. Therefore, while still sojourning
in Phrygia he sent a message to the Emperor saying that
'he was despondent owing to Tribigildus' prowess in war.
Besides, Tribigildus' frenzy could not be endured nor

could Asia be freed from the perils that beset her unless the Emperor could be persuaded to give in to his request. And this was his request: that Eutropius, as the man most responsible for every evil, be surrendered to him, for whatever treatment he might wish to administer.'

18. Arcadius, having heard these things, at once summoned Eutropius and, having stripped him of his rank, dismissed him. He took off on the run to the Christian church, which had been granted by him the right of asylum. But, since Gainas insisted that Tribigildus would not quit his attack unless Eutropius was gotten out of the way, the man was seized (contrary to the law guaranteeing churches the right of asylum) and shipped off to Cyprus under heavy custody. Finally, at Gainas' urgent pressure upon Arcadius to have the man killed, the Emperor's ministers made a mockery of the oath which they had tendered Eutropius when he was dragged out of the church. They recalled him from Cyprus; then, as if they had sworn only that they would not kill him while he was in Constantinople, they dispatched him to Chalcedon and there had him murdered. And so fortune handled Eutropius unexpectedly in both directions: having exalted him to a height the like of which no eunuch had ever attained, it plunged him to death owing to the hatred which the enemies of the State maintained they felt towards him.

Gainas, all were now agreed, was evidently moving toward a revolution, yet he imagined that his plans were a secret. Since he held Tribigildus in the palm of his hand, preëminent as he was in power and authority alike, he slipped into the latter's shoes and made peace with the Emperor; then, having given and received oaths, he returned through Phrygia and Lydia. Tribigildus followed him, leading his troops through upper Lydia by a route that avoided Sardis, the Lydian metropolis. When they had joined forces at Thyatira, Tribigildus was sorry he had not sacked

Sardis, a city which could have been taken easily, totally devoid of relief as it was. Accordingly, he and Gainas decided to turn around and take the city by storm. This decision they would have carried out had not a violent downpour inundated the ground and made the rivers unfordable, thereby cutting off their assault. Then they parted company, Gainas leading his troops into Bithynia, Tribigildus leading his toward the Hellespont; both allowed the barbarians that accompanied them to loot everything en route. After the former had seized Chalcedon and the latter was holding the regions around Lampsacus, extreme peril gripped Constantinople and the Roman Empire itself. Gainas demanded that the Emperor come to him, saying that he would talk with no one else but him. Even to this demand the Emperor gave in: the meeting was held at a place near Chalcedon where there stood a shrine dedicated to Euphemia, a religious martyr, honored for her service to Christ. It was agreed that Gainas and Tribigildus should cross from Asia into Europe and, further, that the State's most eminent men should be delivered over to them for death. These included Aurelianus, who held the consulship that year[1]; Saturninus, an ex-consul; and Joannes, the Emperor's chief confidant, who according to rumor was also the real sire of Arcadius' son. This demand likewise, tyrannical though it was, the Emperor accommodated. Gainas, having seized the men and held them within an inch of their lives at sword's point, was satisfied that they be punished with exile. He then crossed over into Thrace, bidding Tribigildus follow him; thus he left Asia, which got a respite and release from the perils that beset her. Stopping at Constantinople, he discharged hither and yon the soldiery that had served under him, with the result that he stripped the city even of the praetorian bodyguards. To his barbarians he passed on the word by clandestine signals to watch for the departure of the soldiers from the city,

[1]400 A. D.

attack it as soon as it was bereft of military aid, then hand over to himself the full control.

19. Having given his barbarians these injunctions he quitted the city, claiming that his body was war-weary and needed a rest which was unattainable unless he set his life free from all responsibilities. Now, the barbarians he left in the city by far outstripped in number the praetorian soldiery. He removed himself to a suburb five miles from the city; there he awaited the moment when the barbarians remaining in the city should carry out their agreed attack. Gainas was optimistic and, had he not been carried away by his barbaric hotheadedness and jumped the gun, nothing would have prevented the city's passing into his hands. As it was, without waiting for the signal he led his men up to the wall. The guards cried out in terror and a general tumult ensued: women groaned aloud and wailed in confusion as if the city was already done for, until all on the run took their stand against the barbarians in the city and cut them down with swords and stones and whatever other weapons were handy. Then they hurried to the wall and along with the guards shot their javelins at Gainas' soldiery and by every means at their disposal threw back the assault upon the city.

Constantinople thus having escaped danger, the barbarians (more than 7,000 of them) who had been intercepted by the townspeople occupied the Christian church, which is near the palace, securing for themselves sanctuary there. These the Emperor commanded killed on the very spot, because he did not wish it to serve as refuge from a punishment that corresponded to their audacity. Although the Emperor issued this command, not a single person dared to lay a hand on the barbarians or drag them out from their asylum, for fear that they might attempt resistance. Accordingly it seemed best to strip off the roof located over the so-called sacred table. . .[1] The men

----

[1] The passage is mutilated.

entrusted with this task hurled down upon the barbarians lighted kindling and kept this up until all were burned to death. And thus were the barbarians destroyed; but the Christian zealots thought that a great sacrilege had been committed in the heart of the city.

Now Gainas, having been thwarted in his very daring undertaking, openly incited war against the State. Having come to the regions of Thrace he found the cities fortified with walls and garrisoned with the magistrates and townsfolk; these had already had experience in warfare from former attacks and were now massed in full strength for battle. And so Gainas, who observed nothing but grass outside the walls (for the people had taken pains to collect the various crops and animals and victuals of every sort), decided to leave Thrace, make a dash for the Chersonesus and then return to Asia via the straits of the Hellespont. (20) Meanwhile, the Emperor and the Senate by common consent chose as leader for the war against Gainas Fravitta, a barbarian by race but in other respects (not only by disposition but also by deliberate choice and religious practice) a Greek. He already had many conspicuous successes to his credit, having freed from the depredations of bandits the entire East from Cilicia as far as Phoenicia and Palestine. Having accepted command of the troops assigned to him, he opposed himself to Gainas and prevented the barbarians' passage via the Hellespont into Asia. While Gainas was making preparations for war, Fravitta would not tolerate his own troops' being idle, but drilled them continuously. He so built up the soldiers' strength by these exercises that they, having laid aside their former laziness and sloth, bore ill Gainas' delay in offering battle.

Fravitta, then, was busy about these matters in Asia, night and day watching over his own camp and spying out the movements of the enemy; nor was he neglectful of his fleet. For he had a sufficient number of boats for a sea battle, boats known as *Liburnae* (a name derived from an Italian city where the model had first been fabricated). These boats would appear to be as swift as fifty-oared ships but far inferior to triremes. For a long period of time they had not been manufactured, even though the historian Polybius [1] had set forth the measurements of their six banks of oars (the Romans and Carthaginians apparently employed these boats frequently in their wars against one another). (21) Now, when Gainas had forced a passage through the Long Wall into the Chersonesus, he stationed his barbarians along the entire Thracian promontory extending from opposite Parium to opposite Lampsacus and Abydus and the places that make the sea a strait. The commander of the Roman forces was sailing around these places off Asia with his ships day and night on the lookout for barbarian attacks. Gainas, however, owing to want of supplies could no longer endure delay: he felled timbers from the woods in the Chersonesus, fitted them together as precisely as possible, rendered them suitable for conveying men and horses, embarked same thereon, and loosed them with a favoring tide. The rafts could not be guided aright by oars nor would they yield otherwise to the steersman's art, seeing that they had been constructed in bustle and confusion with mere barbarian know-how. Meanwhile Gainas remained on dry land, hopeful that victory was within his grasp, as if the Roman forces would prove no match for his own. The sagacious Roman general, being on the alert, had guessed that this attempt would be made, and ordered his ships to move a short distance out from shore. When he observed the barbarians' rafts being driven at the whim of the waves, he himself was the first to make an attack on one in the front line. He had the upper hand since

---

[1] In a portion of his work that is lost.

his ship was fitted out with a bronze beak: as soon as he
had staved in the raft and hurled missiles upon its occu-
pants, he sank it together with all aboard. At the sight of
their commander's action the marines on board the other
ships imitated it. Some of the enemy were killed by the
weapons, others fell off the rafts and were drowned in the
sea; practically no one was able to escape death. Gainas,
aggrieved at this setback and not knowing what to do after
the loss of so many fighting men, speedily removed his
camp some distance from the Chersonesus back into
Thrace. Fravitta now decided not to pursue the fleeing
Gainas, but regrouped his forces on land, content with the
victory fortune had given him. Nearly everyone accused
Fravitta of being unwilling to give chase to the fugitive
Gainas and of sparing him, together with those who escaped
with him, as a fellow tribesman. But, conscious of nothing
of the sort, he returned to the Emperor, exulting in his
victory and freely acknowledging it as the gift of the gods
whom he cultivated. Indeed he was not ashamed to admit,
within earshot of the Emperor himself, that he venerated
and worshiped the gods according to ancestral custom and
could not bring himself to conform to common practice in
this regard. The Emperor welcomed Fravitta and appointed
him consul. Gainas, on the other hand, having lost the
majority of his troops in the manner stated, with the rest
hastened to the Danube and, finding Thrace laid low as a
result of prior invasions, plundered whatever he came upon.
He was afraid that another Roman army might make pursuit
and attack what few barbarians he had left; at the same time
he regarded as not above suspicion the Romans in his company, and had them one and all killed unaware. Then he
crossed the Danube with his barbarians, intending to return
to his original home and there live out the rest of his life.

22. While Gainas was doing these things Uldes,
currently the chief of the Huns, thought it unsafe to permit

a barbarian who had his own army to make his home above the Danube. In addition, he imagined that he would ingratiate himself with the Roman Emperor by chasing Gainas away, and he prepared to do battle with him. Having collected his forces, he lined them up against him. And so Gainas, who could neither return to the Romans nor otherwise escape the onslaught which threatened, armed his men and engaged the Huns. The armies came to close quarters not once but several times, and Gainas' soldiery stood its ground for a number of conflicts until at length after many had fallen he himself, fighting staunchly and nobly, was killed.

With Gainas' death the warfare ceased. Uldes, chief of the Huns, sent the man's head to the Emperor Arcadius and was honored with rewards. Thereafter he entered upon a treaty with the Romans. However, when affairs took a turn for the worse because the Emperor was devoid of good sense, Thrace again was thrown into confusion. For runaway slaves, along with army deserters, claiming that they were themselves Huns, plundered everything out in the open until Fravitta marched against them and killed as many as he laid his hands upon, thus removing terror from the inhabitants. . . (23) . . .[1] [Aurelianus, Saturninus, and Joannes, upon their return from exile,] fearing that they would be maltreated, disembarked in Epirus and, while deliberating about their own safety, which was rendered doubtful by reason of the magnitude of their transgression, they gave those in their custody an opportunity to escape. Others narrate that these latter won their release by means of money. But, in whatever way they made good their escape, they returned to Constantinople contrary to all expectation and put in their appearance before the Emperor, the Senate, and everybody else.

---

[1] There is missing one entire leaf of the MS. describing events of the years 401 and 402 A. D.

Thenceforth the hatred on the part of the Emperor's wife against John, the Christian bishop [1], increased. She had formerly been incensed at him because he was wont to ridicule her in his public addresses to his congregation. At this time, following the return of Joannes and the others from exile, her animosity against him stood plainly revealed. With all the resources at her command she incited the bishops in every quarter to remove John from office. Among these the first and foremost bishop was Theophilus of Alexandria in Egypt, he who had initiated the attack upon our ancestors' long-standing sacred rites. When a trial was proposed John, realizing that his case would be processed to a vote not at all equitably, left Constantinople of his own accord. The people were quite upset about this (for the man was clever at demogogy) and the city was full of tumult; indeed, already the Christian church had been occupied by the so-called monks. These men abstain from legitimate marriages, and in cities and villages alike they fill up their populous orders with bachelors, good for nothing in time of war or of any other public necessity (not to mention the fact that, proceeding along a certain path from that period right down to the present day, they have appropriated to themselves a great part of the land and, under the pretext of sharing all things with the poor, they have reduced practically everyone to poverty [2]). These men, having occupied the churches, now prohibited the masses from entering for their customary prayers. The people bore this ill, as did the soldiery; both groups alike sought to beat back the monk's audaciousness. To this end at a given signal they set forth

---

[1] Whose epithet was Chrysostom, 'the golden mouth.'

[2] This statement is of a piece with Zosimus' anti-Christian feelings, and is not to be taken seriously; still, it does offer some indication that his *floruit* falls considerably after the events he is here describing: cf. the introduction.

without restraint and indiscriminately kept slaughtering everyone until they filled the church with corpses. Then they chased the runaways and pierced through with spears as many as they spotted in dark garb. Amongst these many happened to perish who because of mourning or some other vicissitude were wearing such raiment. And John now returned to his former undertakings, stirring up similar incidents inside the city.

24. The tribe of sycophants rose to the top as never before. They were forever attending the court eunuchs. If a rich man died, they disclosed his net worth just as if he had no children or relatives. Rescripts kept issuing from the Emperor ordering that the estate of such and such be made over to such and such, and inheritances fell to those who petitioned the Emperor even while children stood by and bewailed the loss of their parents. In short, all that was done was guaranteed to fill the cities with lamentation and to result in unconscionable detriment to every inhabitant. As the Emperor was extremely foolish, his wife was arrogant beyond her sex; on all sides she was exposed to the insatiable demands of eunuchs and of ladies in waiting who got the better of her. So unbearable did she make life for all that to men of sense nothing was more to be desired than death.

As if this were not enough, Constantinople was faced with danger beyond all measure from the following cause. John, having returned after his banishment (as I have said) and agitating the common people against the Empress during his regular church services, when he found himself expelled from his episcopal see and the city as well, took ship and sailed off. His partisans, in their zeal to see to it that no one be appointed to succeed him as bishop, decided that the city must be fired down. Accordingly, during the night they secretly set fire to the church, and towards dawn gathered around outside it, thus escaping detection. By daybreak everybody was aware that the city was already in the utmost peril, for the whole church was burned down and the buildings adjacent to it were being consumed simultaneously, in particular those where a blast of wind started to fan the flame. The fire poured into the house where the Senate customarily assembled, a house which was located in front of the palace and was elegantly, even ostentatiously, fitted out: it was adorned with sculptured works majestic to behold and with colorful marbles which are now no longer mined. It is said that there perished in that fire the very images which had originally been consecrated to the Muses on Mount Helicon and in Constantine's time had been forcibly removed, along with other objects which underwent sacrilege, and dedicated on this site; this calamity portended quite clearly the Muses' aversion from all mankind.

A certain miracle which happened at this time it is not fitting to pass over in silence. The Senate-house of which I have been speaking had before its doors statues of Jupiter and Athena which stood on stone bases, appearing just as they do even today. The former statue is said to be that of Jupiter Dodonaeus, while the latter is said to have been consecrated long ago at Lindus. Now, when the Senate-house had been entirely consumed by the fire and the liquified lead from the roof was dripping down upon these statues and even the building stones, had they not been fire-resistant by nature, would have been rolled against them; when, in short, all this beauty had been reduced to rubble, these statues as well (so common opinion holds) crumbled into dust. Yet when the site was cleaned off and made ready for renovation the statues of these gods alone were seen to have survived the general destruction. This event caused all cultured people to conceive better hopes for the city, as if these divinities would always make provision in its behalf. But let all these matters turn out as seems best to divine providence.

25. All were provoked at the city's calamity, nor did they discover any other cause for it than the proverbial shadow of the ass.[1] While the imperial court was planning the restoration of the devastated buildings word arrived that a great host of the Isauri, who live above Pamphylia and Cilicia in the very rough and inaccessible tracts of Mount Taurus, had formed into marauding bands and invaded the countryside lying below them. Although they had not yet been able to breach the walled cities, they were overrunning the unwalled villages and everything else in their path. These incursions were rendered the simpler because of the preceding sack of the region at the time when Tribigildus and his barbarians had rebelled. When these things had been announced Arbazacius was dispatched as commander to relieve the painful situation in Pamphylia. Having taken a suitable force, he chased the bandits as they retreated back up into the mountains, seized many of their villages, and killed not a few of the leaders. Indeed, he would very easily have subdued them altogether and have furnished the townsfolk complete security had he not been addicted to wantonness and base pleasures, relaxed much of his vigor, and with his grasping hands preferred private wealth to the common weal. When he was recalled to the court on account of this prevarication, he expected that he would have to stand trial. But, after he had offered the Empress part of what he had taken from the Isauri, he not only escaped trial but spent his wealth on the city fleshpots. Thus the depredations of the Isauri continued clandestinely, though not for a while did they attack the neighboring nations openly. . .[2]

---

[1]According to the proverb, he who cannot uncover the offender avenges himself on the unoffending.

[2]A hiatus of disputed length here occurs.

26. Now. Alaric. when he had ravaged all of Greece in the manner described,[1] left the Peloponnesus and the country through which the Achelous River flows. He tarried in the Epirotic region which the Molossians and Thesprotians and others inhabit as far north as Epidamnus and the Taulantians, awaiting the fulfillment of his pact with Stilicho, a pact of the following sort. Stilicho, realizing that those who administered Arcadius' realm were hostile to him, planned to ally Alaric with himself and to annex all the peoples in Illyria to Honorius' realm. Accordingly, having made a compact with Alaric concerning this enterprise. he was waiting for the first opportunity to put it into effect. While Alaric was standing by to follow orders, Rhodogaisus was collecting 400,000 men from among the Celtic and Germanic nations above the Danube and the Rhine and preparing to cross into Italy. The first announcement of this news stunned everyone: the cities had given up hope and Rome herself was perturbed as if in extreme peril. Stilicho, having picked up the entire army encamped at Ticinum in Liguria (it numbered thirty divisions) as well as the allied auxiliaries he had been able to procure from the Alans and the Huns, did not await the advent of the enemy but crossed the Danube himself with his entire force. Having fallen upon the barbarians unaware, in a mass slaughter he cut down their fighting strength to such an extent that almost none of them was spared outside of a very few whom he enrolled in the Roman auxiliary force. Naturally, Stilicho was quite proud of this victory; he returned with his army, having been all but universally crowned because contrary to every expectation he had freed Italy from dread danger.

27. At Ravenna (metropolis of Flaminia, a venerable city formerly, as a Thessalian colony, called Rhene[2]

---

[1]Chapters 5f., above.   [2]As if from the Greek word "flow"; but Ravenna was almost certainly of Etruscan origin.

because waters flow around it on all sides and not because, as the historian Olympiodorus of Thebes [1] says, Remus, brother of Romulus, founded it; this latter cause ought, I believe, to be credited to Quadratus, who in his history of the Emperor Marcus Aurelius talked about the city) — at Ravenna, then. Stilicho was preparing to take his army over to the cities of Illyria and with Alaric's help to wrest them from Arcadius and gain them for Honorius' realm. Two impediments, however, intervened: first, a rumor of Alaric's death was making the rounds and, second, a letter from the Emperor Honorius at Rome was delivered, declaring that Constantinus had embarked upon tyranny, had crossed from Britain, and was in the midst of the trans-Alpine peoples, playing the role of Emperor in their cities. Now, the tale of Alaric's death appeared dubious even before certain men came and told how matters really stood; but what was said about Constantinus' proclaiming himself Emperor received general credence. Accordingly, Stilicho stopped short his departure for Illyria and proceeded to Rome, desiring to take common counsel as to what should be done.

28. Autumn was ended and winter had set in. Bassus and Philippus were appointed consuls. [2] Now the Emperor Honorius, whose wife Maria had died not long before, was seeking the hand of her sister Thermantia in marriage. But to this Stilicho would not [3] consent. Serena kept pressing for the marriage. wanting it to take place for the following reason. When Honorius and Maria were engaged, her mother Serena discerned that the maiden was not yet nubile; nevertheless, she abstained from postponing the wedding even though she considered that [3] to hand over an

---

[1] *Floruit* 425 A. D.; probably the latest source from whom Zosimus drew information.   [2] For the year 408.

[3] Two sentences in this paragraph are mutilated.

immature girl in marital union was nothing other than an offense against nature. She found a woman who knew how to remedy matters of this sort and with her aid brought it about that her daughter would consort with the Emperor and share the same couch with him, but that he would have neither the desire nor the capacity to consummate the marriage. Since then the daughter had died a virgin, and Serena not unnaturally was desirous of a grandchild by the Emperor, fearful lest something of her own great power be lessened. Thus she zealously sought to unite her second daughter to Honorius in marriage; this she accomplished, but the daughter died soon thereafter, having suffered the same fate as her sister.

29. To Stilicho some one brought a report that Alaric had left Epirus, crossed the difficult narrows between the Pannonians and the Veneti, and pitched his camp at Emona, a city lying between upper Pannonia and Noricum. It is not fitting to pass over in silence what is known of this city and how it came to be founded. It is said that the Argonauts, when Aeëtes was pursuing them across the Euxine Sea, came to anchor at the mouth of the Danube. They judged that they could succeed in bucking the river-current and in rowing upstream with the aid of a favorable breeze until they could come nearer to the sea. Having carried out this plan and having reached this point, they left behind as a memorial of their coming the foundation of this city. Then they placed the Argo on scaffolding and hauled her a distance of fifty miles to the sea. Thus did they come to the Italian coast, just as the poet Pisander relates in his work entitled "Heroicae Theogamiae"[1], which embraces the whole of history, so to say. Alaric now set forth from Emona for Noricum by crossing the Aquilis

---

[1] "The Marriages of Heroes to Gods," written in the early third century A. D.

River [1] and climbing over the Apennines. These mountains mark the boundaries of Pannonia and furnish a very narrow passage for those who wish to go over into Noricum, a passage which requires only a handful of men to guard even if a great multitude is trying to force its way through. Alaric nevertheless effected the crossing, and from Noricum dispatched an embassy to Stilicho. He demanded money both for his sojourn in Epirus, which he said he had undertaken at Stilicho's behest, and also for his advance into Italy and Noricum. Stilicho received the embassy and, leaving it behind at Ravenna, he went to Rome, for he wanted to take counsel with the Emperor and the Senate as to what should be done. After the Senate had been convened at the palace and a discussion about whether or not to wage war had been held, the majority voted for war. Only Stilicho and a few others who out of fright agreed with him voted the opposite way, that is, to make peace with Alaric. When those in favor of war asked Stilicho to tell them why he was in favor of peace, and that, too, a peace which would have to be purchased with money, to the disgrace of the good name of Rome, he replied, "Because Alaric spent all that time in Epirus for the Emperor's benefit, to the end that along with me he might make war on the Eastern Emperor, strip Illyria from his realm and annex it to Honorius'." He added that this plan would already have been accomplished had not the delivery of Honorius' imperial rescript interfered with his own departure for the East, the departure in expectation of which Alaric had consumed so long a time there. Upon saying this Stilicho produced the letter, and placed the blame on Serena for wanting the concord between the two Emperors to be

---

[1] There is no such river; the name is probably drawn from Pisander. Indeed, Zosimus' geography in this paragraph with regard to all of Alaric's movements appears badly bungled.

preserved inviolate. Since Stilicho's statement appeared just to all, the Senate decreed that 4,000 gold pounds be given Alaric in the name of peace, the majority voting for this amount not by choice but through fear of Stilicho, so much so that Lampadius, a man outstanding by birth and by worth, let loose this utterance in his native tongue: "Non est ista pax sed pactio servitutis" (i.e., "This is no peace, but a pact of slavery"). When the Senate had been dismissed Lampadius, fearful lest he might suffer for his freedom of speech, took refuge in a nearby Christian church.

30.   Thus Stilicho, having achieved the peace with Alaric, was preparing to set forth on the journey to carry out his plans. The Emperor, however, kept saying that he wanted to go from Rome to Ravenna to review the army and welcome it cordially, especially since so great an enemy had crossed inside Italy. He said these things not of his own motivation but on Serena's advice: she wanted him to be in a safer city so that, in case of a violation of the peace and an invasion of Rome, Alaric would not be able to become master of the Emperor as well. Indeed, she was anxious for his safety because her own safety depended upon his. The Emperor's journey to Ravenna did not meet with the approval of Stilicho, who devised many objections to it. Since the Emperor would not give in but stuck to the idea, at the instance of Stilicho a barbarian named Sarus, leader of a gang of ruffians in Ravenna, created disturbances in front of the city — not that he was really a wilful revolutionary but that he might scare off the Emperor and divert him from his proposed trip. When not even this could change the Emperor's mind, Justinianus, one of Rome's distinguished advocates and a close adviser to Stilicho, with his keen sagacity apparently divined the reasons behind the Emperor's journey as well as the fact that the soldiers stationed at Ticinum were averse from Stilicho and should the Emperor come thither would place

him in danger of his life. Justinianus continually exhorted Stilicho to fend off the Emperor's journey. But when he saw that the Emperor would not heed Stilicho's words he gave up, for fear that he might be sunk in the same fate with Stilicho because of his intimacy with him.

31. A rumor concerning the death of the Emperor Arcadius had earlier reached Rome and now, following the departure of the Emperor Honorius for Ravenna, was confirmed. At this point the Emperor was at Bononia, a city of Aemilia seventy so-called milestones distant from Ravenna, where Stilicho was. The latter was now summoned to check by chastisement the soldiers who had been quarreling among themselves along the way. Stilicho, having called together the mutineers and told them not only that the Emperor had bidden him chastise them but also that he had instructions to decimate their ranks by killing the guiltiest ten per cent., instilled such dread in them that they all dissolved in tears. The general was moved to pity. He promised that the Emperor would be clement, and the Emperor did not go back on that promise. Then they turned their attention to public matters: Stilicho was desirous of setting out for the East and of settling the affairs of Arcadius' son Theodosius, who was still a youth and in need of a protector; while the Emperor Honorius was himself planning to undertake the same mission and to do what he could in the way of stabilizing the young man's realm. Stilicho was displeased with this plan, and deterred the Emperor from it by discussing the prohibitive expense involved in his undertaking it. He said, further, that 'the rebellion of Constantinus made it impossible for the Emperor to be further removed from the administration of Italy and of Rome itself, since already that tyrant had coursed through all of Gaul and was sojourning at Arelate. Besides these matters, which in themselves should suffice to require the Emperor's presence and prudence, there was

the advent of Alaric with his great host of barbarians, who, since he was a barbarian himself and hence untrustworthy, would invade Italy should he find her destitute of aid. The best plan, the plan most advantageous to the State, was for Alaric to march against the tyrant Constantinus, taking with him part of his barbarian troops, backed up by Roman legions with their commanders to share with him the conduct of the war. Finally, he himself would go on to the East if the Emperor would command him to do so and would give him written instructions as to what should be done there.'

The Emperor, judging that everything Stilicho said was all right, gave him letters addressed to the Eastern Emperor and to Alaric, and then departed from Bononia. But for the time being Stilicho stayed put, neither proceeding to the East nor bringing to fulfillment any other of his plans; he did not even transfer to Ravenna or anywhere else the portion of the soldiers that was stationed in Ticinum, for fear that these might gain access to the Emperor and incite the latter to mount operations against him.

32. Stilicho acted thus, conscious of no discord directed either against the Emperor or against his soldiers. But a certain Olympius, a native of the Euxine Sea region who had been honored with a splendid command in the praetorian guard, was covering up, under the guise of Christian piety, great inward malice. Pretending to be a man of moderation, he was wont to converse with the Emperor and would pour into his ear many things against Stilicho that were (if I may speak poetically) soul-destroying: namely, that Stilicho had concerned himself about the expedition to the East for the reason that he could plot the assassination of the young Theodosius and hand over [his Empire[1]] to his own son, Eucherius. With these things he

---

[1]The passage is mutilated.

kept filling the Emperor's ear as ample opportunity arose on the journey. When they got to Ticinum, Olympius visited the soldiers who were ill (indeed, this was the chief point in that specious moderation of his), sowing even among them some such innuendoes as the above. And now it was only the fourth day since the Emperor's arrival at Ticinum when the soldiers were summoned to his quarters. The Emperor appeared before them and was exhorting them to make war upon the tyrant Constantinus. No man made a stir about Stilicho until Olympius was seen to nod to the soldiers, as if to remind them of what he had discussed with them in secret. They, somehow or other beside themselves, cut down in cold blood Limenius, the praetorian prefect among the trans-Alpine peoples, and along with him Chariobaudes, the master of the soldiery in those same regions (these men happened to have escaped from the tyrant and had come to meet the Emperor at Ticinum). On top of them there were murdered Vincentius and Salvius, the former the master of horse, the latter the principal of the school of household slaves. As the sedition increased the Emperor withdrew into his tent and some of the magistrates managed to escape. The soldiers scattered throughout the entire city and killed all the magistrates they could, dragging them forth from the houses into which they had run for cover; they also plundered the city's resources. The evil progressing to the point of i n c u r a b i l i t y, the Emperor threw around him a tunic (no cloak, no crown) and, having appeared in the center of the city, he was just barely able with great effort to check the soldiers' mania. There were killed also as many magistrates as were captured after their flight, including Naemorius, the master of the palatine orders, and Patruinus, the prefect of the treasury, and ... [1] , who was in charge of the Emperor's privy purse, and Salvius, whose office was that of dictating

---

[1] The name is missing.

the Emperor's opinions and has been called "quaestor" since Constantine's time. The last-named, although he threw himself at the very feet of the Emperor, was not able to avoid death. The rebellion lasted until late afternoon, as the Emperor, fearful lest something might happen to him, had withdrawn from the scene. In the interim Longinianus, the praetorian prefect of Italy, was found and put to death. These magistrates, then, were killed by the insane soldiery. There perished also a multitude of passers-by, more than could be readily counted.

33. When these things were reported to Stilicho, who was at Bononia (a city of Aemilia, as aforesaid[1]), they upset him no end. He summoned all the leaders of his confederate barbarians and proposed a deliberation as to what should be done. It was everyone's shared opinion that it would be well that, if the Emperor were dead (indeed, this matter was yet moot) all together, barbarians and Romans united, should attack the soldiers and thus restore all the rest to their senses; but, if the Emperor were still alive and only the magistrates killed, then the ringleaders of the rebellion should be brought to justice. Such were the resolutions of Stilicho and the barbarians he had with him. But when they had learned that no indignity had been done the Emperor's person, Stilicho decided not to proceed with the chastisement of the army but to depart for Ravenna. For he kept reflecting upon the multitude of the soldiers, and he still did not know for certain how the Emperor felt towards him; besides, he thought it neither scrupulous nor safe to let loose barbarians against the Roman army.

34. Stilicho being hesitant on these scores, the barbarians with him wanted to put into effect the plans they had already laid and they undertook to divert him from his current thinking. Failing to persuade him, all the rest decided to stay put until the Emperor should disclose more clearly his

---

[1]Chapter 31 above.

feelings with regard to Stilicho – all the rest, that is, but Sarus, who surpassed the other allies in bodily strength and in reputation. With the aid of the barbarians under his command he killed while asleep all of Stilicho's Hunnish attendants and, having gained possession of his entire baggage train, proceeded to his tent, where they found him speculating about his future course. And so Stilicho, even while his barbarians were in disagreement, made for Ravenna and exhorted the cities where the barbarians' wives and children happened to be to receive no one of the barbarians into their midst. But Olympius, who had by now mastered the Emperor's mind, sent an imperial dispatch to the soldiers at Ravenna, ordering them to arrest Stilicho and detain him in free custody for the time being. Having learned this Stilicho while it was still night entered a certain Christian church nearby. The barbarians with him plus other supporters saw him do this and, under arms together with their slaves, awaited the outcome. After daybreak the soldiers entered the church and swore oaths in the presence of the bishop that the Emperor's orders were not to kill Stilicho but merely to place him under custody. As he was led forth from the church under guard by the soldiers, there was delivered a second letter by the same carrier that had brought the previous one; this letter demanded the death penalty for Stilicho's crimes against the State. In the meantime as Stilicho was being led to his death his son Eucherius had taken flight and was headed for Rome. Stilicho's barbarians and the slaves and other henchmen (their number was not inconsiderable) began a movement to rescue him from death, but Stilicho called off this attempt by employing all kinds of threats and alarms and somehow managed to expose his neck to the sword, a man of greater forbearance than almost all the dynasts of the period. For, although he was wedded to the niece of the elder Theodosius and had been entrusted with the realms of both of Theodosius' sons and for twenty-three years had been a general, he had never once been seen to accept money in exchange for an appointment or to turn to his own private gain the provisioning of the army. He had one son, for whom he set a magisterial limit of the so-called notarial tribunate, securing for him no higher office. That the scholars may not be in doubt about the time of his death, let them know that this occurred on the twenty-third of August of the year in which Bassus and Philippus were the consuls, which was also the year that the Emperor Arcadius met his fate.[1]

35. With Stilicho dead all court affairs were carried on at the discretion of Olympius, who as a matter of fact accepted the title of master (of offices); other magistracies the Emperor distributed among those whom Olympius recommended. Stilicho's close friends and others who appeared to be his partisans were sought out from every quarter. Brought to trial were Deuterius, head of the guard of the imperial bedchamber, and Petrus, tribune of the notarial order; they underwent a public investigation and were compelled to testify about Stilicho. Olympius, having failed to obtain any information which could be used either against them or against Stilicho, had them clubbed to death. Several others also were brought to trial as if privy to Stilicho's plans and were coerced to tell under torture whether they knew of his coveting the throne. When they replied that they knew of no such thing, those who were in charge of the investigation desisted from their undertaking. Now, the Emperor Honorius gave orders that his wife Thermantia be removed from her imperial throne and returned to her

---

[1]This final tribute to Stilicho is in startling contrast to Zosimus' earlier estimates of him, which are based on Eunapius' disparagements. The reason is that ever since chapter 28 above, where the events of the year here referred to began , Zosimus employed as his main source Olympiodorus, whose dislikes centered around Stilicho's wife Serena and, of course, Olympius.

mother, although she was altogether free of suspicion, and that Stilicho's son Eucherius be hunted down and murdered. They found him, to be sure, a refugee in one of the churches of Rome, but owing to the hallowed nature of the spot they let him be. Likewise at Rome Heliocrates, the prefect of the treasury, bore a letter from the Emperor which demanded confiscation of the property of everyone who had filled any magistracy whatsoever during Stilicho's period in office, and was busy collecting the money for the fisc. And, just as if these things did not suffice to sate the evil genius which, heavy-laden with bonds of guilt and godforsaken, was forever upsetting all human affairs,[1] to what had been done before something else was added, as follows:

The soldiers stationed in the cities, when news of Stilicho's death reached them, set upon the wives and children of the barbarians in city after city and, having wiped them out wholesale as if by previous agreement, seized all their belongings. When their relatives heard of their murder they flocked together from all sides, incensed at so impious a violation on the Romans' part of a pledge given in God's name. They unanimously decided to ally themselves with Alaric in the war against Rome, and for this purpose they collected more than 30,000 men who were agreeable to any plan he might make. (36) However, even these did not provoke Alaric to start fighting: mindful of the truce made while Stilicho was still alive, he preferred to continue the peace. He dispatched an embassy, asking that in exchange for a small amount of money the peace be kept and that there be given him as hostages Aetius and Jason, one being the son of Gaudentius, the other the son of Jovius. At the same time he said he would give as hostages some

---

[1]Zosimus here has reference to the *daemones* of the later Neoplatonism, the prevailing creed of the pagan reaction.

noblemen of his own, and on these conditions would live peaceably and would lead his army out of Noricum into Pannonia. But the Emperor rejected the terms upon which Alaric sought peace, even though to settle the present situation satisfactorily he should have done one of two things: either he should have postponed the war by making a moderate outlay of money for a truce or, if he preferred to fight, he should have collected all his military legions, stationed them opposite the enemy approaches, and cut off the barbarian from advancing further. In this latter event Sarus should have been appointed leader and commander in chief of operations not only because in his own right he was, owing to his valor and battle experience, terrifying to the enemy but also because he possessed a force of barbarians sufficient for the job of resistance. But Honorius neither accepted the peace nor cultivated Sarus' friendship nor mustered the Roman army but, pinning all his hopes on Olympius' vows, he became the author of great calamities to the State. For he furnished the army with such leaders as aroused the enemy's contempt, placing Turpilio in charge of the cavalry and Varanes in charge of the infantry and Vigilantius in charge of the body of slaves. Other matters were handled in like manner. And so everyone was in despair, already envisioning the destruction of Italy.

37.   Matters having been conducted in this fashion, Alaric started his march on Rome, sneering at Honorius' preparations. Since it was his intention to undertake so great an enterprise not just on an equal but on a greatly superior footing, he summoned his brother-in-law Ataulphus from upper Pannonia to join him in it (Ataulphus had a force of Huns and Goths that was not to be despised). Yet Alaric did not await his coming: marching ahead he overran in order Aquileia and the cities lying on the far side of the Eridanus River (I mean Concordia and Altinum and, lastly, Cremona). He crossed the river in high festival,

as it were, and meeting no opposition he came to a certain castle of Bononia called Oecubaria. Thence, having passed through all of Aemilia and having left Ravenna behind him, he arrived at Ariminum, a large city in Flaminia. This city also he overran, as well as all the others in the province, and then he entered Picenum, which territory is situated at the end of the Ionian Gulf.[1] From there he set out for Rome, ravaging every fort and town en route; and, had not the eunuchs Arsacius and Terentius, before the barbarians' arrival at these places, started on the run, leading Stilicho's son Eucherius into Rome to be killed in accordance with the Emperor's instructions (instructions which were dutifully carried out), the young man would surely have fallen into Alaric's hands and been saved. When the eunuchs had fulfilled their orders in this regard and also had handed back Thermantia, Honorius' wife, to her mother, they were unable to return via the same road to the Emperor and so took ship and sailed towards the Celts and Gauls. They anchored off Genua, a city in Liguria, and got back safely to Ravenna, where the Emperor was still in residence. Believing it a great boon to the State if he should reward these eunuchs for their manly feats of restoring Thermantia to her mother and murdering Eucherius, the Emperor put Terentius in charge of the imperial bedchamber and made Arsacius Terentius' second-in-command. He had Bathanarius, [who was commander[2]] of the forces in greater Africa and who was married to Stilicho's sister, killed. That province he handed over to Heraclianus, who had cut down Stilicho with his own hand and as his reward received this honor.

---

[1] As in chapter 29 above, so here Zosimus' (Olympiodorus'?) geography with regard to Alaric's movements is questionable. He even uses the mythical name Eridanus for the Padus (i. e., Po) River.

[2] The passage is mutilated.

38.   Alaric was already in the vicinity of Rome and had laid its inhabitants under siege. The Senate began to hold Serena under suspicion as if she had influenced the barbarians to attack the city: unanimously it (together with the Emperor's sister by the same father, Placidia) decided that Serena be put to death as being responsible for the current woes; for, they thought, with Serena out of the way Alaric himself would take leave of the city, there being no one left that he could expect would betray it to him. Now in fact this suspicion was false, for nothing of the sort had entered Serena's head; but she paid the penalty proper to her impiety toward the gods, which impiety I am now going to narrate.   When the elder Theodosius had put down the tyranny of Eugenius, he came to Rome and instilled in everyone contempt for the sacred rites by denying the use of public funds for the sacrifices.[1] Priests and priestesses alike were expelled and the shrines were forsaken, deprived of religious ceremonies. At that time, then, Serena, making light of this, desired to see the temple of the Great Mother. Spying the necklace on the image of Rhea, an ornament worthy of her divine cult, she removed it from the image and placed it around her own neck. And when an old woman, the last of the Vestal Virgins, upbraided this impiety to her face, she mocked her and ordered her attendants to eject her.   As the woman descended she called down upon the heads of Serena and her husband and her children everything and all things that her impiety deserved. But Serena, taking no notice of this, left the shrine sporting the necklace.   Thereafter oftentimes there came a dream by night or a vision by day warning her of her impending death, and several others had visitations very similar to hers.   To such an extent did Iustitia, who pursues the impious, prevail in fulfilling her office that even though Serena knew what was coming she took no precau-

---

[1] Book IV, chapter 59 above.

tions but placed at the disposal of the noose that very neck around which she had hung the goddess' ornament. Stilicho also, it is said, on account of another act of impiety not very different from hers, did not escape Iustitia's mysterious ways. For he had commanded that the gates on the Capitol of Rome be stripped of their great weight of gold, and those who were ordered to fulfill this task found on a certain part of the gates the inscription "misero regi servantur," that is to say, "Woe to the tyrant for whom (these) are preserved." And the upshot corresponded to the inscription, for he ended his life woefully and wretchedly.

39. However, not even Serena's death budged Alaric from his siege, but he encircled the city and all its gates and, by occupying the Tiber River, prevented the sending up of supplies from the harbor. Although the Romans noticed this they determined to hold out as if just about any day they might expect relief to reach the city from Ravenna. But when none arrived they became desperate and decided that the daily ration of cooking grain must be reduced by one-half and thereafter, as their want increased, by two-thirds. And, since no remedy for curing this evil could be devised and their stomachs lacked any kind of sustenance, as was to be expected plague followed upon famine[1] and on all sides there were dead bodies which could not be buried outside the city, for the enemy was guarding every exit. The city was to such an extent a sepulcher of the dead that otherwise it was uninhabited and, even if there had been no shortage of victuals, the stench given off by the cadavers would have sufficed to destroy the living. To be sure, Laeta, the wife of the former Emperor Gratian, and her mother Tisamena managed to furnish the necessities of life to several people inasmuch as the treasury, thanks to

---

[1]The words *loimos* ("plague") and *limos* ("famine") recall the "death-dearth" discussion in Thucydides II. 54, the archetype of all descriptions of plagues.

Theodosius' liberality. granted them a regal banquet table's provisions; as a result of these ladies' philanthropy, at their household some few men appeased their hunger pangs.

40. But as things went from bad to worse and there was danger that the Roman people might resort to cannibalism. having made a trial of every other abomination known to man. they decided to send an embassy to the enemy announcing that 'they were prepared for peace provided the terms were moderate. yet were even more prepared for war since they had taken their weapons in hand and as a result of their continuous handling of them would no longer scruple about fighting'. There had been chosen for this embassy a Spaniard who had attained the rank of proconsul, Basilius; along with him went Joannes, who had once been chief of the Emperor's notaries (or tribunes, as they are called), since he was a friend and acquaintance of Alaric's. Indeed, the Romans did not know for certain whether Alaric was still present and besieging Rome in person, for they were beguiled by a rumor previously circulated that it was another, a partisan of Stilicho, who had incited him[1] to action against the city.

When the envoys reached Alaric they were ashamed of the ignorance which had for so long a time gripped the Romans, but they announced the Senate's business. Alaric listened, above all to the statement that the people were under arms and prepared for battle, and replied, "Thick grass is more easily cut than thin." At this utterance he let loose upon the envoys a big belly-laugh. When they turned to discussions about a peace he employed language that surpassed even a barbarian's insolence, for he said that he would under no circumstances put an end to the siege unless he received all the gold which the city possessed and all the silver, plus all the movables he might find throughout the city as well as the barbarian slaves. When one of the

---

[1]Or, by an alternate reading which makes more sense, "the army."

envoys asked, "If you should take all these things, what would be left over for those who are inside the city?" he answered, "Their lives." Upon receipt of this answer the envoys sought permission to consult with those inside the city as to what should be done. Permission granted, they reported back what words had been exchanged in their mission. Then it was that the Romans were convinced that the man who was making war on them was Alaric, and, despairing of all things that pertain to human strength, they recalled the resources which the city had formerly known in times of crisis and of which they were now bereft because they had violated the ancestral rites.

41.   While they were occupied with these thoughts Pompeianus, the urban prefect, by chance met some men who had come to Rome from Etruria. They said that a certain city, Narnia by name, had freed itself from imminent danger, having evoked by prayer to heaven and by worship in the ancestral manner violent thunder and lightning which drove off the barbarians besetting it. After this conversation Pompeianus was persuaded of the advantage of doing what the pontifical books prescribed. But, since his religion was that which currently prevailed, in order that he might accomplish in greater safety his heart's desire he related everything to the bishop of the city (his name was Innocent). Innocent, placing the salvation of the city ahead of his own religion, secretly allowed him and the priests to do whatever they knew how to do. But when they said that nothing would avail the city unless the customary sacrifices were performed in public, with the Senate ascending to the Capitol and celebrating both there and in the city marketplaces the duly prescribed rites, no one dared to take part in the ancestral ceremonies. Instead they bade the men from Etruria farewell and applied themselves to appeasing the barbarians in every possible way. Therefore they sent the envoys back again and, after an exchange of a great

many words, accepted these terms: that the city pay 5,000 pounds of gold, 30,000 more of silver, 4,000 silk tunics, 3,000 scarlet-dyed fleeces, and 3,000 pounds of pepper. Since the city had no funds in the treasury, absolute necessity demanded that such senators as had resources should undertake to secure these amounts by levy. To Palladius was assigned the task of meting out what payment should be made by each individual according to his substance. He was unable to collect everything completely, either because the owners concealed a part of their possessions or simply because the city had been reduced to penury owing to the exactions of one greedy Emperor after another. The guilt-laden genius [1] which had seized control of human affairs led those who were in charge of this particular business to the utter extreme of wickedness, for they decided to make up what was lacking with the ornaments attached to the gods' images — which of course meant nothing other than the images which had been consecrated by sacred rites and adorned with decorations befitting the fact that they had preserved the city's well-being from of old, and which when the religious rites had been diminished to some extent had become lifeless and inefficacious. Finally, since it was fated that everything having to do with the city's destruction should coincide, they not only stripped the images of their adornment but even melted down some of the gold and silver ones, among them that of Courage, whom the Romans call Virtus. With its destruction there was extinguished whatever courage and virtue the Romans had, just as it had been prophesied by men schooled in divination and ancestral ritual.

42. Accordingly, when the funds had been collected in this wise, it was decided that an embassy should be sent to the Emperor to confer with him about the pending peace and to serve notice that Alaric desired to obtain not money alone but hostages as well, sons of noblemen: 'only on this

---

[1]See note to chapter 35 above.

condition would he enter into an alliance of war with the Emperor (in addition to making peace) and would he march with the Romans against anyone who was of hostile intent towards them.' Since the Emperor also considered it best to make peace on these terms, the moneys were paid over to the barbarians. Alaric granted the urban population a market period of three days, with permission to exit freely through certain gates, plus allowing them to fetch grain from the port. And so the citizenry breathed once again, either selling whatever they had left and buying necessities or acquiring same by barter. The barbarians withdrew from Rome and pitched their tents around certain places in Etruria; thither practically all the slaves that were in Rome kept escaping from the city nearly every day, and kept joining the barbarians until the number of them thus assembled reached 40,000. Meanwhile some of the barbarians strayed away and attacked the Romans who were going down to the port and bringing back quantities of supplies. When Alaric learned of this he earnestly put a stop to it as taking place contrary to his will. And now there appeared to be a moderate letup of evils as at Ravenna the Emperor Honorius was entering upon the consulship for the ninth time and in the East the Emperor Theodosius was entering upon his fourth consulship.[1]

43. At this point the tyrant Constantinus sent eunuchs to Honorius, begging his pardon for having taken the power offered him: "For," he said, "he took it not of his own free will, but it was thrust upon him forcibly by the soldiery." The Emperor, having heard this plea and noting that he could not readily contemplate other wars so long as Alaric and his barbarians were no further removed than they were (besides, he was taking thought for his own kinsmen, Verenianus and Didymus, prisoners of the tyrant; as a matter of fact, his anxiety over them was futile, for they

---

[1]That is, the beginning of the year 409.

had been slain prior to the dispatch of this embassy), yielded to Constantinus' request and sent him an imperial robe in addition. Hereupon he dismissed the eunuchs.

44. Now, the peace with Alaric had not yet been confirmed because the Emperor had neither delivered the hostages nor fulfilled all the other demands. The Senate sent to Ravenna legates, Caecilianus and Attalus and Maximianus, who lamented bitterly all Rome's calamities and exaggerated in tragic fashion the number of the dead. They accomplished nothing by all this, for Olympius confused the issue and contradicted even their colorable statements. And so the legates were dismissed without succeeding in their mission, although the Emperor did supplant Theodorus with Caecilianus in the office of praetorian prefect and he did give orders that Attalus be put in charge of the treasury. Meanwhile, Olympius had no other occupation than to track down on every side those who supposedly knew something about Stilicho. On an information to this effect there were brought to trial Marcellianus and Salonius, brothers in the service of the imperial notaries, whom Olympius handed over to the praetorian prefect. Although their hides were tanned by every form of outrage, they told nothing of what Olympius wanted to hear.

45. With affairs at Rome in no better case than heretofore, the Emperor resolved to remove from their stations in Dalmatia five divisions of soldiers and summon them for guard duty in the city. Their ranks numbered 6,000, and for daring and strength they were the cream of the Roman army. Their leader was Valens, most ready to run any risk. He thought it beneath his dignity to proceed by roads which were not guarded by the enemy. Alaric awaited his approach and set upon him with his entire force. All fell into the hands of the adversary except a hundred men, who with difficulty escaped. Among these last was their leader, who together with Attalus (the man

who had been sent by the Senate to the Emperor) managed to reach Rome unharmed. With ever greater woes being added to the current ones, Attalus entered Rome and relieved Heliocrates of that charge which the Emperor had made over to him at Olympius' bidding. Now this was the task assigned him: to search out and then confiscate the property of those who had been proscribed owing to their friendship [1] with Stilicho. But since he, a man of moderation, considered it an act of impiety to trample upon wretched men and did not carry out a strict investigation (he even told many secretly to conceal whatever goods they could), having proven himself useless for the task he was led away to Ravenna to pay the penalty for his philanthropy towards the down-and-out. And he would by all means have been condemned to die owing to the savagery that then prevailed had he not by chance at this particular time betaken himself to one of the Christian churches. Maximilianus, on the other hand, did fall foul of the enemy and was restored to his father Marinianus upon a ransom payment of 30,000 gold pieces. For as the Emperor deferred the peace by refusing to satisfy the terms agreed upon — he would not turn over to Alaric's custody as hostages [2] the nobly-born — freedom of egress from the city was no longer available to the Romans. The Senate yet again sent emissaries (the bishop of Rome among them) to the Emperor to deal with the peace. Likewise there went along certain barbarians sent by Alaric to protect the emissaries from highwaymen.

After these men had set out for the Emperor, Ataulphus (who, as I narrated earlier, [3] had been summoned by Alaric) crossed the Alps which extend from Pannonia to Venetia. The Emperor got wind of this, and learned that

---

[1] The MS. reading is here defective.
[2] The passage is mutilated.
[3] Chapter 37 above.

he did not have a large force. He commanded all the soldiers that were stationed in the cities, both cavalry and infantry, to fall in with their leaders and go to meet Ataulphus. Olympius, who was leader of the palatine orders, was assigned the Huns who were at Ravenna, three hundred strong. These [caught up with the Goths who had come with Ataulphus and who were encamped around the Italian city[1]] known as Pisae and, having attacked and fallen upon them, killed 1,100 of them with only seventeen casualties on their own side. But when they observed the whole host advancing upon them, fearful lest they be encircled by so many they retreated to Ravenna unscathed.

46. The court eunuchs made charges in the Emperor's presence against Olympius as the man responsible for the calamities that had befallen the State, and caused him to be removed from his office. And he, for fear that he might suffer something yet more serious, took to his heels and fled to Dalmatia. The Emperor sent Attalus to Rome as urban prefect, and, evincing much concern lest any of the funds intended for the treasury be concealed, sent Demetrius to undertake Attalus' former office and to take inventory of all the fisc's holdings. Making many innovations as regards the civil magistracies and otherwise, ejecting those previously in power and supplanting them with others, he placed Generidus in charge of all the soldiers in Dalmatia, in addition to his being leader of those who were garrisoned around upper Pannonia and Noricum and Raetia as far as the Alps. Generidus was by race a barbarian, but he was naturally disposed to every form of virtue; above all, he was incorruptible in matters of money. He still adhered to the ancestral rites, nor would he allow himself to be seduced away from the worship of the gods. When a law was passed forbidding those who were not Christians to wear a belt at court, although he

---

[1]The passage is mutilated.

had at the time of the law's passage the highest military office in Rome he stayed at home, his belt laid aside. When the Emperor asked him, seeing that he was numbered among the magistrates, to assume his appointed station at court, he replied that there was a law which forbade him to wear his belt and, more generally, which forbade anyone who did not venerate the Christian religion to be reckoned among the magistrates. The Emperor then stated that the law might apply to all the rest but not to one who had undertaken so many risks in the State's behalf. But Generidus answered that he could not accept a privilege which tended to dishonor all those who on account of the law had been stripped of their military employment. Indeed, he did not take up his office until the Emperor, impelled by shame and also by necessity, abolished the law altogether, conceding to everyone, magistrate and soldier alike, the right to his own religious conviction.

Following this act of liberality Generidus began to drill his soldiers in continuous exercises, supplying them with their rations (on which he allowed no one to cut back, as had been the custom) while he himself fittingly rewarded the harder workers out of the supplies which the fisc furnished him. In so conducting himself he threw fear into the neighboring barbarians and safeguarded the peoples over which he had been commanded to keep watch. (47) However, at Ravenna the soldiers mutinied and seized the port, shouting in disorderly fashion their demands that the Emperor put in an appearance before them. But he was afraid and hid himself while Jovius, the praetorian prefect who was also honored with patrician dignity, proceeded into the midst of the insurrection feigning ignorance of its cause (even though he himself was held to be its coauthor together with Allobichus, commander of the domestic cavalry). He asked the soldiers to say why they had been induced to take such a step. When they replied that their two leaders Turpilio and Vigilantius, plus Terentius the imperial chamberlain and Arsacius his second in command, must by all means be delivered up to them, the Emperor, afraid of the soldiers' defecting, condemned the leaders to perpetual exile. They were thrown on a ship and were killed by those who were transporting them (this murder had been ordered by Jovius, who feared they might some day return, find out about the plot that had been laid against them, and provoke the Emperor to exact punishment from him). Terentius was banished to the East and Arsacius was ordered to confinement in Mediolanum. (48) The Emperor made Eusebius chamberlain to replace Terentius, and gave Turpilio's former office to Valens. Then, having appointed Allobichus cavalry commander to succeed Vigilantius, he appeared to have put a stop to the soldiers' insurrection.

But Jovius the praetorian prefect, when he had surrounded himself with all the power of an Emperor, decided to send legates to Alaric urging him to come with Ataulphus straight to Ravenna, where the peace would be concluded on the spot. Alaric was persuaded by letters written by the Emperor and by Jovius and proceeded to Ariminum, thirty miles distant from Ravenna; and there Jovius joined him on the run. Inasmuch as Jovius had become Alaric's friend and guest in Epirus, they entered into conversations concerning the peace treaty. Alaric's demands were as follows: that each year he be paid a fixed sum of gold and be supplied a certain measure of grain, and that he and all his followers settle in both Venetias, in Noricum and in Dalmatia. These demands Jovius wrote down in Alaric's presence and dispatched to the Emperor; he also wrote him privately urging that Alaric be appointed commander of the joint forces since by this treatment he might relent somewhat with regard to the bitterness of the treaty terms, making them more bearable and moderate. Upon receipt

of this letter the Emperor condemned Jovius' forward-
ness, and in his letter of reply made it clear to him that,
'although Jovius might decide what was a fair measure of
gold and grain seeing that he was praetorian prefect and
knew what the public revenues could afford, he himself
would never confer either upon Alaric or any of his race
the rank of the office of a general.'

49.   When Jovius received this dispatch he did not
unroll it privately but read it aloud in Alaric's presence.
Alaric found it tolerable up to the point where he discovered that the office of general was denied both to himself
and to his race.   Thereupon, roused to anger, he gave
orders that his barbarians were to march upon Rome
immediately and avenge the insult done himself and his
entire race.   Jovius, however, in a dilemma owing to the
unexpected tone of the Emperor's letter, returned to
Ravenna and, desirous of absolving himself from blame,
made Honorius promise under oath 'of a surety never
again to make peace with Alaric but to be his enemy forever.' He also swore this oath, touching the Emperor's
head, and then he got his fellow magistrates to do likewise.

50.   Following these actions the Emperor summoned
10,000 Huns into an alliance of war against Alaric and,
since he wanted to have provisions on hand for their
arrival, he ordered grain and sheep and oxen brought
from Dalmatia.   He sent men to spy out how Alaric was
making his expedition to Rome.   Finally, he collected his
own forces from all sides.   Meanwhile Alaric had repented of his proposed march on Rome.   He dispatched as
emissaries the bishops of the various cities to admonish
the Emperor 'not to overlook the fact that a city which had
for more than a thousand years ruled over a great part
of the world was being surrendered to barbarians for
sacking; rather than seeing such a mass of buildings

being destroyed by enemy fire he should make peace upon terms moderate in the extreme; the barbarian had no need of power or dignity nor did he any longer crave the provinces previously demanded for settlement purposes, but only the two Noricums, which were situated at the far end of the Danube, were continuously harried by forays, and fetched little revenue for the treasury; in addition, the barbarian would take only so much grain annually as the Emperor considered sufficient and would forego the gold entirely; finally the barbarian wished there to be friendship between himself and the Romans plus an alliance of war against anyone who took up arms and made a hostile move against the Empire.'

51. Such were the lenient and temperate terms proposed by Alaric: everyone alike was amazed at the man's moderation. But Jovius and the other magistrates whose power was second only to the Emperor's insisted that these demands could not be acceded to because all of them had bound themselves by oath never to conclude peace with Alaric — 'Now if the oath had happened to have been made to God perhaps it might have been just possible to overlook it by trusting the divine beneficence to condone the impiety; but since they had sworn by the Emperor's head it was not lawful for them to commit perjury against such an oath' — so dim were the wits of those who, bereft of God's providence, were then conducting the State's affairs.

BOOK VI

Accordingly Alaric, his equitable demands having been thoroughly rebuffed, marched upon Rome with his entire army, intent upon besieging it. At this juncture there came to Honorius a legate from Constantinus (he who had entered upon tyranny among the Celts), Jovius, a man conspicuous for his education and other virtues. He asked that the peace previously[1] agreed upon be confirmed, and at the same time sought the Emperor Honorius' forgiveness for the murder of his kinsman Didymus and Verenianus (he apologized by saying that they had been killed contrary to Constantinus' wishes). Noticing that Honorius was thoroughly unsettled, he told him 'he would be well advised, occupied as he was with problems in Italy, to give in to Constantinus. If he (Jovius) were permitted to go back to Constantinus and announce to him Italy's calamities, he would not long thereafter return with all the Celtic, Spanish, and British forces bringing aid to Italy and to Rome.' And Jovius upon these conditions secured permission to depart.

Celtic affairs have not yet been given above the treatment they deserve; it is right that I relate them now in detail. (2) While Arcadius was still reigning and Honorius and Theodosius were in their seventh and second consulships, respectively,[2] the soldiers stationed in Britain revolted, placed Marcus upon the imperial throne, and submitted to his authority as master of affairs in those regions. Having then murdered him because he did not suit their temperament, they introduced Gratianus, decked

---

[1]Cf. Book V, chapter 44 above.
[2]That is, the year 407.

him out in the purple and crown, and with spears attended him as they would an Emperor. But they became disenchanted with him also, after a reign of four months killing him and handing over the throne to Constantinus. This man, having placed Justinianus and Nebiogastes in charge of the Celtic soldiery, crossed the Channel. When he reached Bononia (a city of lower Germany[1] hard by the sea) he stayed there several days. He won over to his side all the armies as far as the Gallic and Italian Alps, and appeared to have a secure hold upon his realm. At this point Stilicho dispatched an army commanded by Sarus against Constantinus. Sarus marched out his forces against the general Justinianus and in an encounter killed him and the greater part of his soldiery. He gained control of a vast amount of booty and, having learned that Constantinus had betaken himself to Valentia, a suitable refuge for his purposes, he set about besieging it. Nebiogastes, the other troop commander, while conducting peace talks with Sarus, was received by him amicably, but after an exchange of oaths was forthwith murdered, Sarus taking no account of said oaths. Constantinus now appointed Edobinchus, a Frank, and Gerontius, a Briton, as his new generals, men for whose military experience and courage Sarus had respect. After a seven-day siege he withdrew from Valentia. Constantinus' generals ran out after him with all their might and main, and it was only with great difficulty that he escaped. All of his booty he forfeited to the Bacaudae, who met him at the Alps, in exchange for their granting him right-of-way into Italy. Sarus in this fashion returned safely. But Constantinus collected his entire force, determined to set up sufficient garrisons in the Alps. He set up three altogether (in the Cottian, the Pennine, and the Maritime Alps) which shut off all access between Italy and the Celtic peoples. He considered these

---

[1]Actually, it was a Belgic city (modern Boulogne).

matters worthy of such attention for the following reason:

3. Prior to this, when the consuls were Arcadius for the sixth time and Probus,[1] the Vandals had joined forces with the Suebi and the Alans, overrun the trans-Alpine regions and destroyed the peoples. Having wrought much slaughter, they became formidable even to the armies in Britain, which, being afraid they might march against them, they drove to the point of choosing tyrants, the aforesaid Marcus and Gratianus and, thereafter, Constantinus. Against this last[2] the Romans joined fierce battle and gained the victory, slaughtering the greater part of the barbarians; but they did not chase after those who had escaped (else they would have massacred them all to a man) and so gave them opportunity to repair their loss by collecting another host of barbarians worthy to do battle. For these reasons then Constantinus was establishing garrisons in the Alpine regions, so that they[3] might not have free access into Gaul. He also was setting safeguards along the Rhine, which had been neglected since the reign of the Emperor Julian.

4. Having settled matters throughout all Gaul thus, he dispatched to Spain the older of his two sons, Constans, having decked him out in the dress of a Caesar. For he wanted to bring all the Spanish nations under his sway so as both to extend his realm and at the same time to wipe out the dynasty of Honorius' kinsmen there. Indeed, he was growing fearful lest these latter might some day collect a force of soldiers there, cross the Pyrenees and attack him while the Emperor Honorius simultaneously might dispatch his armies from Italy, encircle him on all sides, and remove him from his tyranny. Accordingly Constans crossed over into Spain together with Terentius[4] the general

---

[1] That is, the year 406.

[2] So the MSS.; but Zosimus really means the Vandals, Suebi, and Alans — one of many signs that Book VI was not redacted.

[3] "They" can only refer to the Romans.

[4] Undoubtedly Zosimus meant to write "Gerontius" (cf. above, chapter 3, n. 2, and below, chapter 7, n. 1.

and Apollinaris the praetorian prefect; he had in addition appointed leaders, both civil and military, of the palatine orders.[1] Through the agency of these men he moved against those who, related by birth to the Emperor Theodosius, were upsetting the state of affairs in Spain. Even before they had joined battle with their Lusitanian armies against Constans they recognized that they would be worsted, and so they fielded a host of slaves and farmers and came very close to bringing him into extreme danger. But, frustrated in these hopes, they along with their wives were handed over into Constans' custody. After their brothers Theodosiolus and Lagodius had learned of this, the former fled to Italy, the latter got away safely through to the East.

5. Having accomplished these deeds in Spain, Constans returned to his father Constantinus, bringing with him Verenianus and Didymus. He had left behind the general Gerontius together with his Gallic soldiers to guard the road between France and Spain, even though the soldiers in Spain had begged that this duty be entrusted, according to custom, to them and that the safekeeping of the region not be committed to foreigners. And Verenianus and Didymus, having been conducted before Constantinus, were forthwith killed. Thereupon Constans was again dispatched by his father to Spain, taking with him Justus as general. On this account Gerontius was incensed and, having won over to his side the soldiers in those regions, he raised the Celtic barbarians in revolt against Constantinus, who could not withstand them because the greater part of his own soldiery was in Spain. The barbarians above the Rhine, assaulting everything at their pleasure, reduced both the inhabitants of Britain and some of the Celtic peoples to defecting from the Roman rule and living their own lives disassociated from the Roman law. Accordingly the Britons took up arms and, with no consideration of the danger to

---

[1]The passage is mutilated.

themselves, freed their cities from barbarian threat; likewise all of Armorica and other Gallic provinces followed
the Britons' lead: they freed themselves, ejected the Roman
magistrates, and set up home rule at their own discretion.

6.   Now, the defection of Britain and of the Celtic
peoples took place during Constantinus' tyranny, the barbarians having mounted their attacks owing to his carelessness in administration. But in Italy Alaric, not having
obtained the peace terms which he sought nor having received hostages, again set upon Rome, threatening to take
it by storm unless the citizens sided with him and marched
against the Emperor Honorius. When they hesitated to do
what he demanded, he laid siege to the city and, proceeding
to the port, spent several days in beleaguering it before
emerging its master. Having found the city's entire grain
supply stored there, he issued threats that he would expend
it upon his own army unless the Romans moved swiftly to
carry out his proposals. Thereupon all the senators convened and, having debated the issue, gave in completely to
Alaric's bidding. Indeed, since no supplies were forth-
coming to the city via the harbor, there was no other
recourse available to avoid destruction.

7.   Thereafter they received Alaric's embassy and
invited him to come before the city and, just as they had
been ordered, they set Attalus, the urban prefect, upon the
Emperor's throne and placed the purple and the crown upon
him. Straightway he proclaimed Lampadius his praetorian
prefect and Marcianus his urban prefect. He handed over
one military command to Alaric himself and the other to
Valens, who had previously been leader of the Dalmatian
legions, and similarly he filled the other magistracies in
order. Then he marched off with his imperial bodyguard
to the palace, under many unfavorable omens. The following
day he entered the Senate and delivered a harangue teeming
with arrogance, boasting that he would procure for the

Romans the entire world, and other things even more grandiloquent. At such statements the Deity would almost certainly take offense, and not long afterwards the man was toppled.

The Romans were in transports of delight because they had obtained magistrates who were successful, experienced administrators, especially the consul Tertullus. Only the family known as the Anicii were aggrieved that all things seemed to be going well for the commonweal, since they alone, possessing the riches of nearly everyone, were unhappy when the populace was happy.

Alaric had advised Attalus, correctly, to send a good-sized force to Africa and Carthage for the purpose of dissolving Heraclianus' rule, lest some impediment to his undertakings come from that quarter (Heraclianus was a partisan of Honorius). But Attalus did not heed this admonition, instilled as he was with hopes raised by seers and persuaded that he would become master of Carthage, indeed, of all Africa, without a struggle. And so he did not dispatch Druma[1], who with the force of barbarians at his disposal could very easily have put down Heraclianus from power; but, thinking Alaric's plan of secondary importance, he entrusted the command of the soldiers in Africa to Constans and sent off with him no fighting force worth mentioning. Meanwhile, with the situation in Africa still in doubt, he took it upon himself to march against the Emperor, who was at Ravenna.

8. The latter was thoroughly terrified. He had sent an embassy asking for a joint reign between himself and Attalus; Jovius, Attalus' appointed praetorian prefect,[2]

---

[1] This man is mentioned again in chapter 12, below, as if for the first time — one more instance of the fact that Book VI did not undergo redaction (cf. above, chapter 3, n.2)

[2] *Contra* chapter 7 immediately above, where Lampadius is stated to be Attalus' appointee.

replied that Attalus would not leave Honorius even the name of Emperor nor yet a sound body, but would mutilate some part of his person and banish him thus maimed to an island. Everyone was horrified at the arrogance of this statement, and the Emperor Honorius was poised for flight, for which purpose he had brought together into the harbor of Ravenna no small fleet of ships. Six cohorts of soldiers had brought the fleet to anchor, cohorts totalling 4,000 soldiers who had been expected while Stilicho was still alive but now for the first time had arrived from the East. Honorius, as if aroused from deep torpor, upon their arrival from the East put them in charge of guarding the walls and decided to remain in Ravenna for the time being, until the situation in Africa clarified itself: 'then, if Heraclianus should come off the victor and affairs there be in safe hands, he would wage war against Attalus and Alaric with his entire army; on the other hand, if those whom he had sent to Africa should be defeated, he would set sail in the ships at his disposal to Theodosius in the East and abdicate from his Western Empire.'

9. This was the state of Honorius' affairs. But Jovius, who as I have already related had been sent on an embassy to Honorius, began to entertain thoughts of betrayal as the Emperor worked on him through agents. Accordingly he told the Senate, addressing to it certain indecorous words, that he would not carry out his mission further. He said that 'it was altogether right and fitting to send barbarians to fight Heraclianus, since those who had been dispatched to Africa had failed of success and since with Constans killed their cause for hope in that region was shaken.' Attalus was stirred to anger, and indicated through informants what had to be done: fresh troops were sent to Africa with money to bolster the situation there. When Alaric learned what had happened he was displeased and began to despair of the fortunes of Attalus because the

latter facilely undertook unprofitable ventures owing to his folly and lack of organization. With these thoughts in his mind he decided to withdraw from Ravenna, even though he had originally intended to persist in the siege until he captured the city. Indeed, he was exhorted to this change of action by Jovius, who, realizing that the leader sent to Africa had failed, turned around completely to Honorius' side and incessantly spoke ill of Attalus in Alaric's presence, anxious to persuade him that Attalus, once his Empire was secured, would lay plots first against him and then against all those related to him by race.

10. But Alaric was willing still to abide by his oaths of allegiance to Attalus. When Valens, the master of the horse, was killed after falling under suspicion of treason, Alaric attacked all the cities of Aemilia that had refused to accept promptly Attalus' rule. He brought over with no trouble at all every one of them except Bononia, which he besieged for several days but could not capture as it held firm. He then proceeded to the Ligurians and compelled them to recognize Attalus as Emperor. Honorius, however, wrote letters to the cities in Britain urging them to be on their guard, and he distributed rewards to the soldiers from moneys supplied him by Heraclianus. Thus he gained complete relief, having won over the good will of the soldiers on every side.

11. Heraclianus held all the harbors of Africa under full guard, and so neither grain nor oil nor any other necessities of life were being conveyed to the port of Rome. A famine fell upon the city more severe than the preceding one, the market speculators hiding whatever they had for sale in the hope of eventually appropriating everyone's money by getting any price they might choose to set. The city had come to such a pass that at the circus games those who hoped to taste the contestants' corpses let out

the following cry: "Pretium inpone carni humanae," that
is, "Set a price on human flesh."

12.   At this point Attalus arrived at Rome and con-
voked the Senate, laying before it a plan. Nearly everyone
agreed that barbarians should be sent to Africa along
with Roman soldiers and that the command of these forces
should be given to Druma,[1] a man who had already de-
monstrated very many proofs of trustworthiness and good
will.   Only Attalus plus a few others dissented from the
majority opinion, since he wanted no barbarian dispatched
with the Roman army. Thereupon Alaric looked to Attalus'
downfall, having long since been made the more ready
for this by Jovius' incessant accusations.   Putting his
scheme into execution, he led Attalus out in front of
Ariminum, where he was staying, removed his crown and
stripped off his purple (these he sent to the Emperor
Honorius), and reduced him before the eyes of all to private status.   However, he did keep him and his son Am-
pelius at his own house until, peace having been concluded
with Honorius, he could obtain safety of life and limb for
them both.   The Emperor's sister Placidia was also
staying at Alaric's house, filling the role of a hostage,
as it were, but enjoying altogether dignified, indeed,
regal courtesy.

13.   This, then, was the situation in Italy. Constantinus, however, having crowned his son Constans and
raised him from a Caesar to an Augustus, installed him
in the office of praetorian prefect, removing Apollinaris
therefrom.   Meanwhile Alaric set out with his troops for
Ravenna in the hope of making a firm peace treaty with
Honorius; but fortune, advancing down the road leading
to the ruination of the State, found another impediment to
dash that hope.   For Sarus, who had allied himself with
neither the Emperor Honorius nor Alaric, was by chance

----

[1]See the note to chapter 7, above.

staying with a small force of barbarians in Picenum, and Ataulphus, who was angry with him as a result of some long-standing grievance, was en route with his entire army to that very region. Sarus, having been made aware of his approach and thinking that the mere three hundred men he had would be no match to do battle against him, decided to flee to Honorius and to ally himself in common cause against Alaric.

INDEX

INDEX

261

THE ROMAN EMPIRE
at the time of
Zosimus: Circa 475 A.D.